The Future of Services Management

Edited by
Colin Armistead

First published in 1994

Kogan Page Limited
120 Pentonville Road
London N1 9JN

British Library Cataloguing in Publication Data

A CIP record for this book is available from the British Library.

ISBN 0 7494 1064 7

Typeset by Saxon Graphics Ltd, Derby
Printed and bound in Great Britain by Biddles Ltd, Guildford and Kings Lynn

The Future
of Services
Management

Titles in the Cranfield Management Research Series include:

The Challenge of Strategic Management
Corporate Strategy and Financial Decisions
Strategic Marketing Planning
Strategy Planning in Logistics and Transportation
Making Sense of Competition Policy
European Developments in Human Resource Management
Executive Redundancy and Outplacement
The Challenge of International Business
The Future of Services Management
Advances in Consumer Marketing

These books are available from all good bookshops or directly from
Kogan Page Ltd, 120 Pentonville Road, London N1 9JN.
Tel: 071 278 0433 Fax: 071 837 6348.

CONTENTS

5

Contents

LIST OF FIGURES

LIST OF TABLES

List of Tables

11

THE CRANFIELD MANAGEMENT RESEARCH SERIES

The Cranfield Management Research Series represents an exciting joint initiative between the Cranfield School of Management and Kogan Page.

As one of Europe's leading post-graduate business schools, Cranfield is renowned for its applied research activities, which cover a wide range of issues relating to the practice of management.

Each title in the Series is based on current research and authored by Cranfield faculty or their associates. Many of the research projects have been undertaken with the sponsorship and active assistance of organisations from the industrial, commercial or public sectors. The aim of the Series is to make the findings of direct relevance to managers through texts which are academically sound, accessible and practical.

For managers and academics alike, the Cranfield Management Research Series will provide access to up-to-date management thinking from some of Europe's leading academics and practitioners. The series represents both Cranfield's and Kogan Page's commitment to furthering the improvement of management practice in all types of organisations.

THE SERIES EDITORS

Frank Fishwick
Reader in Managerial Economics
Director of Admissions at Cranfield School of Management

Dr Fishwick joined Cranfield from Aston University in 1966, having previously worked in textiles, electronics and local government (town and country planning). Recent research and consultancy interests have been focused on business concentration, competition policy and the book publishing industry. He has been directing a series of research studies for the Commission of the European Communities, working in collaboration with business economists in

12

France and Germany. He is permanent economic adviser to the Publishers Association in the UK and is a regular consultant to other public and private sector organisations in the UK, continental Europe and the US.

Gerry Johnson
Professor of Strategic Management
Director of the Centre for Strategic Management and Organisational Change
Director of Research at Cranfield School of Management

After graduating from University College London, Professor Johnson worked for several years in management positions in Unilever and Reed International before becoming a Management Consultant. Since 1976, he has taught at Aston University Management Centre, Manchester Business School, and from 1988 at Cranfield School of Management. His research work is primarily concerned with processes of strategic decision making and strategic change in organisations. He also works as a consultant on issues of strategy formulation change at a senior level with a number of UK and international firms.

Shaun Tyson
Professor of Human Resource Management
Director of the Human Resource Research Centre
Dean of the Faculty of Management and Administration at Cranfield School of Management

Professor Tyson studied at London University and spent eleven years in senior positions in industry within engineering and electronic companies.

For four years he was a lecturer in personnel management at the Civil Service College, and joined Cranfield in 1979. He has acted as a consultant and researched widely into human resource strategies, policies and the evaluation of the function. He has published 14 books.

THE CONTRIBUTORS

Haider Ali gained his BSc in Monetary Economics from the London School of Economics. Having launched a publishing venture on graduation, he subsequently joined the doctoral programme at the Cranfield School of Management. After a year on the programme he has submitted his MPhil thesis, *Marketing through Network Leverage*, a study of the market entry methods of small businesses. Material based on this work has been presented at conferences in the UK, Europe and the US. He is currently transferring to Imperial College (University of London) to complete his doctorate. Haider brings to his research his past and current business experience and has also made use of the experiences of the hundreds of small business owners who have attended his training seminars at enterprise agencies in North London.

Colin Armistead BSc PhD Cert Ed, Senior Lecturer in Operations Management and Head of the Operations and Project Management Group at Cranfield School of Management. He is also the Research Director for the Centre for Services Management in Cranfield and Joint Director of the Service Operations Management Research and Development Club. Colin's research interests are in the formulation of operations strategy, the design of service delivery systems and the re-engineering of service business processes, and the management of capacity, quality and resource productivity in service organisations. He has a specific interest in customer service and support.

Colin has been involved with training managers in a wide range of organisations on general management programmes, and specific programmes relating to operations management and the management of services. He has acted as a consultant to service organisations on matters concerned with the formulation and operational implementation of service strategy and the re-design of service process.

Colin is the author of a number of books and articles on the management of services including *Customer Service and Support*, co-authored with Graham Clark and published by Pitman (1992). A forthcoming book is *Inspired Customer*

Service, co-authored with David Clutterbuck and Graham Clark, to be published by Kogan Page.

James Arrowsmith BA MA, Research Associate in the Department of Management at the Manchester Metropolitan University, where he is currently researching issues relating to age and employment. He graduated from the University of York with a degree in Politics, where he developed his interest in European employment and social policy issues. James' Masters degree (Industrial Relations) was obtained from the Industrial Relations Research Unit at the University of Warwick Business School, where he developed research interests in the industrial relations of occupational safety and health. Current interests relate to the development of 'service unionism'; trade union member recruitment strategies; and the nature and direction of EC policy on worker representation and participation. Particular research initiatives include an examination of the dynamics of older worker employment.

Peter Barrett MSc PhD FRICS, Director of Policy Coordination in the Department of Surveying, University of Salford. He has been researching the management of the professional construction firm for many years. Peter is a chartered building surveyor with nine years' experience in practice before moving into the academic world. He is Chairman of the Research Committee of the Royal Institution of Chartered Surveyors (RICS), a member of the RICS QA skill panel and the RICS representative on the Research and Development Committee of the Construction Industry Council.

Peter is a member of the international Working Commission 88 (Quality Assurance) of the Conseil International du Batiment. He is also a member of W-65 (O+M of Construction) of the CIB, within which he leads CON*FIRM*, an international research group, with membership from around twenty-five countries, which concentrates on the management of the *construction firm*.

Graham Clark, Director, Executive MBA Programme, Lecturer in Operations Management, Cranfield School of Management. Following a career in engineering and manufacturing management, Graham joined the faculty of Cranfield School of Management in 1986 and apart from the normal teaching commitments has carried out research in after sales service, quality management, and service operations strategy. The main focus of his research has been on after sales customer support, and he is the author of a number of research reports and articles on the subject. He is co-Director with Colin Armistead of the Service Operations Research and Development Club, which has recently sponsored surveys on service recovery and unconditional guarantees.

He is co-author (again with Colin Armistead) of *Customer Service and Support*, published by Financial Times/Pitman.

Brett Collins is Chairman of the Marketing Group and Principal Lecturer at the Royal Melbourne Institute of Technology, Australia. Prior to this, he lectured in

Marketing at the Graduate School of Management, University of Melbourne, and at Deakin University. He has 15 years' experience in sales, manufacturing, marketing, corporate planning and general management, and is active as a consultant to companies and government bodies. His teaching and research centre . on marketing management, financial mathematics, marketing decision analysis and business strategy. He has published widely in academic and professional journals.

Colin Fletcher is Professor of Educational Research at the University of Wolverhampton. He read Social Sciences at Liverpool and holds a Diploma in Industrial Administration and a Phd in Organisational Studies. He has taught research methods at universities and polytechnics and specialises in doctoral studies. The author of books on methods and education and a national authority on community education, he acts as a consultant to schools, education authorities and voluntary organisations. He developed practitioner research at Cranfield with key professionals in the public and voluntary sectors.

Richard Kay is Chief Executive of the Rainer Foundation, a national voluntary organisation working with young people. After service in the public sector, in the Royal Hong Kong Police and as Deputy Governor of an English Borstal, he has spent the last 17 years working in senior management positions in the voluntary sector. His research into the 'theories-in-use' of chief executives of voluntary organisations led to the award of a PhD from the Cranfield School of Management in 1992.

Simon Knox is a Senior Lecturer in Consumer Marketing at the School of Management, Cranfield University. After graduation, he followed a career in the marketing of international brands with Unilever plc. After a spell in detergents, Simon moved to convenience foods as marketing manager for UK instant soups. Since joining Cranfield, he has published over 40 papers in the area of consumer behaviour and branding. Simon is the Research Director of the Centre for Marketing Relationships.

Hervé Mathe is a Professor of Service Management at the University of Lausanne and at ESSEC in Paris. He has been a visiting professor at Cranfield, SDA Bocconi in Italy and the Harvard Business School as well as a management consultant with Arthur D Little in Cambridge, Massachusetts. His most recent published books include *Managing Services Across Borders* (1991), *Strategic Marketing for Service Industries* (1993) and *Integrating Service Strategy in the Manufacturing Company* with R D Shapiro (1993).

Ann McGoldrick BA MA Cert Ed PhD, Senior Lecturer in Human Resource Management in the Department of Management at the Manchester Metropolitan University and Director of the MSc in Management by Action Learning and Research programme. Her previous work includes appointments as Research Fellow and Lecturer in the School of Management at the University of Manchester

Institute of Science and Technology, contributing to a range of Organisational Behaviour and Psychology courses. She has published widely in the areas of Human Resource Management and Organisational Behaviour, including *Early Retirement*, Gower Press, 1989. Currently her research interests include the implications of demographic change and economic circumstances for human resource planning, employment of disadvantaged workforce groups and resourcing issues for the future.

Joseph Nellis was formerly on the staff of the universities of Keele and Loughborough and since 1984 he has worked at Cranfield School of Management as a Senior Lecturer in Business Economics. He is currently the Director of Cranfield's Full-Time MBA Programme where he teaches on the School's full range of post-graduate and post-experience management courses. He is co-author of eight books and over 100 business and academic journal articles. His current research interests include the impact of deregulation on the financial services sectors in UK and Europe and the UK housing market dealing with house prices, affordability, mortgage finance and economic forecasting. He was jointly responsible for the research and development of the UK's leading house price systems reported by the Halifax and Nationwide Building Societies. He has regularly been appointed as an advisory consultant to HM Treasury, the Department of the Environment and the Central Statistical Office.

Adrian Payne is Professor of Services Marketing and Director of the Centre for Services Management at Cranfield School of Management. He has practical experience in marketing, market research, corporate planning and general management. His previous appointments include positions as CEO for a manufacturing company and senior appointments in corporate planning and marketing. He teaches on many international executive courses and consults and researches worldwide. His current research interests are in strategic marketing and management in service industries, customer service, corporate acquisitions, global competition and developing market-oriented organisations. He has published over 30 journal articles.

Cynthia Perras is a management consultant with the Center for Service Excellence at Arthur D Little, Inc, the international management consulting firm headquartered in Cambridge, Massachusetts. Her interest in services management was ignited by stimulating MBA course work at Harvard Business School, as well as by personal experiences in the health care industry.

Susan Segal-Horn BA MA MBIM Sloan Fellow, Lecturer in Strategic Management. Susan is responsible for developing international business strategy at Cranfield School of Management and teaches across a range of MBA and corporate programmes. She also acts as a consultant and facilitator for strategy workshops with a range of commercial companies, public sector organisations and professional service firms. Her research focuses on strategy in international service industries, particularly international growth and globalisation issues, on which she is a regular speaker at international conferences. Her publications include work on the internationalisation of retailing; managing professional service firms; strategies for coping with retailer buying power; strategic groups in the European food industry; managing services across borders; and global service delivery for international service firms.

Keith Thompson is a lecturer in Marketing and Management at Silsoe College, Cranfield University, where he lectures in international marketing and buyer behaviour. His academic work is founded on many years' experience in marketing management, notably with IBM and Spillers. His research interests are in the areas of international (especially pan-European) competitive advantage in food retailing and manufacture, and he regularly publishes and contributes papers to marketing conferences on food marketing and related subjects.

He has recently taken on the role of secretary of the Chartered Institute of Marketing's Agrifood Group Executive, of which he is an active member.

Jeff Watkins is Director of the Centre for Professional Development at the University of Bristol. His latest publication is 'Managing the transition – A comprehensive study of the changing use of IT in the retail financial services sector'. He is course leader on the IT management module of the Manchester Business School/University of Wales distance learning MBA. He has recently carried out two major research surveys on the major changes currently affecting the professional workforce and on the changing career patterns of professional people. The results of the first survey are published in a 100 page book entitled *Evolution to Revolution: The pressures of professional life in the 90s*. The results of the second survey will be published in 1994.

PROLOGUE: THE FUTURE OF SERVICES MANAGEMENT RESEARCH

Colin Armistead

INTRODUCTION

Research in the management of services has been developing fast during the last 10 to 15 years. There have been a number of reasons for this growth. It is perhaps of interest to identify some of the major changes in the world of services management which have caused management researchers to take a greater interest, and for managers in services to look to academics for ideas on how they might manage their organisations better. The major factors are:

- The increase in the proportion of people employed in service organisations. In the UK the proportion of the working population employed in services in 1971 was 52.5 per cent and this had increased to 71.9 per cent by 1992 (Social Trends, 1993). Comparable figures for other countries are the US 70.9 per cent, Japan 58.7 per cent and the EC 60.9 per cent, all at 1990 (Eurostat, 1993).
- The change in the pattern of employment, with more women in the workforce and an increase in the number of part-time workers.
- The global spread of US service firms like McDonald's, American Express, and DHL, who have influenced the expectations of consumers and the behaviour of indigenous companies.
- The attempt by many companies to differentiate themselves on the basis of service quality. This phenomenon is also increasingly applicable to manufacturing companies in markets where products are very similar. Examples exist for car and domestic white goods manufacturers.

- The adoption within the quality movement of the concept of the internal customer in all types of firms and organisations. The result has been an increased awareness of the management of internal services.
- The championing of the service ethic as a route to success by managers and investigators. The 'moments of truth' of Jan Carlzon of Scandinavian Airline Systems and Tom Peters' service stars are illustrations.

All these changes have had a profound effect on management researchers. First there has been a realisation that, while a particular service sector has specific skills attached to it, there are generic aspects of services management which apply in all circumstances in managing service encounters. This has led to attempts to classify services more by the nature of the service interaction than by the service product. At the same time researchers have been exploring the detail of specific service sectors, for instance financial and professional services which have changed radically in scale and scope.

The output from services management research may at times appear confusing to practising managers. Where should they look for up-to-date guidance? Concentrating only on literature which relates to their own industry sector would be too limiting. Taking specific service issues such as the management of service quality would start to give a greater breadth of experience across sectors, but it is not the complete answer. This book does not pretend to provide a complete solution to the problem. However, it is an honest attempt to present managers with the results of current research which give strong pointers to the ways in which services will be managed in the future across the services sector and within manufacturing organisations.

A ROUTE MAP FOR THE BOOK

In putting together a book of this type the editor is faced with the unenviable task of trying to satisfy both the generic and the specific in a manner which is useful and readable. I have tried to structure the book in a way that gives managers a view of some important developments which apply across the services sector and also more detailed results from a number of specific service sectors. The reader may then move back and forth throughout the book rather than taking the chapters in the printed sequence. Each chapter includes a summary of the work and the messages or lessons which the research has for practitioners. As all the research is recent these lessons form the basis for managers to approach the delivery of their services in the future.

As an introduction to the text I have included a review of the recent history of research in services management. The reader will appreciate that this picks up the generic themes and contributions from various management science disciplines, including strategic management, marketing, human resources and operations management. These themes are then illustrated by the research reported in the chapters included in the part dealing with generic aspects of services management. In this part I have included two chapters on the globalisation of services, because I believe that, even if managers are not involved in organisations which currently have a global dimension, the spread of new service approaches and products has an influence on other service providers and consumers in ways which ultimately affect all service providers. The chapter by Susan Segal-Horn makes this point very strongly with case histories from international retailers Benetton and Toys 'R' Us, financial service provider American Express and travel company British Airways. The success of globalisation strategies is shown to rely heavily on strong marketing of brands, a commitment to customer service and the development of information systems. The accompanying chapter by Hervé Mathe and Cynthia Perras gives a perspective from the experience of US firms globalising their offering. This has led to a five-step approach being proposed for all service companies which are wishing to expand globally. These steps include the proposition that service firms should consider a global strategy before the event rather than after the fact, and the realisation that such expansion will require the organisation to be capable of learning and adapting during the expansion stage and then managing the mature service operation.

The issue of the marketing of services has been central to the development of the concept of services management, and researchers from this functional area have been among the most active. The two chapters which I have included give two perspectives on the research. The first, by Haider Ali, addresses the issue of the marketing of services for a large and small service organisation and the understanding of customer-perceived risk for service providers. The management of this perception can lead to a greater trust being established between the customer and the service providers which may produce more purchases on the part of the customer. The development of trust may be facilitated by networking and the role of gatekeepers. This chapter reflects the shift in marketing emphasis from *transaction marketing* to *relationship marketing*, where there is a recognition that successful marketing does not just address existing customers but takes into account other markets which affect the overall success of the enterprise. These include new customer markets, supplier markets, influencer and referral markets, employment markets and internal markets.

The role of internal marketing is developed in the chapter by Brett Collins and Adrian Payne. As the concept and practice of internal marketing involves people within the service organisation, it has direct implications for managing human resources. The authors suggest that HR managers can gain effectiveness by adopting a market rather than product orientation for their policies. A consequence of such a change is a clearer segmentation of customers for different types of policies.

The theme of human resources is continued in the chapter by Ann McGoldrick and James Arrowsmith, who address the issue of developing human resources in the service sector in the future with the potential of using 'older workers'. The authors show through the experience of a number of service organisations in the public sector, retailing and financial services that the use of older workers can bring benefits in employee motivation, absenteeism, retention and standards of customer service. However, where the potential of older workers has led to success, the organisation has considered its older workers as a significant part of a human resource strategy and has not been simply updating its equal opportunities policies.

The role of service workers in achieving consistent service quality is one of the three most important dimensions of customer service reported in the chapter on research into the role of capacity management. Graham Clark and myself show that across the services sector in the UK insufficent attention is given to the management of capacity to meet demand and consequently service quality suffers in uncontrolled ways. The features of customer service which are most important to customers, namely the reliability of the service, the attitudes of service staff and the ability to recover from mistakes, are the ones which suffer to the greatest extent. We propose approaches which service managers may take to improve their management of resource capacity and service recovery.

The final part of the book reports research from specific service sectors. It is not possible in a book of this length to represent all sectors. However, I have tried to include a report of research in some of the most important service sectors which have experienced great change and where change is likely to continue in the future. These are food retailing, financial services and professional services. The chapters should give the reader an appreciation of the work which is being carried out within sectors and the messages which emerge. Even if your experience is from outside the sectors included you may well find that the lessons presented strike a chord.

The chapter by Simon Knox and Keith Thompson discusses the influence of the Single European Market on manufacturers and retailers in the grocery market. There are strong echoes in this chapter of earlier ones dealing with global strategy for service firms, because the story told is about the dangers and consequences of complacency in the face of expanded markets and new competitors. The reluctance of UK retailers to expand into the rest of the EC is considered to be unwise as continental retailers like Aldi and Netto make inroads into UK markets. The authors make suggestions about how UK retailers might respond.

There are two chapters on financial services. The first, by Joe Nellis, examines the changing structure and role of building societies in the financial services sector. The impact of the changes in the industry has been felt particularly at branch level and the research points towards two areas which need to be managed more effectively in the future. These are the management of the link between head office and the branches and the management of staff expectations. It is likely that one would find similarities in other areas of financial services including banking and insurance, if not in other service organisations which rely on a network of branches to deliver their services.

The second chapter, by Jeff Watkins, addresses the question of the changing role and work patterns of professionals in the financial services sector and reports research involving HR directors and professional groups. The results show a move towards professionals working in networks which require them to adopt more flexible work patterns. The lessons for managers are for them to establish where the value is added in their business processes, what mix of technical, managerial and political skills are required by the new professionals, and to seek to outsource those parts of the service which contribute little to the knowledge core of the organisation.

The theme of the professional is carried over in a more specific manner to Peter Barrett's chapter which considers professional firms in the construction industry and the management of service quality. The adoption by professional service firms of quality standards like BS 5750 is suggested to involve a consideration of the role of quality management at the level of the firm, the development of appropriate standards and the impact on improving working practices within the industry. Professional service firms and their clients can gain from adopting the quality assurance approach by focusing attention on discussing performance with clients.

The final chapter, by Colin Fletcher and Richard Kay, gives an opportunity for the public sector and commercial services perhaps to learn something from the non-profit making voluntary sector. This sector, while not being profit seeking, does have to compete for funds for charitable purposes. The research centres on the metaphors adopted by the chief executives of voluntary organisations when discussing their role. The authors found that executives employed a richness in their use of metaphors and that a *journey* was a metaphor commonly employed to describe successes and failures in organisations.

CONCLUSION

Reflecting the diversity of research in services management in a single text is not an easy task. I have tried to present a balance of approaches and perspectives on the subject from a number of management disciplines and from within specific service sectors. There are bound to be gaps, but these are less evident when there is a richness in the messages which are included. I am indebted to the contributors and I consider the messages they give are strong pointers to where service managers should be directing their attention in the future.

Colin Armistead
May 1993

References

Eurostat (1993) *Basic Statistics in the Community* 29th Edition, Brussels.
Government Statistical Office (1993) *Social Trends 23* HMSO, London.

Part One

GENERIC ASPECTS OF SERVICES MANAGEMENT

1

THE JOURNEY TO DATE: LESSONS FROM PAST SERVICES MANAGEMENT RESEARCH

Colin Armistead

OUTLINE

Research into services management has developed considerably during the last 15–20 years. In this time researchers have tried to examine some of the generic aspects of managing services as well as carrying out detailed studies of different service sectors. This chapter attempts to identify some of the main themes covered and bring out the main issues for researchers which affect the way practitioners operate. The chapter is divided into seven sections covering:

- *Concepts and frameworks for services* including some of the factors which identify the service process and the search for a generic model for all service organisations.
- *Service strategy*, explaining the approaches which are being suggested for developing and implementing service strategy, both at a competitive strategy level and in formulating a service operations strategy through the characterisation of a service task.
- *Service delivery* and the tools and techniques which are available for analysing service delivery, for reviewing resource allocation, and developments in the area of business process re-engineering.
- *Service quality* has often been viewed as the driver for change in many service organisations and consequently it is important to identify why and where failure can occur in the capability to deliver consistent service quality.

27

- *The service encounter* forms the focus for all service operations and understanding the fundamentals of the encounter in any service allows the formulation of the corresponding management process.
- *Service people* are the most important and costly resource for most services. It is important that their worth is recognised and steps taken to prevent a cycle of failure developing which leads to disaffected staff, poor service quality, dissatisfied customers, and the loss of profitability of the service firm. The role of empowerment is much talked about but not always fully understood and inevitably the development of empowerment must be accompanied by changes in organisational culture.
- *Internationalisation of services* is growing although the factors which facilitate the process are less well understood than for manufacturing companies. Some of the salient research is identified.

In a chapter of this length it is not possible to go into detail and consequently a comprehensive reference list is provided to guide the reader into areas of interest.

INTRODUCTION

Research in services management has evolved as a general discipline over the last 20 years from a study of individual service sectors towards attempts to view the production of services as a generic set of activities which have common features and hence common messages for service managers. One of the main drivers of this change has been the increase in the service sector in developed countries and in the US in particular, and the global spread of US service companies such as American Express, Disney and McDonald's. Indeed in the early days most of the literature on services management emanated from that country. In recent times there has been an increase in contributions from European researchers.

The search for generic aspects of services management does not mean that the separate demands of the individual constituents of the service sector have been abandoned as areas of research. Many studies continue to be focused on service sectors like professional services, public services, hotel and catering, financial services, and retailing. The mix of approaches is reflected in the individual contributions to this book.

Much of the generic work in the early days centred on establishing differences between the production of goods by manufacturing and the delivery of services in order to define the nature of services. Services tend to be intangible, simultaneously produced and consumed, and customers participate in their production. The intangibility of services makes it difficult for managers, employees and customers to assess service output and service quality. Coproduction and consumption mean that there is no decoupling of the two, which makes the management of matching supply and demand more difficult with the associated consequences for managing efficiency and service quality. The participation of customers in the service production to any extent makes it difficult to maximise efficiency and the consistency of service quality and means that service managers must influence the behaviour of both customers and service employees for the successful delivery of services.

A consequence of these attributes has been the recognition that the traditional approaches to management research, which had its origins in concepts based on manufacturing firms, were no longer sufficient. Many of the approaches which have been developed for services management stress the need to include contributions from strategic management, operations management, marketing, and organisation and human resource management.

Perhaps the main thrust of the investigation of services management in the recent past has concentrated on ways to improve the quality of services. The importance of consistent delivery of service quality and customer satisfaction has increasingly been linked with achieving higher levels of customer retention, which in turn has been shown to be correlated with increased profitability. An important factor in the achievement of high levels of customer satisfaction where consistency of service quality is good has been shown to be the way in which service providers recover from mistakes. It is also proposed that this capability is in turn a prerequisite of being able to offer and deliver unconditional guarantees of service or service pledges. The role of front-line staff in all these processes is recognised, particularly in labour-intensive services where relatively unskilled and poorly paid staff are employed. There is also a need to address the cycle of failure in services caused by the lack of recognition of the value of such staff, exemplified by the failure of management to recruit, train, support and reward these groups. The results of the cycle of failure are staff who are poorly motivated to serve customers and who hence deliver poor quality service, high staff turnover as employees are disaffected by their employment and so leave, and higher costs caused by constant recruitment and retraining.

CONCEPTS AND FRAMEWORKS FOR UNDERSTANDING SERVICES MANAGEMENT

The search for a generic taxonomy for services has been the subject of a large number of articles. As yet there is no one taxonomy which is widely accepted as being a rigorous representation of the differences exhibited across the service sector. One of the earliest attempts identified services along a scale between pure services and quasi-manufacturing based on the mix of intangible and physical features of the service package, so that professional services are classified as pure services and distribution as quasi-manufacturing. Other attributes include:

- the degree of contact and participation required of the customer in the production of the service;
- the length of time the service encounter takes to produce the service;
- the extent to which the service is customised in contrast to a standard service;
- the extent to which a service is delivered by equipment as opposed to service people;
- the degree of discretion or autonomy a service provider has in the service encounter to manage the process;

- the extent to which most of the added value in the service production is created with the customer in a front office environment or remote from the customer in a back room;
- the extent to which the service is concerned with the product (ie what is delivered) or with the service process itself (ie how it is delivered).

An attempt has been made to combine these attributes into a single model to characterise three types of services, professional services, service shops and mass services (Fitzgerald *et al*, 1991), based on empirical results from a detailed examination of 12 different service organisations. The three types of services are defined as follows:

> *Professional services* are high contact organisations where customers spend considerable time in the service process. Such services provide high levels of customisation, the service process being highly adaptable in order to meet individual customer needs. A great deal of time is spent in the front office and contact staff are given considerable discretion in servicing customers. The amount of time and attention provided for each customer means the ratio of staff to customers is high. The provision of professional services tends to be people based rather than equipment based. Emphasis is placed on the process rather than the product. The large proportion of professional staff, the heterogeneity of tasks and the fuzziness of the means – end relationships imply that employees are given greater autonomy: under these conditions organisational control is effected by short chains of command and subjective organisational structure — shared values and culture — complements observable structure such as work group size and set procedures.

> *Mass services* have many customer transactions involving limited contact time and little customisation. Such services are predominantly equipment based and product orientated, with most added value in the back office and little judgement applied by front office staff. Here means – end relationships are clear; the mainly non-professional staff have a closely defined division of labour and follow set procedures.

> *Service shops* are characterised by levels of customer contact, customisation, volumes of customers and staff discretion which position them somewhere in between the extremes of mass and professional services. Service is provided by means of a mix of front office and back office activities, people and equipment, and product/process emphasis.

The purpose of a taxonomy of this kind is to provide a template against which to investigate the management issues for appraising the most appropriate service delivery for a given service strategy and for investigating the operations management, organisational and human resource issues, and the context for marketing services.

SERVICE STRATEGY

Two main approaches have been taken to the development of service strategy. The first has followed closely the work of Michael Porter (1980, 1985), employing his techniques for evaluating the business environment by way of an evaluation of political, environmental, social and technological factors (ie PEST), the strength of competition using the five forces model of power relationships, and the basis for competitive advantage. The second approach to service strategy has been directed at establishing a blueprint for service delivery in terms of a service operations strategy.

The Porter models have proved useful tools for considering the influence of the PEST factors on the five competitive forces, namely the power relationship between the service firm and its customers and suppliers, the intensity of the rivalry between service firms operating in the same market sector, the barriers to entry, and the threat of substitute services. Consideration of the PEST factors and the five forces simultaneously creates a dynamic model for evaluating key changes and the issues which arise as the result of these changes for service managers.

Porter suggested general directions for competitive advantage for all firms based on a strategy of differentiation, low cost, or a focused strategy in niche markets. Others have questioned the simplicity of this view, notably Mathur (1988) who is at odds with Porter on the basis of cost competitiveness alone as a sustainable strategy and encourages an assessment of the differentiation of a service product package based on differentiation of the product or of the service. He develops this view of differentiation by suggesting a further investigation of the way the product and service can be differentiated. So the product is evaluated on content and image and the service on expertise and what Mathur refers to as personalisation (ie the way in which the service is delivered). Bowman and Johnson (1992) have taken the view that the Porter approach to competitive advantage being either on the basis of differentiation or low cost is wrong. The proposition they make is for strategies which are based on differentiation, efficiency (ie low cost) or a hybrid of the two. The three strategic directions have been confirmed by research into the perceptions of managers in firms of the relative importance of differentiation and efficiency in their strategy.

The second approach to service strategy is one which can be classed as service operations strategy. Here the aim is to provide a blueprint for the service delivery system. Illustrative of the development of a service operations strategy are the models proposed by Heskett (1986) and Armistead (1990). Heskett links the service concept and the service delivery. The service concept, an idea propounded by Sasser *et al* (1978) and Lovelock (1984), represents the service product consisting of the core service and the product surround. So a hotel is conceptualised as a core service of rooms and beds with food and leisure activities representing the service surround. Heskett talks of the operating strategy in terms of the policies and practices for managing the service business, but does not develop these in detail.

A more prescriptive solution to the definition of service operations strategy has been developed by Armistead (1990) and refined by Armistead and Clark (1992a). Here the basis for the service strategy is a definition of a service task which takes account of customer requirements for the service, service demand, resource productivity targets, and operating constraints. The customer requirements are expressed as customer service dimensions which lead to differentiation and also those dimensions which are referred to as sensitive hygiene factors. The hygiene factors are aspects of the service package which a customer would expect to find but when absent or poorly delivered may lead to loss of business. Resource productivity targets identified in the service task are those on which service managers will control the business. A clear definition of demand factors is considered fundamental to the service task, as they are an essential input into managing capacity. They should reflect the trends in service volume, the variety of services, and the variation in the level of demand over time and any variation in the nature of demand with time changes. Constraints in the service task restrict the ability of service managers to make changes. Constraints may be financial or linked to the availability of resources. It is proposed that the service task is used to define an existing service operation, ie the *now* state, and the blueprint for a *future* situation against which changes in the service delivery system can be evaluated. Experience with service firms has shown that the characterisation of service tasks is at times taxing as it requires information to be gathered in ways which may not fit with existing information systems. Nevertheless, perseverance with the process leads to an increased understanding of what needs to be achieved in the future and a characterisation of the existing state of affairs.

SERVICE MARKETING

Service marketing research has been at the forefront of service management research. Many of the concepts for service management and managing service quality have being propounded by marketing specialists. These contributions are dealt with in other sections. Of concern here is the work concerned with the marketing process for services. Perhaps the largest shift has been in the change from traditional *transactional marketing* to *relationship marketing*, described by Christopher *et al* (1991) in the following terms:

Transaction marketing

- A focus on a single sale.
- Orientation on product features.
- Short time scales.
- Little emphasis on customer service.
- Limited customer commitment.
- Moderate customer contact.
- Quality is primarily the concern of production.

Relationship marketing

- A focus on customer retention.
- Orientation on product/service benefits.
- Long time scale.
- High customer service emphasis.
- High customer contact.
- Quality is the concern of all.

A consequence of this change of view is the concept of a wider audience for the marketing process. Rather than the marketing process involving only customers, whether they are existing customers or potential new customers, other audiences are now envisaged. These are *supplier markets* for materials or services, *employee markets* for new staff, *internal markets* for existing staff, and finally *influencer and referral markets* consisting of those agents who may assist or hinder the process of gaining new customers or keeping existing ones.

SERVICE DELIVERY

The creation of tools for developing service delivery systems has perhaps been one of the main elements for investigation. Clearly there is a strong association between the way in which a service is produced and the characterisation of the service as discussed earlier. The terminology used by writers reflects an analytical approach to the topic mirroring the manufacturing antecedents of much of the work. However, it is interesting to observe the management discipline to which writers are aligned in their approach. A large proportion of writers are marketeers, which perhaps is explained by the closeness of marketing and operations in the delivery of services especially in the front office environment of a service business. The management of the service encounter is an integral part of the service delivery, and most of the researchers in this aspect of service delivery have been from a human resources discipline; this is described in a subsequent section in more detail. The operational elements of the control of service delivery with regard to the management of quality, resource productivity and capacity attract the attention of operations specialists. In this section some of the most useful tools for service delivery are considered.

The early articles on service delivery systems talk of '*servunction*' systems, drawing a parallel between manufacturing production and service delivery. Developing this idea, Shostack (1984) introduced the concept of '*service blueprinting*' as a technique for detailing the process of delivery, allowing the passage of the customer through the service to be identified and linked to actions taken by the service operators in both the front office and back room environments to deliver the service. Integral to the process is the identification of a line of visibility between aspects of the service delivery system which the customer is in contact with or aware of. The concept of service blueprinting has been extended by Gummerson (1991) to that of 'service mapping', by which means he suggests that increased detail can be accommodated.

More recently the technique of business process re-engineering (BPR) (Hammer, 1990) has become a topic of growing interest for researchers and practitioners. While writers in the area do not always make the link between previous work on service delivery, it undoubtedly exists. Perhaps the reason for the omission arises from the information systems discipline base of many business process re-engineering authors, be they researchers or practitioners. It is undoubtedly the case that the approach of BPR brings together a number of strands of thought. Those which seem of most relevance seem to overlap the strategic and the operational.

The strategic roots of BPR lie in the *'value chain'* concept, introduced by Porter (1980, 1985), which allows the critical resources in a firm to be identified. While the model was developed for manufacturing firms it has application to services, albeit with some changes. One suggestion for adapting the value chain concept more successfully to services are the resource activity mapping techniques developed by Armistead and Clark (1992b). This identified main business processes and the key resources and activities which are entailed in each process. This approach is close to the concept of key competences for competitive advantage which Stalk *et al* (1992) have demonstrated for a number of service firms.

It is interesting that many of the proponents of BPR have been from service organisations with large back office activities. These have proved both costly to operate and unresponsive to customer needs, often because they span a number of traditional functional areas in firms with their own structures and processes which may operate around conflicting goals. The application of BPR allows processes to be simplified and aligned more closely with customer process flows. In the application of the technique service blueprinting or service mapping techniques have a place in identifying the major customer processes involved in the total service delivery. Perhaps the wheel has turned full circle, as one might argue that there is nothing new in BPR which has not been written about in the service literature or in traditional O & M (Organisation and Methods) texts. However, such a dismissal may lead to missed opportunities for an approach which can bring about change for the good in large service organisations.

The importance of operational control of service production should be self evident. However, as is shown in the chapter on capacity management later in this book, service managers on the whole do not seem to be sufficiently aware of the importance of capacity management as the fulcrum on which consistent delivery of service quality and attainment of productivity targets rest. Perhaps it also in part explains why service productivity has received so little attention from researchers, despite the growing importance of the topic for practitioners in times of recession and restructuring of major service industries, including financial services and health care.

SERVICE QUALITY

The focus of the largest proportion of services research has undoubtedly been on service quality. The reasons for this perhaps lie in the TQM movement of the last ten years and the attempt by many service organisations to gain competitive advantage by way of improvements in service quality and customer satisfaction. The view of service excellence being equated with the ability to deliver consistently on service quality has been reinforced by the appearance of service firms among the winners of quality awards, including the Malcolm Baldrige National Quality Award in the US and the Deming Quality Award, and no doubt to be followed by the European Quality Award. However these are only part of the story and an attempt is made here to identify how a number of factors of service quality are coming together.

The definition of quality of service has engaged researchers. The product-based definitions were found to be inappropriate although associated. Gronroos's (1984) simple concept of service quality comprising two components is a useful starting place. He proposed that service quality is made up of *technical* and *functional* quality, technical quality being what is received and functional quality the way in which it is received. While simple in concept this model does not provide adequate definition. The detailed interpretation of service quality which has gained greatest acceptance comes from the work of Berry *et al* (1990). These researchers suggest a number of dimensions for service quality arrived at from research with focused groups of users of services, namely tangibles, reliability, responsiveness, competence, courtesy, credibility, security, access, communications, and understanding the customers. These ten dimensions were subsequently grouped into five main dimensions of tangibles, reliability, responsiveness, assurance and empathy.

The same researchers investigated the reasons for the failure to deliver consistent service quality and established what has become known as the '*gap model*' for service quality. Basically they propose that the inability of a service organisation to deliver service quality rests with five gaps, which are briefly described as follows:

- The gap between customer expectations and service managers' perception of what is required caused by a lack of meaningful marketing research.
- The gap between the service management's perceptions and the service quality specifications set to achieve service quality, caused by indifference, resource constraints or market conditions.
- The gap between the service quality specifications and the service delivery gap, caused by incapable processes, systems, and perhaps front line service providers.
- The gap between service delivery capabilities and external communications, caused by over-promising in promotion.
- The gap between customer expectation and perceived service, which is a component of all the other gaps.

The researchers have developed a technique referred to as SERVQUAL to investigate these gaps in a number of service industries. While there has been debate among academics about the technique, the concept provides practitioners with a model for investigating failures in their service quality delivery.

Another factor linked to service quality and customer satisfaction is the correlation between profitability and customer retention over time. If the proposition is accepted that customer satisfaction is most likely to occur with consistent delivery of service quality and customer retention is the likely outcome, then ensuring consistency in service quality should become paramount for service organisations. This has further implications for management. Even the most capable of service delivery systems may at some point fail and if failure occurs when the customer is engaged in the delivery process the process of recovery assumes a major significance. There is a strong association between the way in which service recovery takes place and customer satisfaction. Actions which exacerbate the failure in the eyes of customers needless to say lead to low levels of customer retention. Consequently the proposition is that service organisations should include strategies for dealing with service recovery in their approach to service quality.

Researchers are beginning to investigate service firms which seek to gain competitive advantage by giving meaningful if not unconditional service pledges or guarantees. The ability to make such offerings without giving away the shop must require service providers to be capable of consistent quality and to be able to recover well when failures occur, no matter whether the customers are the principal cause of failure.

THE SERVICE ENCOUNTER

Closely allied with work on service delivery and service quality is the question of managing the service encounter. Many managers in services are now familiar with the concept of 'moments of truth' used by Jan Carlzon of the airline SAS to describe the 50,000 service encounters a day between staff and customers. Research in the area of managing the service encounter has been carried out predominantly by behavioural scientists and those from an HR discipline.

There are perhaps three key factors to be borne in mind when looking at the subject of service encounters. First, they involve front-line service staff who are referred to as '*boundary spanners*' because they transcend the interface between the service organisation and its customers. Secondly, in this role front-line staff are viewed by customers and Lovelock (1984) suggests they become in the customer's eyes a '*service trinity*', selling the service, running the service organisation and being linked to the success of the service. Thirdly, boundary spanners can often feel isolated and neglected and left to cope with demands of customers on their own, which results in burnout showing itself in poor staff morale, high levels of turnover and poor service to customers.

It is against this background that research into managing the service encounter is set. Czepiel *et al* (1985) have provided insights into the nature of service encounters by recognising that they are interactions which are different from other types of human interactions. They have identified a number of features of service encounters:

- Service encounters are purposeful.
- Service providers are not for the most part altruistic.
- Prior acquaintance is not required.
- Service encounters have a narrow focus.
- Customer and service provider roles are well defined.

Recognising the special features of service encounters makes it possible to design the management of service encounters. This is especially important for mass services where the front-line service providers are often not highly skilled and may work on a part-time basis. Work has been reported on the use of service scripts for service staff. The dangers of the 'have a nice day' approach are now well appreciated as being inadequate in themselves if there is no other substantial aspect to the service encounter.

While not being prescriptive, one approach to the service encounter is to appreciate the event from both the customer's perception and that of the service organisation. Customers' perceptions may be influenced by a number of factors including the purpose of the encounter, the importance the customer attaches to the encounter, the perceived risk, and the costs involved. Recognising what the customer brings or needs to be trained to bring to the encounter and the outcome which is expected provides a starting point to decide what front-line staff need to put in and what support is required from the back room. Obviously the development of information systems can assist with the provision of information in a form which is readily accessible to the front line.

While research has been carried out on the design of the service encounter, it still remains an area for further work.

SERVICE PEOPLE

Research into human resource issues for services does of course have features associated with the last section on managing the service encounter. However the issues are wider and three key themes can be identified in the current literature:

- the treatment of service staff, particularly those who are regarded as low skilled and low paid;
- the consideration of the concept of empowerment of service staff;
- the whole issue of managing cultural change, which is recognised as being fundamental to any radical changes in the way in which service delivery is carried out or where substantial improvements in service quality are being sort.

Regarding the treatment of service staff who may carry out repetitive tasks with little support and be low paid, Schlesinger and Heskett (1991) have identified how what they refer to as the cycle of failure caused by dissatisfied staff, resulting from poor training and support and high staff turnover, leads through to poor customer satisfaction and in consequence a loss of customer loyalty and a reduction in potential profitability. These researchers advocate a change to a virtuous cycle brought about through a concentration of the service managers on recruitment and training support, recognition and reward. They claim that few service companies know the cost of high staff turnover which if reduced could offset the cost of increased training and rewards. Other researchers focus on the skills required by high contact staff, including interpersonal skills and coproduction skills, referring to the ability to involve customers in the production of the service almost as partial employees.

The concept of empowerment has become topical. However, the meaning of the term is often not well defined in service organisations. At a general level empowerment can be seen as the controlled transfer of power from management to employees in the long-term interest of the business as a whole. Nevertheless, this definition begs the question of what aspects of power and to what ends. Clearly many service organisations require the use of strong procedures in the interests of safety and security, and procedures may in themselves be seen as inhibiting empowerment. There is also the issue of people's own motivation to assume greater control of what they do and when they do it. Alpander (1991) proposes that understanding what employees want is key to the empowerment process. He suggests five categories of needs relevant to the work situation which must be taken into account: economic security, belongingness, recognition, control and self-worth. Moreover, achieving empowerment means managers must have a clear vision of new ways of operating and be willing to train and support staff in making the change. The claimed benefits from empowerment link with increases in participation in an improvement in service delivery, particularly when there is the need to recover from failure. Empowerment is an area which requires more investigation to demonstrate the appropriate strategies for service managers to follow.

Clearly moves to empower staff are part of a cultural change programme for service organisations. The management of cultural change has been an area of investigation for a number of researchers who have developed models to analyse the process. One which has some power for the understanding of organisational change has been developed by Johnson (1992) in the form of a *cultural web*. At the centre of the web there is the cultural paradigm, which is a statement of those factors an organisation holds true and which drive the actions of people both individually and collectively. Reinforcing or weakening the paradigm there are six contributing factors. These are:

- *Organisational structure* which describes the actual structure of the organisation using terms like hierarchical, flat or functional.
- *Power structures*, which describe where the power lies to block or enable things to happen. It may be perhaps with a board of directors or with a group of middle managers.
- *Control systems* are the formal systems for controlling the business, such as management accounting and quality management systems.
- *Rituals and routines* are the way things actually get done.
- *Symbols* are of status and reward.
- *Stories and myths* are the campaign stories of failure and success, reward and punishment.

The message in managing cultural change is that the central paradigm can be changed by managers by envisaging change, but that other components of the web may then be in conflict with the new paradigm. Change will only result when all the dissonant components are addressed.

INTERNATIONALISATION OF SERVICES

Research into the internationalisation of services is to a large extent still in its infancy. However, as there are an increasing number of global service companies and others looking to expand their business beyond national boundaries, the approaches which are followed and the resulting benefits gained should be a fruitful area for investigation. The chapter in this book by Segal-Horn reviews much of the work in the field and proposes new models for service managers founded on the potential for competitiveness based on economies of scope, economies of scale or a combination of the two, and recognising possible changes in corporate culture and economic and technical capabilities. The way in which services become international will depend also on the nature of the service and the opportunity to capitalise on technological strengths. The three approaches to expansion would seem to be following existing customers and learning from them, buying local operations, and creating replicas or new versions of existing national service operations.

CONCLUSIONS

Services management has been investigated by researchers from across the management disciplines. It has been demonstrated that researchers are interested in seeking an understanding of the generic aspects of managing services as well as investigating specific service sectors. This is likely to continue and should be supported, as there is a richness to be gained from the dual approach.

References

Alpander, G G (1991) 'Developing managers' ability to empower employees', *Journal of Management*, Vol 10, No 3.

Armistead, C G (1990) 'Service operations strategy: Framework for Matching the service operations task and the service delivery', *International Journal of Service Industry Management*, Vol 1, No 2.

Armistead, C G and Clark, G R (1992a) *Customer Service and Support: Implementing Effective Strategies*, Financial Times/Pitman Publishing, London.

Armistead, C G and Clark, G R (1992b) 'The value chain in service operations strategy: Resource activity mapping', Cranfield Working Paper SWP 22/92, to be published in *The Service Industries Journal* 1993.

Berry, L L, Zeithaml, V A and Parasuraman, A (1990) 'Five imperatives for improving service quality', *Sloan Management Review*, Summer.

Bowman, C and Johnson, G (1992) 'Surfacing competitive strategies', *European Management Journal*, Vol 10, No 2.

Christopher, M, Payne A and Ballantyne, D (1991) *Relationship Marketing*, Butterworth Heinemann, London.

Czepiel, J A, Solomon, M R, Surprenant, C F (1985) *The Service Encounter*, Institute of Retail Management/Lexington Books, New York.

Fitzgerald, L, Johnston, R, Brignall, S, Silvestro, R and Voss, C, (1991) *Performance Measurement in Service Businesses*, CIMA, London.

Gronroos, C (1984) 'A service quality model and its marketing implications', *European Journal of Marketing*, Vol 18, No 4.

Gummerson, E (1991) 'Service design and quality: Applying service blueprinting and service mapping to railway services', Proceedings of a Workshop on Quality Management in Services, European Institute for Advance Studies in Management, EIASM, Brussels, May.

Hammer, M (1990) 'Reengineer work: Don't automate, obliterate', *Harvard Business Review*, July– August.

Hart, C W L, Heskett, J L and Sasser, W E (1990) 'The profitable art of service recovery' *Havard Business Review*, July–August.

Hart, C W L, Schlesinger, L A and Maher, D (1992) 'Guarantees come to professional service firms', *Sloan Management Review*, Spring.

Heskett, J L, (1986) *Managing in the Service Economy*, Harvard Business School Press.

Johnson, G (1992) 'Managing strategic change — Strategy, culture and action', *Long Range Planning*, Vol 25, No 1.

Lovelock, C H (1984) *Services Marketing*, Prentice Hall, Englewood Cliffs N J.

Mathur, S S (1988) 'How firms compete: A new classification of generic strategies', *Journal of General Management*, Vol 14, No 1.

Porter, M E (1980) *Competitive Strategy: Techniques for Analysing Industries and Competitors*, Free Press, New York.

Porter, M E (1985) *Competitive Advantage*, Free Press, New York.

Sasser, W E, Olsen, R P and Wyckoff, D D (1978) *Management of Service Operations*, Allyn and Bacon, Boston.

Schlesinger, L A and Heskett, J L (1991) 'Breaking the cycle of failure in services', *Sloan Management Review*, Vol 17, Spring.

Shostack, L G (1984) 'Designing services that deliver', *Harvard Business Review*, Jan–Feb.

Stalk, G, Evans, P and Schulman, L E (1992) 'Competing on capabilities', *Harvard Business Review*, March–April.

2

ARE SERVICE INDUSTRIES GOING GLOBAL?

Susan Segal-Horn

OUTLINE

The debate on global competition has given little attention to service industries. Service industry characteristics such as close local control of quality and interaction with the customer made them unsuitable candidates for global strategy. However, competition in service industries is changing. A combination of structural, market and technological changes has provided a shift in the potential for globalisation as a competitive strategy available to, and appropriate for, service firms. This chapter reviews the major causes of these changes. It also discusses new sources of competitive advantage specific to large international service firms.

Important issues addressed include:

- cultural homogenisation and the emergence of global markets;
- political and economic pressures;
- the impact of information technology on services;
- sources of economies of scope in services.

The implications of this work for managers of service firms are as follows:

- Competitive strategies developed under one set of structural and market conditions must be reviewed when the conditions which gave rise to them have changed.
- Service firms which compete only in their domestic markets, and will not be entering international markets in the future, will still be affected by the rise of international competition in services. This is because even firms which have no intention of entering other international markets are likely to find themselves

in competition with international firms which have already entered, or are about to enter, their domestic market. This will change the basis of competition within domestic markets irrespective of the prevailing strategies of individual firms.

- Services have been a successful competitive arena for Western firms and for UK firms in particular. If the shift towards globalisation of services is not understood and acted upon, this success may be eroded in the same way that leadership in manufacturing industries such as motorbikes, television and cars has already been eroded or lost altogether.

INTRODUCTION

The potential for globalisation as a competitive strategy available to service industries is still poorly recognised. It is a view which attracts criticism and hostility. Evidence remains piecemeal and often anecdotal. For every service company which is reconfiguring its business globally, there remain a dozen which are not. However, it is the contention of this chapter that the race for pre-eminence in international services trade has already begun. The historical pattern of competition in manufacturing industries can be seen repeating itself in the service sector. Those companies which have recognised at an early stage the trend to internationalisation of services, and have begun to reorganise their businesses accordingly, are likely to be most strongly placed to meet future developments.

A global industry is one in which rivals compete against each other on a worldwide basis. Firms operating in global industries are characterised by high levels of coordination and integration of activities across national markets (Porter, 1986; Prahalad and Doz, 1987; Bartlett and Ghoshal, 1989). It is not a definition commonly thought appropriate to service industries, which have been most often conceived of as 'fragmented' industries, populated by many small firms and lacking powerful market leaders (Porter, 1980). This is because service industries were characterised by low entry barriers, diseconomies of scale, close local control, high personal service and 'image' content, where service delivery is at the point of sale to the customer or client (Sasser *et al*, 1978; Normann, 1984; Daniels, 1985; Albrecht and Zemke, 1985; Heskett, 1986; Hindley *et al*, 1987; Carlzon, 1987; Heskett *et al*, 1990). However, the nature of international competition in service industries has shifted as a result of recent structural, market and technological changes. Global manufacturing companies are increasingly being supported by global service companies (Enderwick, 1989). Some of the problems inherent in the management of global service delivery, the key implementation issue faced by global service companies, are being addressed by greater sophistication of management practice and innovative use of technology.

The literature on global strategy (Harrigan, 1984; Hamel and Prahalad, 1984, 1985, 1989; Ohmae, 1985, 1989; Kotler *et al*, 1985; Stopford and Turner, 1985; Doz, 1986; Porter, 1986; Telesis/PSI, 1986; Bartlett and Ghoshal, 1986, 1987; Ghoshal, 1987; Prahalad and Doz, 1987; Franko, 1989; Yip, 1989 and 1992) has taken its evidence overwhelmingly from manufacturing industry. It provides a range of views concerning both how to manage global expansion successfully and also the goals and critical features of such global strategies. The literature largely consists of extending the basic framework for the analysis of competitive advantage developed by Porter (1980, 1985, 1986) to global competition. This approach is of only limited use in regard to service industries since it concentrates on the ground common to both manufacturing and services, rather than the service delivery issues of particular importance to services.

This chapter addresses the changing nature of international competition in service industries. It is argued that product and market evolution, developments in information technology, economic and cultural homogenisation of markets, and political and economic deregulation have combined to change the competitive environment for service industries. It is now possible for world market leaders to emerge and reshape the potential sources of competitive advantage in their sector.

THE GROWTH OF THE SERVICE SECTOR

The service industries are significant to the developed economies in terms of output, jobs and trade balances (Riddle, 1986; Tucker and Sundberg, 1988; Enderwick, 1989; Porter, 1990). Increasing internationalisation of services is likely to be encouraged by international agreement to reduce service trade barriers in the troubled Uruguay Round of GATT. Demand growth has recently begun to flatten out as market penetration, industry concentration and rationalisation take their course, both nationally and internationally. Domestic industry restructuring has been accompanied by expansion into world markets by some of the larger firms. This process is already well advanced in airlines, financial services, professional service firms, software and advertising agencies. It has also progressed some way in retailing, telecommunications and media such as broadcasting and publishing.

Growth in services is built on three factors:

1. increased demand for services by both firms and households;
2. the separation of service suppliers;
3. the standardisation of service delivery processes.

Increased demand by households for new types of services has arisen from the changed socio-demographic structure of the advanced economies. Dual-income families, single-person households, affluent older consumers all represent significant and attractive market segments. They often have special needs for which new service offerings are being specifically designed, such as high-income investment packages or off-season holidays for the over-60s. With regard to corporate demand, the consumption of existing services as well as the design of new services have been affected by specialisation, sophistication and internationalisation. For example, banks and airlines are among many service suppliers offering corporate business travel management systems, while established services like executive recruitment have become international markets.

43

Growth has also come from more specialist service suppliers replacing service provision previously carried out in-house. The most common examples of this practice have occurred in commercial cleaning and catering. However, firms like EDS, the US technology and facilities management company, have grown rapidly, nationally and internationally, as an external supplier of information technology (IT) design and management for client companies. Rajan (1987) calls this 'externalisation'; Porter (1990) calls it 'de-integration'. In the UK it has become known as 'contracting out' and has grown sharply alongside the UK government's privatisation programme as part of a general search for efficiencies in the provision of public sector services. Growing capital intensity and rising productivity of specialist service companies (both mostly IT-related) make internal service provision increasingly inefficient. This is exacerbated by the ability of large service firms to standardise and replicate facilities, methodologies and procedures across locations. Specialisation and standardisation are leading to high quality provision at lower cost to the client company or customer, in such different service businesses as car repair (eg exhaust, brake and tyre centres) or consultancy packages for executive compensation.

THE SPREAD OF GLOBAL COMPETITION IN SERVICE INDUSTRIES

The factors underlying the changing pattern of international competition are familiar and well documented (Levitt, 1983; Ohmae, 1985; Porter, 1986; Winram, 1987; Douglas and Wind, 1987). For services, as for manufacturing, there is no single force pushing for globalisation. Instead the following combination has changed the service industry environment:

- cultural homogenisation;
- the removal of industry barriers via deregulation;
- the development of information technology;
- service industry concentration.

Cultural Homogenisation and the Emergence of Global Markets

There has been a lengthy and vigorous debate surrounding the validity of the argument that an increasing similarity exists between certain groups of consumers within global markets. The debate centres on the question of the desirability of standardising products or services for broadly defined international market segments. The belief in consumer homogeneity is controversial, since it coexists with the view that fragmentation rather than homogenisation may more appropriately describe international consumer trends. Much discussion has taken place over the opportunities for, and barriers to, such standardisation (Kotler, 1985; Quelch and Hoff, 1986; Douglas and Wind, 1987; Link, 1988; Jain, 1989). It was triggered by Levitt (1983) and predicated on the convergence of markets as a result of economic and cultural interdependences across countries and markets. He argued that the new communications technologies are a key influence in the growing homogenisation of markets, reducing social, economic and cultural differences, including old-established differences in national tastes or preferences. This process has meant that companies need to examine any growing similarities between consumer preferences.

Market segmentation based on lifestyle has been around for a long time (Sheth, 1983). However, the argument for global markets does not mean the end of market segments. It means instead that they expand to worldwide proportions. The retail chain Benetton has built its whole strategy on precisely these assumptions, as shown in the example on p46. Certainly there is some adaptation of such things as colour choice for different domestic markets, but this adaptation occurs around the standardised core of Benetton's 'one united product' for its target market segment worldwide.

Globalisation offers the advantage of economies of scale for a segmented marketing strategy. Ohmae (1985) speaks of the 'Californianisation' of the young within the Triad of regional trading blocs (Europe, Asia Pacific and North America), forming a massive lifestyle-related segment. Socio-demographic change, higher incomes, smaller households, concern for health and environment, preference for greater choice and control, are developments which have been taking place at varying rates across the world and are viewed by many writers (Thorelli and Becker, 1980; Levitt, 1983; Jain, 1989; Ohmae, 1989) as a driving force behind the emergence of cross-market segments, providing opportunities for more international strategies. Nelson (1989) has indicated that there is an observable trend towards the concept of 'open citizenship'. People who share this attitude exhibit a positive identification with their own country, yet at the same time consume, and are influenced by, worldwide products and trends such as films, the arts, ethnic foods and popular music. Not only do such influences operate in OECD (Organisation for Economic Cooperation and Development) countries, but Jain (1989) believes that the same patterns of consumption characterise pockets of consumers within LDCs (Less Developed Countries) and NICs (Newly Industrialised Countries), such as in India.

Some of the most vehement rebuttal of the standardisation approach occurs with regard to international marketing activities. This is largely because of the critical role performed by the marketing function in the close tracking of consumer preferences, which must, by definition, be carried out as close to the markets as possible. However, this function can now be performed as well or better by IT, for example retailers' electronic point of sale (EPOS) data capture technology.

In fact considerable standardisation of international marketing has occurred for some time (Sorensen and Weichmann, 1975; Takeuchi and Porter, 1986; Jain, 1989). As Stopford and Turner (1985) concluded: 'even if the case for global brands is somewhat oversold, there is an obvious case that consumer-oriented companies can internationalise general marketing strategies'. This does not necessarily mean providing the same product in all countries, but offering local

Benetton

Rationale behind globalisation

- European domestic markets are relatively small and a successful concept can reach saturation coverage fairly quickly.
- The development of 'lifestyle retailing' based on clear segmentation of the target market is the perfect platform for global marketing.
- The success of 'lifestyle' retailing is indicative of similar international market segments.
- There is in some real sense a proprietary technology — not in a technical sense, but in the interrelationship with the other elements of the strategy which gives a sustainable competitive edge as it is not easily imitated.
- International systems provide the channel for fast response to shifts in consumer demand and risk-free low inventory.

The strategy

- Putting fashion on an industrial level.
- To develop one product line of sufficient breadth to accommodate the needs of particular markets and stores: 'one united product'.
- 'I am speaking of a new business reality which is extra-European in scope' (Luciano Benetton, 1982).

Putting the strategy into operation

- The concept: vertical integration, from design through manufacturing and distribution to retailing.
- The offering: 'paletted' good design and colours of universal appeal.
- Innovative merchandising: making space and inventory more productive.
- Control over store design and location further to control other elements in the service concept.
- Inventory is replaced by information systems linked to factories.
- Inventory risk elimination: produce to firm customer orders.
- Financial risk elimination: agency 'franchising' for capital investment in stores while retaining strategic control.
- Logistics network: rapid access to information on demand.
- Innovatory manufacture to allow 'customised' batch production in response to demand.

Source: L'enterprise Logistique, 1991

adaptations around a standardised core. Just as Benetton balances standardisation with some local adaptation, so Pizza Hut protects the core elements of its brand by copyrighting its individual product brand names (such as Perfect Pizza). It also ensures standardisation across markets by operating a strict specification of product ingredients. However, the Pizza Hut concept is adapted to suit local needs in differing ways. Some elements of the menu (such as desserts) will vary, as will store design and even the way in which products are served to the customer. This illustrates the point made by Quelch and Hoff (1986) that the relevant issue in international marketing 'is not whether to go global but how to tailor the global marketing concept to fit each business'.

Since lead times for securing markets are becoming shorter and shorter, it makes sense to minimise the gap between the launch of new services across international markets. For example, the 1989 UK launch by American Express of its 'Optima' credit card occurred shortly after its test launch in the US market. Global competition increases the need for rapid worldwide roll-outs of new services, especially since new services are often more transparent in the market-place than new products. This high visibility to competitors as well as customers leaves them more open to speedy imitation.

Many service industries are competing in mature markets where competition is fierce and demand is at replacement level only. The financial services market, for example, is heavily oversupplied. Demand for services may be rising only in a few segments within an industry, such as higher value-added food products and fresh produce in grocery retailing, or media purchasing, corporate identity work and public relations in the advertising industry. Although industry restructuring via mergers and acquisitions may initially provide new ways of addressing changing patterns of demand or of removing overcapacity in an industry, restructuring has its limits. Redefining target markets as global markets or global segments provides opportunities for growth and a way out of mature domestic markets.

Deregulation and Protectionism: Political and Economic Pressures

Despite the social, cultural and technological changes behind the development of global market segments, there are additional economic and political pressures on governments to create barriers to this increasing transnational flow of goods. Protectionist policies such as quotas or tariff barriers create constraints on global competition. Such government protection is most likely to occur in industries that are 'salient', ie those that affect government policies regarding defence, regional development or employment. However, they may also occur as a response to a severe imbalance in the volume of international trade between nations (as between Japan and the US, and Japan and the EC in the 1980s). The very need for artificial trade barriers is evidence of the strength of international demand by consumers for international goods and services.

Deregulation is a deliberate attempt to improve the efficiency of markets by opening them up to increased competition. It has been most visible in the world financial markets, where the removal by governments of fixed commissions and ceilings on foreign ownership has shifted competition from service to price and triggered mass exits from the industry through either mergers or business failure.⌉ The same process occurred in the 1970s in the US when President Carter deregulated the airlines in order to encourage competition. The short-term effect was to encourage many new entrants. The longer-term effect was a massive shake-out in the industry, leaving a few internationally competitive 'supercarriers' and higher entry barriers. The same effect is likely in the European airline industry as the EC 'open skies' directives agreed in 1991 begin to be implemented.

The two policies exist in relation to each other. Fierce international competition and the changed economic structures of many industries lead to the devastation of many firms or indeed entire sectors in their home markets (Hamel and Prahalad, 1985), resulting in political pressure for protection. Under this continuing cycle of events, global companies have to operate as what Ohmae (1985, 1989) calls 'true insiders', honorary citizens perceived as direct investors in each 'home' market in which they operate.

The service industries are relatively new to the influences of deregulation and protection (the unique regulatory structure of the international airline industry being one exception). They have been less generally visible and their effect on jobs and the balance of trade less well understood publicly than manufacturing industry. By and large they have also been growth industries, where jobs were being created rather than lost and where no dependent, historically long-established constituency of communities existed (as in shipbuilding, textiles, steel or mining). There has consequently been little political volatility in the shake-out of any significant group of service workers, as in the financial services sector in the late 1980s. In addition, jobs that have been lost in significant numbers in services (eg in banking, retailing, medical support services) have been largely (though not always, eg bank middle management, security analysts) low level, female and often part time (Rajan, 1987). This is also now becoming increasingly true of jobs likely to be created in many service industries in the 1990s, where full-time service jobs lost in the recession of the early 1990s are frequently being replaced by part-time posts, eg in retailing.

The Effect of Information Technology

The speed and scope of technological innovation have affected service industries at least as much as manufacturing. Information technology (IT) has been a driving force for international expansion in services. IT increases a company's ability to coordinate its activities nationally and internationally. It can provide powerful opportunities to boost service performance. IT has also increased capital requirements, thus raising entry barriers. Efficiency and the ablity to compete in service companies now require high levels of capital investment in systems that produce reliable, rapid and low unit cost results (Levitt, 1986). In the US retail sector, for example, Lusch (1987) states that any new entrant 'would need state-of-the-art retail technology, including a high-impact merchandising information system'. Without electronic support systems it is now impossible to compete effectively in many markets, such as multiple retailing, travel and financial services. Large-scale network effects are very important in service industries, more so than in manufacturing, since additional links increase the attractiveness of the service to the consumer (eg in how many places can I use my credit card?)

Table 2.1 illustrates the relationship between information systems and the changes that have occurred in competitive strategy in service businesses.

Table 2.1 Systems technology — changing the nature of the offering

American Express	Response times
	New products
	Distribution channels
	Add-on services
Benetton	Responsive merchandising
	Inventory elimination
	Customised production
	Credit management
British Airways	Yield management
	Exclusion effect
	Vertical integration

As technology changes, so do the possibilities for service delivery and consumer expectations with regard to that service, as in the seat reservation systems now appearing in UK cinemas or the more extensive service offered to a multinational client by a global bank such as Nomura or Citibank, as compared to what a single-country operator could offer. 'The combination of cost-reduction and increasing capability of IT results in a broader range of applications' (FAST, 1986) so that IT systems can be the basis of service add-ons which differentiate the company and its offerings, as well as locking the customer in to further purchases. For example, American Express uses its worldwide systems network and database to offer customers holiday and business travel arrangement services or privileged theatre bookings. It is also able to set and monitor high service standards such as fast response times for any international card inquiry from any service outlet.

Benetton was one of the earliest retailers to realise the benefit of using electronic point of sale (EPOS) systems. Benetton used EPOS both to eliminate the cost of holding inventory and replace it by real sales information and to be able to use the information on sales for decisions about current production. IT can help develop switching costs that tie in suppliers and customers and shut out competitors, blocking their access to the market. Airline reservation systems which lead to better ticket sales for the airlines which own the system, or EPOS systems linking retailer and manufacturer, are obvious examples of what FAST (1986) refers to as the 'exclusionary effect'. IT not only changes cost structures and service offerings, but markets also become more 'transparent' (Rada, 1987) as access to information and databases grows.

Technological change can change the economics of an industry. British Airways (BA) is already an international megacarrier and it is looking for continuous improvement in its utilisation of high-technology capacity-planning .software, together with vertically integrated reservation and distribution systems which connect the airline to worldwide hotel chains, car hire firms, theatre ticket agencies, etc. These moves are aimed at better exploiting its global service distribution network. BA has joined with United Airways, KLM and Swissair in the 'Galileo' project, a worldwide reservation and distribution system (rival to the 'Amadeus' consortium, which has itself recently linked up with its erstwhile rival 'Sabre' owned by American Airlines). Such systems, when in place in travel agents or airline outlets (offices, airports), ensure the airline owning the system a profit, even if the customer buys a ticket on another airline, since a booking/usage fee is charged for each transaction.

Service Industry Restructuring: From Fragmentation to Concentration

Service industries have traditionally been defined as 'fragmented' industries (Porter, 1980). By this is meant an environment in which many firms compete, but which lack clear market leaders with significant market share. It is this absence of market leaders with power to shape the industry which Porter stresses as being the most important competitive feature of fragmented industries. Financial, health, leisure and recreation services, retailing, distribution and 'creative' businesses were considered to conform to the fragmentation stereotype. The reason for this is that these industries possessed many of the characteristics by which fragmented industries are defined, including:

- numerous small firms providing services on a localised basis;
- high personal service content;
- high labour content;
- hard to routinise;
- the service must be delivered at the point of sale to the customer (at the customer's location or the customer must come to the service);
- low entry barriers;
- low economies of scale;
- close local control.

While most or all of these characteristics applied to service industries in the past, and some such as personal service still do, to a very large extent consolidation and vertical integration (eg banks/estate agencies/insurance; airlines/hotel chains) have occurred as a result of fundamental changes in many of the key factors listed above.

Service industries have been undergoing a prolonged process of concentration and rationalisation for the last 20–30 years, although the pace has certainly hotted up over the last 5–10 years, as witnessed by the emergence of very large firms in insurance, banking, distribution, communication, consultancy and business services, fast food, leisure companies and retailing. Even very traditional professional services such as law, accountancy and surveying already contain international firms of great size (eg Clifford Chance, Arthur Andersen, Jones Lang Wootton respectively). They market a global brand of quality and service delivery. Consultancy firms such as McKinsey have been doing this for some time. Mergers and acquisitions have been commonplace and even increasing across all these groups (the accountancy 'Big 8' became the 'Big 6' during 1989–90), but they have not noticeably experienced difficulty in re-creating their image and service delivery standards. Service concepts can and do 'travel'.

To illustrate this view some data from the retail sector may be helpful, since it was for many years the received wisdom that retail concepts were highly market specific and did not travel. Tables 2.2 and 2.3 give some indication of the range of global coverage in international retailing. .

Table 2.2 Indicative Triad coverage — international retailers

Retailer	Trading bloc presence		
	N America	Europe	Asia Pacific
Bally (Germany)	*	*	*
Benetton (Italy)	*	*	*
Body Shop (UK)	*	*	*
C&A (Netherlands)	*	*	*
Carrefour (France)	*	*	
Delhaize (Belgium)	*	*	
IKEA (Sweden)	*	*	*
Marks & Spencer (UK)	*	*	*
Toys 'R' Us (US)	*	*	*
Tengelmann (Germany)	*	*	
Tandy Corp (US)	*	*	
McDonald's (US)	*	*	*
Mitsukoshi (Japan)	*	*	*
Takashimaya (Japan)	*	*	*

Source: Segal-Horn and Davison, 1992.

Despite such well publicised early failures as Marks & Spencer's poor entry into the Canadian and French markets, the international spread of retailing is now proceeding rapidly. Retail concepts can be exported, although competition becomes even fiercer when international firms enter well defended domestic markets. Often it transforms the style of competition in that domestic market, as when Toys 'R' Us entered the UK children's market and triggered a major competitive response resulting in the launch by Boots of their 'Childrens World' concept.

Table 2.3 Indicative Triad coverage – speciality retailers

Retailer	Trading bloc presence		
	N America	Europe	Asia Pacific
Dunhill (UK)	*	*	*
Gucci (Italy)	*	*	*
Joseph (UK)	*	*	*
Louis Vuitton (France)	*	*	*
Mappin & Webb (UK)	*	*	*
Ralph Lauren (US)	*	*	*
Wedgwood (Ireland)	*	*	*

Source: Segal-Horn and Davison, 1992.

A final point to be made in refuting the 'fragmented' stereotype of the service industries concerns the positive benefits that can be derived by service companies operating internationally. The company may be able to serve its clients better; indeed it may be the customer who internationalises first, with the service company following to keep important clients. This was the main trigger factor for much of the concentration in the advertising industry worldwide. Firms such as Saatchi & Saatchi or Interpublic needed to build international networks of agencies to service international clients. It is interesting to note that, alongside the problems of Saatchi & Saatchi and also of WPP in servicing the debt created by their acquisition programmes, there was a significant increase in global advertising handled by international agencies. From 1976–87 the proportion of world advertising handled by international agencies grew from under 13 per cent to 22 per cent (Sheppards and Chase, 1987). Perhaps more important still is that the 13 per cent in 1976 was handled by 12 agencies, whereas the 22 per cent was shared by 7 agencies, showing far greater concentration despite the problems of combining size, creativity and client management.

By expanding internationally, the image of the company may be enhanced, not only in the eyes of its customers but also in the eyes of its staff and potential staff it might wish to attract and retain, a factor of exceptional importance in professional service firms and 'creative' businesses where the staff are the service. This is an important element in the service industry's 'quality wheel' (Heskett, 1986), with high-level employee motivation contributing to high-level customer satisfaction. Efforts to reproduce the success formula in other international markets can sometimes reveal the basic character of the service concept more clearly, thus contributing to streamlining the service management system in the home market as well.

Across all sectors reviewed, the current structure of service industries no longer fits the pattern of 'fragmented' industries. They have in fact become significantly concentrated and capital intensive with increased barriers to entry.

Global Competition in Service Industries

Globalisation as a concept has been developed with a focus on manufacturing. Most of the current literature on global strategies is based on evidence from the manufacturing sector, favourites being cars, motorcycles, construction and agricultural machinery, watches, textiles and consumer electronics (Altshuler *et al*, 1984; Hamel and Prahalad, 1985; Kotler *et al*, 1985; Doz, 1986; Cvar, 1986). The best documented global market development for a service industry is that for financial services. Attention has been given to deregulation and the effect of the 24-hour financial market-place on international banking and financial services (Arthur Andersen, 1985; Channon, 1986; Hamilton, 1986; Sobel, 1987; Walter, 1988). Yet little real analysis has occurred of the routes to creating global strategic capability or the common denominators in such capability which are emerging more generally for service industries.

Service industries are those whose output is not a physical good or product and where added value is derived from such factors as concept, image, quality of service delivery, reliability, convenience and flexibility. This underpins an essential difference in the significance of globalisation in services as opposed to manufacturing. For manufacturing industries the sources of global advantage come mainly from comparative advantage, eg in factor costs; economies of scale in production, marketing, distribution, logistics and purchasing; mobility of production; or any combination thereof (Porter, 1980). This means that manufacturing is concerned with the most effective ways of moving the product to the market. In service industries, globalisation means that a mobile customer base (often literally mobile, eg the tourist, the shopper, the business traveller) experiences an identical product wherever it goes at each access point or transaction. Service delivery is about controlling the quality of the offering at the point of sale to the customer. In service industries the customer can move to the product. It is for this reason that American Express labels its core charge card (and traveller's cheques and travel shop) business: 'Travel Related Services' (TRS). The TRS market is the international traveller for whom the TRS core concept — the 'global servicing concept' — has been developed. As the example on p54 shows, the aim is to provide a standard quality service to the targeted customer, wherever that service is taken up (American Express, 1983/85/86/88/89/91).

This approach is a common one in service industries. It is highly visible in the airline industry whose travel offices, lounges and staff uniforms are identical worldwide. This is not only to communicate more clearly with the market but, as the British Airways example on p55 stresses, to overcome internal power and culture blockages among worldwide staff and offices, which have a crucial role in worldwide consistency of service delivery. Similarly the international hotel chains (Hilton, Sheraton, Intercontinental) undertake to make the traveller's experience of Tokyo, London, Milan or Sydney as similar as possible.

In some very real ways, services do travel and can be re-created globally more easily than products, since what is being re-created is the concept and the quality of its delivery. One aspect from which service industries benefit is what van

---

American Express

Rationale behind globalisation

- Deregulation: the opening up of international markets to international competition.
- Interactive IT systems networks providing 24-hour global trading (collapse of geographical time-zone, regulatory and market boundaries).
- Creation of financial conglomerates through merger and acquisition.
- Technology-generated new products.
- International presence crucial to future growth.
- Internationalisation of institutional investment portfolios.
- Scale of investment (eg in systems and key staff) and capital base required to compete effectively favours large players.
- Global coverage required to remain competitive and retain clients and staff.
- Industry concentration across existing boundaries.

The strategy

- World leader in integrated financial and travel-related services.

Putting the strategy into operation

- Focus on customer needs.
- Strong, quality brand names.
- Multiple distribution channels.
- A family of companies (cross-selling).
- Careful selection of clear, profitable target markets ('only the most prestigious but also the most valuable' (Amex 1986 annual report)).
- Enter market segments with market share leadership potential.
- Uniform level of customer service at outlets.
- Uniform quality at outlets.
- Global marketing must be backed up by global service delivery and service levels.
- Ability to introduce products quickly.
- Sophisticated global marketing and global systems network.

Source: L'enterprise Logistique

Mesdag (1987) calls 'the age symptom', of usage and acculturation. Some products are associated with long-established national usage patterns, which make them less amenable to international adaptation. However, offerings related to newer, and therefore less firmly established, usage patterns, have more global potential. It can be argued that for this reason services generally need fewer adaptations for global markets than do manufactured products, particularly since fewer predetermined assumptions exist with regard to usage of advertising, consultancy, credit

---

British Airways

Rationale behind globalisation

- Deregulation: unique regulatory industry structure under attack.
- Advances in IT systems and communication networks.
- Need for consistent global competitive position.
- Scale of investment (eg in planes, landing slots, IT) required to compete favours large players.
- Global route structure required to remain competitive.
- Industry concentration: international 'megacarriers'.

The strategy

- A global distributor: linking routes, distribution systems, channels and outlets to provide a worldwide service distribution network.

Putting the strategy into operation

- Product upgrading.
- Global advertising.
- Consistent corporate identity.
- Service training focus on customer needs.
- Continuous visible commitment to customer service.
- Control of routes and transit or access hubs.
- Forward vertical integration via CRS (Computer Reservation System) in retail outlets.

---

card facilities or automated teller machines.

Managing domestic markets independently becomes more difficult as firms find ways of gaining advantage from working globally and forcing others to do the same, or risk being relegated to small niches in local markets which may themselves become indefensible.

CHANGING THE APPROACH TO THE CUSTOMER

Service industries have some important characteristics which distinguish them from manufacturing industries. Among the most widely recognised are the 'intangibility' of the service offering and the simultaneous production and consumption of the service (Sasser *et al*, 1978). The nature of a service offering may therefore best be understood as an 'experience' or 'outcome'. The successful management of a service business thus becomes the management of the quality of the experience for the customer or client. It is this quality of customer experience, often known as 'the moment of truth', by which service quality is measured (Normann, 1984; Carlzon, 1987). This would be equally true of a firm of accountants as for a restaurant. Thus for service industries, control of the offering at the transaction point with the customer or client is critical. When the service network is extended globally, the management of outcomes for the customer faces obvious quality control problems in accurately reproducing the service concept in different cultural, political and economic environments and ensuring consistency in the quality of the offering at all transaction points.

Most large service firms have met these requirements for consistency through standardising their offering. This has in turn meant that service businesses have grown in particular sorts of ways. Carman and Langeard (1980) argue that profitable growth strategies for service firms are based on 'multisite development' which exploits the 'duplication of a well-conceived system'. Duplication is carried out by means of standardisation. Standardisation requires clarity in the core service concept.

In strategic terms, core concepts can either be about playing the same game better than your competitors, or about changing the rules to challenge the conventional wisdom about product and market directly. A challenging core concept should focus on identifying the objective function of the offering for the customer, rather than on existing approaches to satisfying customer needs. Given the structural, market and technological changes in service industries described above, there exists an opportunity for challenging the conventional wisdom in many service sectors.

Table 2.4 The core concept – changing the approach to the customer

	Global core concept	Industry standard
American Express	Integrated travel related services	Individual product offerings
Benetton	One 'united' product	Fashion ranges
British Airways	Global distributor	World's best airline

Table 2.4 illustrates the change in approach made by Benetton in clothing, American Express in financial services and British Airways in travel. Benetton targeted young leisurewear and developed a style of offering based on image and design. This image has been reinforced consistently over 30 years in their retail outlets and advertising campaigns. It has enabled them to achieve low-cost manufacturing and distribution efficiencies combined with high margins relative to the sector. American Express was a pioneer in understanding the connection between travel services and financial services. The largest part of Amex's growth has come from developing financial products, like the traveller's cheque and the charge card, which serve both sets of needs for a specific target market segment — the business traveller. British Airways has exploited its route network, systems network and software, distribution outlets and customer databases to provide integrated worldwide travel services, including as many added-value items such as insurance, hotel reservations or car hire as the customer requires.

In strategic terms, these redefinitions of the business by each of the firms discussed, have amounted to changing the rules of the game by which firms compete in their industry. In developing and clarifying their international strategies, these firms have pioneered new ways of thinking about how their customers may actually use the service, and have thereby redrawn the boundaries of their industry.

Transfer of the Service Offering

In their analysis of growth strategies for service firms, Carman and Langeard (1980) conclude that, for a service firm, international market expansion represented high risk. The characteristic of simultaneous production and consumption means that services have to be reproduced directly for the customer and immediate on-site quality control is expected, whether for a fast food outlet, a management consultancy or an advertising agency. Learning has to take place at the same time as service delivery, with acceptable quality achieved from day one. The need to maintain the quality level of a new service in international market expansion therefore carries a high risk.

However, the authors also argue that geographic market expansion is more appropriate for service businesses than market expansion based on new socio-demographic segments. This is because services have to be conceptualised for a specific market segment, and cannot be marketed to new consumer segments without disrupting the original service interaction and service delivery. There-fore, while accepting the assessment that international expansion does pose more risk for service businesses than for manufacturing businesses, globalisation of services based on the identification of common international market segments represents an opportunity for continued geographic market expansion of the existing core service to the *existing* consumer segment across national bound-aries. As such, it is a lower-risk approach to international expansion for a service firm.

SOURCES OF ADVANTAGE IN INTERNATIONAL SERVICE INDUSTRIES

Sources of competitive advantage within service industries are changing. One of the most helpful ways of exploring the potential sources of advantage from increased international concentration in service industries is outlined in Table 2.5, using the concept of economies of scope. This concept is used to explain economies arising from integration, ie the simultaneous supply of inputs common to a number of outputs. In other words, economies can be derived from the range of '... business activities engaged in by the modern business enterprise' (Teece, 1980). Resources acquired or developed for one purpose may be utilised for additional purposes at no extra cost.

Table 2.5 Scope economies available to service industries in global product and market diversification

| | **Sources of scope economies** | |
	Product diversification	**Market diversification**
Shared physical assets	Flexibility to produce multiple service offerings	Global brand name
Shared external relations	Using common distribution channels for multiple services	Service multinational customers worldwide
Shared learning	Sharing software development or expert teams	Pooling knowledge developed in different markets

Source: Author's adaption of Ghoshal, 1987.

Ghoshal (1987) argues that a diversified firm should be able to benefit from sharing costs across products and markets by joint use of different kinds of assets. For example, global oligopolies are developing in which successful firms are able to achieve economies of scope in international information systems and product policy throughout the regional 'Triad' trading blocs. The pursuit of economies of scope is described by Ghoshal as 'a search for internal consistencies within the firm and across its different activities'. This reinforces the necessity for clarity in the core concept and avoidance of a multiplicity of unrelated core service offerings. The costs of forcing 'internal consistency' onto businesses which are not naturally related can be too high in terms of, for example, inflexibility, customer and staff dissatisfaction, or managerial resource.

Table 2.5 suggests some sources of economies of scope available to international service businesses. Many of these are IT related. This should not be altogether surprising, since IT has played such a significant role in transforming service industries from fragmentation to concentration. Shared physical assets as a source of economies of scope for services should include IT and brand names. IT can simultaneously achieve a high degree of segmentation of activities and lower costs, as hardware and software development are allocated over a broader base of applications, or as entirely new services utilise established networks for little additional cost (FAST, 1986; Rada, 1987). For Benetton, IT is the lifeline by which inventory has been replaced by information for merchandising, supply and distribution. For successful retail chains IT is central to fast response times, cost reduction, inventory control, distribution and supply networks, monitoring of sales and consumer demand, improved customer service and tighter margin management.

IT has created opportunities for economies of scope by breaking down many of the traditional boundaries in the service industries, for example between hotels, theatres and car hire companies or between traveller's cheques and insurance services or holiday bookings. American Express has developed differentiated travel services for corporate customers through the use of IT. Services include arranging travel and monitoring individual expenses. Computers search for the lowest airplane fares, track travel expenses for each cardholder and issue monthly statements. Both British Airways and American Express use IT to set standards of service levels and then monitor them worldwide.

Brand names are a powerful shared asset which service companies have underutilised. Global companies can capitalise on their brand franchise by rapidly expanding across product categories. The American Express 'blue box' logo gives brand acceptability to financial planning programmes, travel agencies, travel management services, banking and credit facilities, all derived from the global brand dominance of its charge card and traveller's cheques.

Ghoshal (1987) defines shared external relations as relations with suppliers, distributors, customers, governments or other institutions. Distribution channels in service industries are used increasingly intensively. Outlets, whether travel shops or banks, are multipurpose. Airports offer retail and financial services as well as travel. Retail stores and sites offer financial and leisure provision as well as merchandise.

Many multinational companies (eg Fiat, Philips, Shell, BA) have consolidated their worldwide advertising into one agency for greater consistency and ease of transfer of ideas and information among country offices and headquarters. Single agencies with global networks provide more centralised control over external relations with customers, suppliers, government agencies, etc. British Airways' 'Supercare' advertising campaign made imaginative use of the theme of staff initiative. Taken together with the revamped corporate logo, uniforms and design, clear signals about service standards were being given to customers, suppliers and staff worldwide.

Shared learning has become extremely important as service industries have become more concentrated and more competitive. Pooled knowledge can cover such diverse assets as software development, staff expertise or scarce ideas for new offerings. BA has developed software to monitor passenger profiles per flight, per route, and across fare ranges to manage load factors (passengers per aircraft) for maximum yield. Monitoring sales gives flexibility in seat transfer between fare classes, just as systems for fuelling, servicing, scheduling, crew usage, route design and so on increase resource capacity utilisation. All the systems which bring productivity gains also enable improvements to be made in the services available to customers, either in quality or range or both, across BA's entire route network. A completely different example of shared learning is provided by the creation of flexible professional teams in professional service firms, able to draw on functional expertise combined with a variety of special skills and project experience. This development is in the early stages in the major accounting and consulting firms, despite the conservative effect of partnership structures on flexibility. It is largely driven by greater sophistication of client needs and the high cost and scarcity of large teams of specialised professionals.

CONCLUSION: SERVICE INDUSTRIES AND GLOBAL COMPETITION

The main issues driving the spread of global competition in the service industries may be summarised as:

- the emergence of global market segments for global products and services;
- political and economic policies (such as deregulation) which intensify international competition, for both aggressive and defensive reasons;
- the service industries are information intensive and therefore major elements of the offering are transferable across market boundaries;
- service industries have become significantly concentrated and capital intensive with increased barriers to entry;
- the potential for economies of scope in service industries has transformed the cost structure for some service firms;
- very large firms have emerged in the service industries competing across both national and traditional industry boundaries.

As a result of these changes, service industries are going through a period of rapid evolution which is changing the nature of competition between service firms. This chapter has considered changes in the structure and environment of service industries, which have created opportunities for globalisation strategies to be adopted more widely by service companies. Some service companies have already leveraged existing strengths to establish identifiable worldwide market presence. It is argued here that this trend will be accelerated by the combined impact on service industries of global market segmentation, reductions in structural barriers to international trade through deregulation, growing concentration of service industries and the far-reaching effect of IT on every aspect of service businesses.

Economies of scale and scope are now available in service businesses. New types of competition in services have emerged which require high resource levels. Opportunities for building world market share in services threaten to erode the position of currently strong domestic competitors. Historically, service industries have been strong in Western economies. They are significant in terms of output, wealth and jobs. Many of them still offer considerable growth potential. However, increasingly, as earlier in manufacturing, service companies are facing fierce competition from international new entrants in their domestic markets. Significant changes have already occurred in banking and financial services, airlines, hotel chains and retail stores. Large European, North American and Japanese firms now often find themselves in direct competition both when attacking new markets and in defending their own domestic and regional markets.

Structural changes in an industry necessitate strategic change by the firms in that industry. If existing brand strengths, distribution networks and service expertise are not utilised as platforms for building world market share when such opportunity arises, the result may be lost market opportunities abroad and a gradual erosion of domestic markets to new international competition.

References

Albrecht, K and Zemke, R (1985) *Service America!*, Dow Jones-Irwin, Homewood, Illinois.

American Express Annual Reports, 1983, 1985, 1986, 1988, 1989, 1991.

Altshuler, A et al (1984) *The Future of the Automobile*, George, Allen & Unwin, London.

Arthur Andersen & Co (1985) *The Decade of Change: Banking in Europe — The Next 10 Years*, London.

Bartlett, C A and Ghoshal, S (1986) 'Tap your subsidiaries for global reach', *Harvard Business Review*, November–December.

Bartlett, C A and Ghoshal, S (1987) 'Managing across borders', *Sloan Management Review*, Summer/Fall.

Bartlett, C A and Ghoshal, S (1989) *Managing Across Borders*, Hutchinson, London.

Carlzon, J (1987) *Moments of Truth*, Ballinger Publishing Co, Cambridge, Mass.

Carman, J and Langeard, E (1980) 'Growth strategies for service firms', *Strategic Management Journal*, Vol 1, pp 7–22.

Channon, D F (1986) *Bank Strategic Management and Marketing*, Wiley, Chichester.

Cvar, M R (1986) 'Case studies in global competition: patterns of success and failure' in Porter, M (ed) *Competition in Global Industries*, Harvard Business School Press, Boston, Mass.

Daniels, P (1985), *Service Industries — A Geographical Appraisal*, Methuen, London.

Douglas, S and Wind, Y (1987) 'The myth of globalisation', *Columbia Journal of World Business*, Vol XXII, No 4, Winter.

Doz, Y (1986) *Strategic Management in Multinational Companies*, Pergamon Press, Oxford.

Enderwick, P (1989) *Multinational Service Firms*, Routledge, London.

Forecasting and Assessment in Science and Technology (1986), 'Structural impacts of telematics on automobile, textile and clothing industries', European Commission FAST Occasional Paper No 10, July.

Franko, L (1989) 'Global corporate competition: who's winning, who's losing, and the R&D factor as one reason why', *Strategic Management Journal*, Vol 10, pp 449–474.

Ghoshal, S (1987) 'Global strategy: an organising framework', *Strategic Management Journal*, Vol 8, No 5.

Hamel, G and Prahalad, C K (1984) 'Creating global strategic capability', Discussion paper, London Business School.

Hamel, G and Prahalad, C K (1985) 'Do you really have a global strategy?', *Harvard Business Review*, July–August.

Hamel, G and Prahalad, C K (1989) 'Strategic intent', *Harvard Business Review*, May–June.

Hamilton, A (1986) *The Financial Revolution*, Viking/Penguin, Harmondsworth.

Harrigan, K (1984) 'Joint ventures and global strategies', *Columbia Journal of World Business*, Summer.

Heskett, J L (1986) *Managing in the Service Economy*, Harvard Business School Press, Boston, Mass.

Heskett, J L, Sasser, W E and Hart, C W L (1990) *Service Breakthroughs*, The Free Press, New York.

Hindley, B, Kierzkowski, M, Norman, V D, Strandenes, S P, Sapir, A and Waelbroeck, J (1987) 'International trade in services: comments' in Giarini, O (ed) *The Emerging Service Economy*, Pergamon Press, Oxford.

Jain, S (1989) 'Standardisation of international marketing strategy: some research hypotheses', *Journal of Marketing*, Vol 53, January.

Kotler, P (1985) 'Global standardisation — courting danger', Panel Discussion, 23 American Marketing Association Conference, Washington, DC.

Kotler, P, Fahey, L and Jatusripitak, S (1985) *The New Competition*, Prentice Hall International, Englewood Cliffs, NJ.

Levitt, T (1983) 'The globalisation of markets', *Harvard Business Review*, May–June.

Levitt, T (1986) *The Marketing Imagination*, The Free Press, New York.

Link, G (1988) 'Global advertising: an update', *The Journal of Consumer Marketing*, Vol 5, No 2, Spring.

Lusch, R (1987) 'A commentary on the US retail environment' in Johnson, G (ed) *Business Strategy and Retailing*, Wiley, Chichester.

Nelson, E (1989) 'Marketing in 1992 and beyond', *Royal Society of Arts Journal*, April.

Normann, R (1984) *Service Management: Strategy and Leadership in Service Businesses*, Wiley, Chichester.

Ohmae, K (1985) *Triad Power — The Coming Shape of Global Competition*, The Free Press, New York.

Ohmae, K (1989) 'Managing in a borderless world', *Harvard Business Review*, May–June.

Porter, M (1980) *Competitive Strategy*, Free Press, New York.

Porter, M (1985) *Competitive Advantage*, The Free Press, New York.

Porter, M (1986) *Competition in Global Industries*, Harvard Business School Press, Boston, Mass.

Porter, M (1990) *The Competitive Advantage of Nations*, Macmillan, London.

Prahalad, C K and Doz, Y (1987) *The Multinational Mission*, The Free Press, New York.

Quelch, J A and Hoff, E J (1986) 'Customising global marketing', *Harvard Business Review*, May–June.

Rada, J F (1987) 'Information technology and services' in Giarini, O (ed) *The Emerging Service Economy*, Pergamon Press, Oxford.

Rajan, A (1987) *Services — The Second Industrial Revolution?*, Butterworths, London.

Riddle, D I (1986) *Service-Led Growth: The Role of the Service Sector in World Development*, Praeger, New York.

Sasser, W E, Wycoff, D D and Olsen, M (1978) *The Management of Service Operations*, Allyn & Bacon, London.

Segal-Horn, S and Davison, H (1992) 'Global markets, the global consumer and international retailing', *Journal of Global Marketing*, Vol 5, No 3.

Sheppards & Chase (1987), *Advertising Agencies*, September.

Sheth, J (1983) 'Marketing megatrends', *Journal of Consumer Marketing*, No 1, Summer.

Sobel, A (1987) *Creating and Sustaining Competitive Advantage in the Global Securities Market*, The MAC Group (UK) Ltd, London.

Sorensen, R and Weichmann, U. (1975) 'How multinationals view marketing standardisation', *Harvard Business Review*, May–June.

Stopford, J M and Turner, L (1985) *Britain and the Multinationals*, John Wiley/IRM, Chichester.

Takeuchi, H and Porter, M (1986) 'Three roles of international marketing in global strategy' in Porter, M (ed) *Competition in Global Industries*, Harvard Business School Press, Boston, Mass.

Teece, D (1980) 'Economies of scope and the scope of the enterprise', *Journal of Economic Behaviour and Organisation*, Vol 1, No 3.

Telesis/P S I (1986) *Competing for Prosperity*, Policy Studies Institute, London.

Thorelli, H and Becker, H (1980) 'The information seekers: multinational strategy target', *California Management Review*, Vol XXIII, No 1, Fall.

Tucker, K and Sundberg, M (1988) *International Trade in Services*, Routledge, London.

van Mesdag, M (1987) 'Winging it in foreign markets', *Harvard Business Review*, January–February.

Walter, I (1988) *Global Competition in Financial Services*, Ballinger, Cambridge, Mass.

Winram, S C (1987) 'The opportunity for world brands' in Murphy, J M (ed) *Branding: A Key Marketing Tool*, Macmillan, London.

Yip, G (1989) 'Global strategy . . . in a world of nations?', *Sloan Management Review*, Fall.

Yip, G (1992) *Total Global Strategy*, Prentice Hall, Englewood Cliffs, NJ.

3

THE CHALLENGES OF GLOBALISATION IN THE SERVICE INDUSTRY

Hervé Mathe and Cynthia Perras

OUTLINE

In the same way that companies the world over recognise and indeed are participants in the accelerating pace of investment in services, numerous firms find themselves grappling with fundamental questions about whether, and how, to offer their services globally. Companies need to address certain basic issues to help assess international competition in their sector, to clarify their motivations and identify appropriate strategies for globalisation. This process further entails making organisational adjustments, determining whether a service is best standardised across all markets or differentiated, and choosing the best mix of services.

This chapter offers frameworks to guide the globalisation process, as well as concrete examples of the various options firms have chosen. It is based on a research project on the globalisation of the service sector (see Table 3.1). The research indicates that global strategy design must be formulated around clearly defined motives and incentives, as well a thorough identification of competitive advantages and evaluation of disadvantages and risks.

In deciding whether to differentiate or standardise a service, and in determining the appropriate service mix, it is important to discern if your service may benefit from retaining its foreign and hence exotic appeal and can therefore be standardised around the world; or whether it must be adapted to local tastes or customs. These decisions can affect both core and peripheral services. Furthermore, even the definition of 'quality' can differ from one location to another.

The level of existing competition influences the entry strategies and learning approaches of a service provider in new markets and will determine which option — organic, internal growth; acquisition; alliance, or joint ventures — makes the most sense given both the environment and the organisation. Based on its particular circumstances, a firm may best decide to learn by following existing customers, while in other cases buying local players or forming alliances will prove most prudent.

Table 3.1 1990–1993 research project on the globalisation of the service sector – sample of the companies studied

---

Insurance and financial services industries

- AGF
- Allianz
- AXA
- BNP
- Generali
- Matuschka
- PFA
- Société Générale
- State Street Boston
- UAP
- Victoire
- Visa International
- Winterthur

Transport, airline companies, express carriers

- Air France
- British Airways
- Allianz
- Calberson
- CGM
- Chep
- Chronopost
- DHL
- EMS
- Federal Express
- PHH
- Royal Mail Express
- Ryder
- Swissair
- TNT
- UPS

Hospitality, restaurant chains and vacation centres

- Accor
- Club Med
- Dunkin' Donuts
- Eurodisney
- Marriot
- McDonald's
- Meridien
- Sodexho

Professional services and consulting

- Arthur D Little
- Cap Gemini Sogeti
- CompuServe
- MAC Group
- McKinsey
- Ove Arup
- Publicis
- Russell Reynolds

Organisationally, successful global expansion of a service firm must be driven by a special corporate spirit. Finding the most appropriate dynamic for network building, allocating decision-making power and profit responsibility as best fits the firm's situation, and defining the best integrative devices to spread the corporate culture appear to be key organisational aspects of globalising services.

Finally, as a service moves into a mature phase, sustaining it depends increasingly on developing first-class information and reporting systems, balancing flexibility through planning and organisational systems, and keeping personnel on board, loyal, and motivated. Ever-improving information and communication technologies offer service firms this possibility throughout the service lifecycle and can be particularly helpful in managing the maturity phase.

INTRODUCTION

Between 1986 and 1990 in the US, average annual foreign investment in service businesses totalled $26 billion compared with the $28 billion going into manufacturing. In 1992, services accounted for 20 per cent of total world trade and, notably, 30 per cent of US exports. With services currently the fastest growing component of international trade, it seems safe to say that the benign period during which service companies were relatively sheltered locally from foreign competition is most definitely over, even in industries such as utilities or telecommunications which used to be, but no longer are, protected by regulations and monopoly status.

Despite this trend in services, or more likely because of its rapid acceleration, numerous service companies attempting to design their global strategy still have difficulty addressing certain basic issues, such as:

- How to understand the forces affecting international competition in a given service sector.
- How to define the appropriate learning processes and market entry dynamics when internationalizing a service whose value relies heavily on a global network.
- How to decide between high international standardisation and high local differentiation in the mix of basic services delivered to geographically different markets.
- How to formulate an effective global approach to service quality that will enhance employees' motivation.

Organisational issues are no more easily solved when service firms are struggling with their global development. Analysing the alternatives to internal, organic growth for international expansion, such as joint ventures, strategic alliances and mergers, requires a clear evaluation of the risks and opportunities associated with each option, which might differ substantially from one country to another. Rather than uniformly superimposing the domestic organisational structure that has presumably served it well, the globalising service company must link its organisational structure to its international strategy.

Faced with the promising but somewhat daunting task these issues raise in terms of becoming an international service provider, what preparation should a company undergo before it takes that step?

In general terms, a service company which wants to expand globally has to go through a five-step process including:

- a global strategy analysis and design, although service firms very often work on defining the international strategy after the fact, while they already operate in multiple foreign markets;

- a more or less flexible definition of the product lines, ie are the services provided transnational or local;
- a learning process: how to operate as a newcomer in this particular foreign market; how to coordinate service operations globally;
- an expansion process: how can reliable international networks and systems for service delivery be efficiently developed;
- a phase of managing the mature service operation: how to keep market share and the best human resources on board when products are mature.

Certain critical success factors correspond to each of these steps, as do potential traps.

MOTIVES AND INCENTIVES FOR PURSUING A GLOBAL STRATEGY

One of the prime motivations that explains why service companies are now working so hard to develop activities beyond their own borders is that they are being forced by competition to go global. In various service industries, from fast food restaurants to telecommunication operators, competition at home has made it harder for the traditional players to increase their domestic profits, whereas demand for their services abroad allows many to earn a higher profit margin. McDonald's, the world's largest restaurant chain, has seen its core US business, which still accounts for almost 60 per cent of profits, begin to wilt, while its international operations are thriving (*Business Week*, 21 Oct 1991). This more favourable international environment is illustrated by the French appetite for the Big Mac, which sells in France for nearly four times its US price despite a personal income differential that would suggest otherwise. In 1995, there will be as many McDonald's restaurants outside the US as within. Average profitability of a European operation is twice what it is in the US, and McDonald's, which runs 1500 restaurants domestically, has already opened more than 910 sites in Japan. In Switzerland, the company is experimenting with operating its first restaurant-cars in the railways managed by government-owned CFF (McDonald's, 1993). It took seven years to prepare the opening of the gigantic McDonald's in Beijing, China, while in Moscow, 40,000 people applied for a job in the Pouchkin Plaza restaurant. Figure 3.1 compares the company's domestic and international operations.

Bell Canada Enterprises recently acquired a 20 per cent share in Mercury, the second largest British operator in the telecommunications service business. Previously Bell Canada had taken an 80 per cent stake in East London Telecom and a 30 per cent share in Videotron Holding. Given that these two companies control about 60 per cent of the cable-based teledelivery system in London, it seems clear that Bell is investing jointly with Cable & Wireless, the main owner of Mercury, in order to take advantage of the growing market in telecom-televideo cable systems. As a matter of fact, strategic alliances are the most frequent type of response explored by telecom companies in their attempts to operate globally. However, it is worth noting that some of the most significant attempts at joint ventures did not work out, such as British Telecom's with Nippon Telegraph and

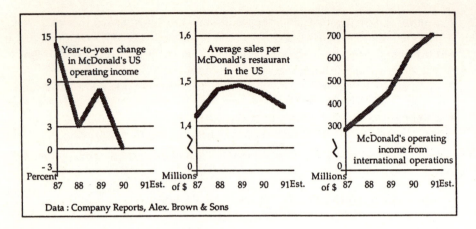

Source: *Business Week*, 21 Oct 1991.

Figure 3.1 Comparison between domestic and international operations at McDonald's

Telephone, or AT&T's with Olivetti. Because of the deregulation occurring in the industry in numerous countries, former local monopolies are now facing aggressive competition at home. At the same time, corporate customers operating branches or offices in different countries are now looking to their providers of telephone services to take into account their global needs. Such was the case with Sprint, which was the first to set up its own commercially available international private networks. As early as summer 1991, Unilever signed Sprint to manage its entire European data network, connecting offices in 18 different countries. As Bert Roberts, head of rival MCI, expressed quite clearly: '*International expansion is critical to our ability to continue to gain domestic market share*' (*The Economist*, 19 Oct 1991).

If the motivations seem clear, strategies for becoming global very often remain quite confused. In the insurance business, for instance, many companies chose what they saw as the most expedient path to international growth rather than focus on improving their profitability. Especially in Europe, most of the big players attempted to buy, at any price, operations outside their home base during the late 1980s. As a result, even Allianz, the German giant, has losses for 1992 — for the first time in its entire history. French companies have been especially active in this process of internationalisation. UAP spent more than $5 billion acquiring foreign companies since 1987, including half the amount for the buyout of Victoire-Colonia in Germany. Numerous economists and industry specialists question the relevance of such an astronomically high price. Other companies followed the same path, paying serious money for unhealthy operations abroad which now generate losses at the corporate level (*Les Echos*, 15 and 16 Jan 1993). Opting for the most risky move, AXA invested mostly in Equitable Life, a North American player. This time the value of the acquired company was calculated on the basis of 50 per cent of its net assets while, in Europe, the basis was 1.2, sometimes 1.5 times the net assets of the firms bought by UAP, AGF, or GAN.

On the other hand, the third largest Swiss insurance company, Winterthur enjoyed a very comfortable profit level in 1991 due to its operations abroad. With more than $4 billion of premiums in Europe and $1 billion in the US, the Swiss group should reach a total of $10 billion in premiums in 1992. In Europe its business grew 24.8 per cent in 1991, with exceptional performance in the UK (+67 per cent) and in Austria (+66 per cent). Winterthur has been running operations out of Switzerland, for Europe, as well as in the US for more than 20 years. When every other large European group was rushing to acquire anything available on the market recently, Winterthur adopted a much more prudent attitude, buying just a few healthy but often small and focused operations. Experience sometimes pays, at least in the near term. The future will show if expertise will be more decisive than size for the success of insurance companies. Figure 3.2 and Table 3.2 illustrate the situation in the insurance sector.

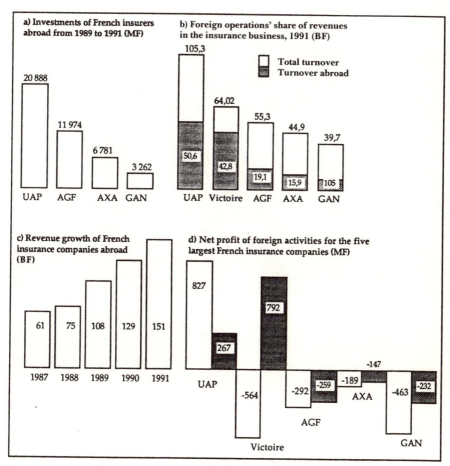

Source: FFSA and *Les Echos*, 15 and 16 Jan 1993.

Figure 3.2 International development in the insurance industry: the five largest French companies

Table 3.2 European activities of four national leaders in the insurance sector

Germany	Italy	France	Britain	Spain
Allianz (2) Biggest in Europe, began expanding actively in 1986. Ready to expand to Eastern Europe. Total price inc. ≅ 1600 (1).	2102 Bought 51.5% of RAS 1984–87, second largest insurance co. with network in Germany and France.	311 Unclear position with CNM. Good foothold with RAS.	1163 Bought 100% Cornhill 1986.	345 (1) Signed cooperation agreement with Banco Popular 1988. Bought 51% Ercos 1989 ($60m. pr.inc. 1989).
861 Even larger network in German-speaking Europe (Austrian-Hungarian ancestry).	**Generali** (3) Leader in home market, Europe's fastest growing. Ready to expand to Eastern Europe. Total price inc. ≅ 8000 (1).	1405 Bought 17% Compagnie du Midi 1988 (owns Equity & Law of B. Merged AXA-Midi, $6.9bn. pr.inc.1988).	637	245 (1)
134 Bought 34% Gpe Victoire 1989 (controls Colonia Group, $4 bn. pr.inc. 1989).	122 Bought Allsecure 1989 ($134 m.pr.inc. 1989).	**UAP** State-owned firm. Impressive operation in Belgium (Royale Belge). Operations in Ireland, Holland, Greece. Total pr.inc. ≅ 8500 (1).	n/a Bought 25% of Sun Life 1988 ($1.3 bn.pr.inc. 1988).	138 (1) To buy Gesa 1990 ($20.5 m.pr.inc. 1989).
	101 Joint venture with Benetton 1988, restructured with L'Abeille (Groupe Victoire) 1990.		**Prudential** (1) Operations in Ireland and Belgium. Big organization in the US. Moving slowly but surely and prudently on Continental Europe, total pr.inc. ≅ 8200 (1).	

(1) Premium income, 1988, in $ million.
(2) More than twice as big as its next largest domestic rival.
(3) Twice as big as its next largest domestic rival.

Source: based on *The Economist*, 24 Feb 1990.

THE 'ADAPTABLE' SERVICE-PRODUCT?

Internationalising a service company brings many issues to the fore. For instance, should a service become highly standardised or, on the contrary, is it necessary to accentuate its differentiation in various settings? Is the failure to establish a uniform quality standard worldwide an indication of: poor management or a good understanding of national cultural differences? Should each country or even groups of countries be assimilated into a profit centre, or is it possible to identify more appropriate units of measurement for economic performance?

If, in fact, a product can be differentiated in terms of the mix of basic service, level of quality and economic objective, one question remains: is there such a thing as a 'global service'? In fact, there are probably three categories of basic services for which the global perspective appears crucial. Table 3.3 shows the different possibilities.

Table 3.3 Services provided locally or transnationally by local or multinational providers

	Local service provider	**Multinational service provider**
Local service product	Local service provided locally for domestic market	Local service provided by multinationals in various countries
Transnational service product	Transnational service provided locally only	Transnational service provided internationally

Services have frequently been defined as economic activities that provide time, place and form utility while bringing about a change in or for the recipients of the service (Riddle, 1986). Following this approach, one can define the local service product as activities produced and consumed in a given place with no special relationship with international operations. It can be provided by a local service provider, such as a one-site family restaurant, or by a multinational service provider, such as insurance groups offering life insurance or home protection coverage in different countries through different firms operating under different brands and with almost no connection with one another. On the other hand, transnational service products provide value when mobilising an existing international network, such as international credit card systems or express mail. They can be provided by local players, such as a national post office or a local bank, but always by means of an alliance program like EMS for the mail, or Visa Group for the credit card system. Or they may be delivered by truly multinational service operators, such as DHL or TNT for the package express business, or American Express and others on the financial side.

(As companies globalise, the importance of attention to customers' needs remains paramount. Take, for instance, the competitive car rental industry. Avis found in the 1970s that if a customer living in the UK rented a car in Spain, the bill would be sent to his home requesting payment in pesetas to be sent back to Spain. At the time, very few Britons travelled to Spain and even fewer rented cars. Those that did were a minority who more or less coped with the hassle of foreign exchange and posting payments to foreign parts. However, as intra-European travel grew, Avis began to get more and more letters complaining about the awkward billing and payment procedures. The tide of customer opinion prompted Avis to change its billing procedures so that customers renting abroad could settle their bills at home, in their home currency and post their payments to a local address. *'This is just one example of a procedure which we radically reformed based on what our customers were saying through complaints,'* according to Alun Cathcart, Chairman and CEO of Avis.)

Operating in different regions of the world, a service company often discovers that the mix of services that must be designed in order to be successful, including sometimes the nature of core and peripheral products themselves, may significantly differ from one location to another. In fact, it can be true even in the case of 'transnational service provided internationally', although one might naturally believe that the mix of this type of service would be identical everywhere it is offered. If we look briefly at the expansion of the express delivery service in Europe, we find that the reason DHL has been so successful is not because it can mobilize more capital (Sparks and Mathe). When Federal Express and UPS, for instance, began to enter the European market, the first factor for them was the need for capital — lots of it. TNT, an Australian-based company, spent about $2 billion to acquire 72 aircraft. In the early 1980s, when FedEx began building a delivery system within Europe, they had no doubt it would lead to tremendous success, given the growth potential of the market. On 18 March 1992 FedEx announced the sale of its intra-European business to two of its rivals, after a $193 million net loss in the third quarter ending February 1992. The company had already decided to contract out its domestic service in Asia (*The Economist*, 21 Mar 1992). DHL, in contrast, saw its revenues increase at twice the industry rate in 1992, partially due to its successful operations in Europe. However, the mix of services they offer there differs from what they provide in the US. DHL offers more and more freight forwarding, inventory control, sophisticated billing and invoicing, start-up of delivered products and many other back-office functions (*Business Week*, 22 Feb 1993). In 1992, the non-transport logistics-related services provided by DHL accounted for one-third of its $2.8 million revenue, while the same activities represented one-tenth of FedEx revenues for that period. As a result, when Toyota Motor Corp needed to contract with a carrier to get parts from key Japanese suppliers to its plants in Burneston, England the speediest way possible in order to meet tough just-in-time delivery schedules, they turned to DHL International. Currently most of the players in this industry are putting together service packages which take into account local needs, but some of them have been more flexible than others, and faster in adapting their original, home-country designed mix of basic services.

Observation of such situations raises a new question, whether there are basic differences in approaches to selected services in Europe and North America, and Japan as well for that matter, reflecting tendencies:

- in Europe, towards 'service-mix' strategies and customised, comprehensive services surrounding customers, as opposed to:
- standardised, fragmented services in North America with greater responsibility placed on the consumer to assemble a complete service package.

If designing services so that the mix of components can differ from country to country stands as a crucial issue, quality issues might also be addressed from a similar perspective. In many European hotels of very high calibre the waiter, bell-boy, maid etc, are instructed to avoid talking to the guest. In fact, only head waiters will talk to a guest in the dining room, while service standards require other personnel on the floor to be extremely discreet, almost invisible. An American frequenting one of these top hotels would consider this service quality inferior and unsatisfactory because of a cultural expectation that 'good service' equals friendly, warm, hospitable people (Leven, 1983). Similarly, it is not unusual to hear a top executive of a French or German company complain because a flight attendant in first class on a given US airline called them by their first name. In Switzerland, it can take ten years of a common professional life before two managers, or professionals, at the same level of responsibility start to use each other's first name. Clearly, criteria and standards for service quality must be defined, in part, relative to different local expectations and sensitivities.

Some basic questions must be considered. For example, how do issues of cultural emphases on egalitarianism (as in Scandinavia), class system (as in Japan, England or France), meritocracy (as in North America), or multiple systems (as in Switzerland or Italy among others) influence the way successful quality service plans are designed and delivered? Indeed, to what extent might some services have an opportunity to be standardised internationally, because they are purchased with the expectation that they will reflect their cultural origins?

Questions of organisation also arise. Since economic situations and cost drivers also differ for service businesses region to region, and even significantly from one country to another in a given region such as South East Asia or even in Europe, determining the right profit centre will depend on where added value for the customer is generated, producing income and profit for the provider. In addition, decisions have to be made concerning a company's priorities: do we want to provide the same mix of services everywhere? Or do we wish to deliver the same level of quality everywhere? Or do we run operations to generate a consistent level of profit everywhere? As an analogy, consider the manufacturing environment, which is characterised by both assembly lines and flexible manufacturing systems, but with standardised output. The level of investment required to put together an advanced, flexible solution can be astronomical; what are the equivalents for service establishments? Answers probably differ based on the special characteristics of the service-product: transnational service provided locally only, or local service provided by multinationals. Tables 3.4 and 3.5 summarise some thoughts regarding these aspects of the adaptability of service-products.

Table 3.4 Providing value-added services internationally probably means the following

Doing the right things in each operating location: differentiating the mix of standardised basic services	*Producing higher quality at a competitive price: differentiating quality criteria and performance levels in various countries*	*Generating added value and thereby income and profit: identifying the right cost drivers in each location and defining the right profit centre*
• What is core and what is peripheral in a service product? • What are the right basic services to be delivered? • What is the appropriate combination in each place? • What should be the order of priority in these combinations? • What is the cost associated with the flexible design and delivery of services?	• How to define quality standards? • Is it relevant to apply the same standards everywhere? • What are the relationships between the level of quality and customer satisfaction and retention in various local situations? • What are the relationships between the level of quality and associated cost in various local situations?	• What are the cost drivers of the activity? • Are the cost drivers the same in any local situation? • What is the price elasticity in each local situation? • What should be the appropriate measurement units for local economic performance? • What should be the appropriate profit centres and where should they be located?

Table 3.5 Priorities for the focus of the local service

Global characteristics	Components of the local 'service offer'		
	Mix of basic service	Quality service	Profitability
Transnational service provided locally only	2. Competitive advantage	3. Important but less of an absolute priority	1. Motive
Transnational service provided internationally	1. Motive for developing the network	2. Competitive advantage in the global market	3. Global approach and management for profitability
Local service provided by multinational	3. Customers usually don't compare from place to place	2. Competitive advantage in the local market	1. Motive

IDENTIFYING THE APPROPRIATE LEARNING PROCESS

Making correct decisions implies that cultural factors, as well as the evaluation of political risks, are carefully considered from the outset. Moreover, the competition faced in each country should be carefully studied to assess the intensity of the rivalry between different local competitors. It is also necessary to identify the level of maturity of the target markets. Often successful approaches in new markets are due to the recognition of appropriate learning processes in the various markets.

In the consulting business, for instance, McKinsey opened their first European office in Geneva in the mid-1950s; they believed they could explore the market by themselves and then generate new clients. Two years later, they had to close this operation because of the lack of activity. Going it alone and learning from the experience seems not to be appropriate in the consulting business. At the same time, the British and Dutch BP Group operating in the US hired McKinsey to solve a problem concerning their home base in London. For two years, a consulting team had to work mainly in England and McKinsey realised that they actually had to run an office in London because of this assignment. They built local credibility from the success of this project and redesigned their European strategy on this basis. In this case, following existing customers abroad and learning from them turned out to be the appropriate way of developing their ability to operate as a service organisation in another region. In the home appliance retailing market, Darty, the main French player, started an operation in Spain in the mid-1980s. Applying the same core concepts and techniques which had made them an outstanding success at home, Darty had to close the Spanish operation after six months because of their inability to secure a customer base. Disappointed by this first experiment abroad, they then decided to buy a 40 per cent share in a Belgian firm operating in Benelux in the same market. They found that by doing so they were in a position to learn better, faster and more efficiently how to expand their business outside France. The story became even more interesting when Kingfisher, a giant in British retailing, announced in February 1993 its acquisition of Darty in order to develop activities on the continent, especially France and then Spain and Germany, as well as spreading Darty's outstanding know-how in after-sales service and customer satisfaction throughout their group. Finding the most efficient learning process is what the whole story is all about.

One of the crucial issues at the heart of international operations is deciding what types of decisions should be made at the corporate level and what responsibility should be retained at the local level. At Hilton International, hotels can be broken down into the following categories: one-third are wholly owned by Ladbroke, one-third are owned on a split-equity basis, and one-third are management contracts. Properties are not franchised, and policies are formulated for the most part at corporate level.

Hilton International hotel owners or managers all pay for global marketing. The corporate headquarters tracks almost every area of expenditure. There is an internal reference document — a manual to give information about every hotel, so salespeople can have information about each hotel worldwide. If a Columbian has questions about the hotel in Hong Kong, the local salesperson in Columbia should be equipped to give that information. The point is that every sales employee is charged with selling the *whole* company (including of course his or her own local hotel).

However, not all standards are global ones. *'You don't tell hoteliers in Hong Kong they should offer free coffee because no one pays for coffee in hotels in Columbia,'* said Geoffrey Breeze, Corporate Vice President of Marketing for Hilton International. *'We believe "locals know best".'*

The general manager in each Hilton International is responsible for the profit and loss of that hotel. He or she may be called on to modify certain areas according to corporate standards, or they may be called on to partake in a promotion designed by corporate headquarters. For instance, certain hotels pacificipated in a promotion with British Airways club, where if BA passengers went into a Hilton they received a free bathrobe or a free bottle of champagne. The programme did not require a large number of guests to cover the costs, except in Hong Kong where it costs $60 a bottle for champagne. As such a promotion would be just one of hundreds being put together all over the world, including and benefiting the Hong Kong Hilton, there is every chance of achieving equilibrium of return. If not, the hotel's general manager, who retains profit responsibility, has every right to protest and ask for remedial action.

The complexities of global competition mean that companies have to break free of many conventional notions of organisation and structure. One of the biggest challenges the delivery service UPS ran into when starting operations in France in 1987 was keeping faithful to its hiring practices. UPS, since its inception in 1907, has always promoted management from within. All its managers are expected to begin literally at the bottom — as truck drivers. But hiring baccalaureate holders in France to start as a truck driver as part of a management programme was definitely a hard sell. Since UPS needed to get its local French offices up and running as soon as possible, it essentially had no time to convince students who were not interested in driving a truck to enter the management programme. Therefore it had to settle for management-level personnel starting off at management level — a practice that would never have occurred in the US.

On the other hand, sometimes in entering new markets both core concept and corporate culture may be strengthened, since efforts to reproduce a successful formula abroad can focus in on its basic characteristics more clearly, thus contributing to streamlining the service management system in the home market. The company's image may be enhanced, not only in the eyes of its customers but also in the eyes of its staff and potential staff it might wish to attract.

Figure 3.3 introduces the characteristics of the three generic learning processes which seem to be adopted by service companies when expanding globally. Based on the results of our field survey, a series of critical success factors as well as some explanations for failure in the learning stage are proposed.

EXPANSION MODE AND MANAGEMENT OF MATURITY

Beyond knowing how to establish new operations in various countries and how to coordinate activities at a global level, new questions arise. How does a company build a mature network of branches or partners which fit with its global ambitions? How can a firm develop an efficient and well coordinated system, or series of related systems for service delivery worldwide? And how does an organisation maintain its competitive position and keep its best people on board once the focus shifts from the fun of opening new offices to the pressures of productivity improvement and cost control?

Characteristics of the Learning Process		
Following existing customers and learning from them	Buying local operations or cooperating	Going it alone and learning from the experience
Critical success factors • Close and loyal customer - supplier relationships, commitment to partnership • Outstanding international coordination systems • Appropriate for professional type of service especially	• Requires investment, needs for capital • Smart and sensitive integration of acquired companies (we have to learn from them) • Appropriate for "factory type" service	• Requires time and patience • Hiring local well-respected executive • Appropriate for services based on adaptable mix or values
Some explanations for failure • Inconsistency of the mix and quality level of the service worldwide • Inappropriate when serving decentralized customers who work very much in accordance with local culture	• Insufficient level of investment • Incompatibility between companies' core product and/on cultures • Strong and immediate generalization of corporate procedures	• Pressure for short-term return • Try to export original culture to locally accultured markets • Lack of loyalty from local executives, agents and employees

Figure 3.3 Success and failure of the learning process for service companies expanding operations globally

Furthermore, when a new company enters a competitive market late, after other companies have established name recognition, infrastructures, etc, there are only a few options to build infrastructure, obtain employees and so on. One can either buy existing companies, form franchises or set up a joint venture.

A franchise operation provides a way to overcome the problems of creating an international network and establish contacts in more remote countries. It also permits closely integrated administrative control, since there would be a strong contractual relationship between the two parties *vis-à-vis* the local office and the foreign office.

Joint ventures have been a recent development within the express industry (express transport of goods, primarily focusing on mail and parcels but also including parts or other large items). This not only provides a larger capital base from which all parties can draw, but may also provide a blend of expertise in special technical areas such as knowledge of marketing logistics, computer systems, or simply some operational aspects of the express industry.

As an industry becomes global, so does its labour market. To retain key staff worldwide, it is important to maintain a strong corporate culture. Airlines make the strongest possible use of corporate indentity, from coordinated uniforms to the interior colours and design of the aircraft. Not only does this provide differentiation, but also internal focus for the staff. As for preserving the loyalty of team members and human resources, issues of geographic mobility of executives, of homogeneity — or not — of remuneration systems, evaluation procedures and training programmes must all be considered in the process of designing the international strategies of large service companies.

Accor, the second largest hospitality company with revenues of $8 billion in 1992, employs 140,000 people in 127 countries. With French roots, Accor stands as a truly multinational group, still focusing primarily on the European market. Efficiently managing human resources is definitely seen as one of the major success factors for a company of that size operating virtually all over the planet. Their main objectives are developing professionalism and motivation among employees, building flexible and reactive administrative structures and processes which emphasise the respon-sibilities of employees, and communicating clearly defined corporate values. On a regular basis, and because of a rate of turnover in the industry of 60 per cent, the Group has to hire about 4000 people a year and 14,000 employees are trained in the Accor academy, the company university and training centre, every year. The cost of losing one regular employee is estimated at close to the equivalent of 30 weeks' salary, so managers are sensitised, and appraised, on the issue of hiring well and keeping people on board. In some divisions, training is organised in such a way that everybody in the most far-flung hotel can participate in the programme by means of an interactive video series with simultaneous translation. Compensation is managed with creativity and imagination to respond to the company's global dispersion, taking into account disparities across operating locations. For example, the level of taxation for the same income can vary from 17 to 60 per cent sometimes more, from place to place. Personal situations, age and citizenship, among other criteria, are taken into consideration when defining whether this employee needs more help to pay college tuition which is so expensive in the US for his three children, which will be paid directly by the company; or if another is more willing to invest in a nice cottage on the French Riviera for up coming retirement. Performance remains, of course, the main differentiating factor for calculating compensation, with collective incentive for low-level personnel and individual incentive for high-level managers.

Adapting organisational structure to the special requirements of managing the maturity phase of a multinational service provider is certainly a second quite crucial effort to be undertaken. Cap Gemini Sogeti stands as the prime customised software maker in Europe, also controlling a significant market share in the US. Given the changes in the computer industry, especially the downsizing of information management within the company due to the broad use of the PC, CGS decided to redesign its administrative structures drastically. The new system retains only three layers of responsibility: each Strategic Business Area will cover a given practice or technical skills, as well as a given territory. For instance, the SBA in the US covers all the group activities in North America as well as the chemical and energy practice worldwide, the UK-based SBA handles the British Isles market jointly with the financial services practice, and so on. Each of the seven SBAs runs a group of roughly 3000 employees which is itself split into seven divisions and then in seven operating units of 70 people each. Better global coordination and efficient local management are expected from the new organisation.

There is also an ever-increasing need to provide greater amounts of information to customers who are believed to be more demanding, not only with regard to the quality of service, but the level of information provided. This seems to be particularly true in the express transport market, for instance. It is becoming more and more important to be computerised, to be able to track and trace items in transit quickly and efficiently. There is also a trend towards more electronic data interchange.

The costs for marketing are considerable. Extensive advertising is needed to create initial awareness in a new market. Currently, there are substantial sums of money being earmarked for this purpose. These companies may well increase their promotional activity, drawing on their extensive resources to support advertising campaigns. It is a widely held opinion throughout the industry that there will be a major price war within the next couple of years, conducted by leading integrated operators. This will tend to squeeze out less efficient operators.

Table 3.6 Critical aspects of internationalising a service organisation

---

Global strategy design
- Motives and incentives for global strategy.
- Identification of competitive advantages.
- Evaluation of disadvantages and risks.

'Adaptable' definition of the service-product
- Differentiation of the mix of standardised basic services, and/or
- differentiation of quality performance, and/or
- differentiation of profit objectives per region.

Learning process
- Learning from following the existing customers, and/or
- buying local players, or cooperating, or
- going it alone (organic growth).

Expansion process
- Expansion driven by special corporate spirit.
- What is the most appropriate dynamic for network building?
- Definition of integrative devices and how to spread the corporate culture.

Management of maturity
- Developing first-class information and reporting systems.
- Balancing flexibility and productivity through planning and organisational systems.
- Keeping personnel on board, loyal and motivated.

CAN TECHNOLOGY MAKE A DIFFERENCE?

Looking to the future, technology will continue to provide service companies with new competitive weapons. For instance, professional service firms conducting business internationally face opportunities to offer their worldwide clientele both high quality and lower costs by taking advantage of ever-improving technologies. The costly inputs of highly paid consultants, who typically travel far and wide; frequently create costs which do not necessarily seem to provide added value to the clients. The latter are less willing to cover travel expenses, or might gladly pay but are frustrated by the unavailability of the specialists they need — another 'cost'.

As a service to its clientele (but of course also as both a cost-control measure and a marketing device), the technologically advanced consulting company can use video-conferencing, satellite linkage and other voice/image/data processing modes to tap its global network of expertise. A properly planned organised and coordinated approach can leverage the firm's key resource — knowledge — and decrease the need to move bodies around the world. Such an approach can also be applied to technical support in high tech industries when only a few, very well qualified engineers can diagnose the origin of breakdowns in advanced devices such as medical equipment, radar systems and so on.

Returning to the five-step development process which we proposed at the beginning of this chapter and developed throughout, Table 3.6 summarises a number of critical aspects to consider when internationalising a service-product.

References

McDonald's (1993) *Capital*, January.

Riddle, D I (1986) *Service-Led Growth: The Role of the Service Sector in World Development*, Praeger, New York.

Sparks, D and Mathe, H, 'Survival of the quickest: the challenges of the international express market in Europe' in *Managing Services across Borders*, L'Entreprise Logistique/Groupe ESSEC, Cergy-Pontoise.

Leven, M (1983) *Emerging Perspectives on Service Marketing*, AMA, Chicago.

SERVICE QUALITY AND SERVICE RECOVERY: THE ROLE OF CAPACITY MANAGEMENT

Colin Armistead and Graham Clark

OUTLINE

Service quality has become an issue for most service organisations. While gains have been made through quality programmes in some cases, research and anecdotal evidence suggest that they have not always been as great as expected. The reasons for the failures may in part lie with the extent of the organisational cultural change required in many instances. However, we consider that problems may also be because of a failure to recognise the importance of managing capacity to meet short-term demand and the consequent effect on service quality.

This chapter reports the result of a survey conducted among service quality practitioners across the services sector to investigate:

- the measures taken to improve service quality and their effectiveness;
- the most important dimensions of service quality to win customers;
- the way in which capacity is managed to match demand;
- the effect on service quality of running out of capacity;
- the actions taken by service organisations to recover from mistakes.

The findings from the survey are as follows:

- The respondents from the survey might have been expected to be representative of some of the best companies at managing service quality. However, even though they demonstrate the use of many of the modern techniques of service quality management, including Total Quality Management (TQM) and customer care programmes and the achievement of quality standards such as BS5750, the effectiveness of these approaches is perceived to be limited.

- *Reliability* of service, the *attitude* of staff to their interaction with the customers, and the ability to *recover* from mistakes, whether they are of the customers' making or due to errors on the part of the service organisations, are perceived to be the most important dimensions for winning and keeping customers.
- Management of capacity to meet demand seems to take little account of the danger zone when demand exceeds capacity. The dimensions of service quality which suffer at these times correspond to the most important dimensions of quality, ie reliability, attitudes of staff, and ability to recover from mistakes.
- There is little evidence of measurement including 'early warning signals' of when operations are running out of capacity or effective plans being made to manage well in these circumstances.
- When mistakes are made there is little evidence of service organisations trying to put things right immediately and making sure the customer is satisfied with the action being taken.

The following lessons are evident from this research:

- The ability to deliver service quality consistently is linked to the effectiveness of capacity management.
- Understanding what happens to service quality as capacity runs out and being proactive mean:
  — having measurements which give early warning signals;
  — planning what actions to take to reduce the damage to service quality;
  — taking action to minimise the occurrence of capacity shortfalls by forecasting demand and building flexibility into service delivery.
- Service recovery is perceived to be an important dimension of service quality in winning and keeping customers. Hence there should be an emphasis on recovery strategies which repair the damage at the time of the failure and leave the customers satisfied with the actions taken. This requires measurements to be taken of customer satisfaction related to failures caused by lack of capacity or other factors.

INTRODUCTION

Service quality and customer service have been investigated by a large number of researchers in Europe and the US in recent years. Many organisations have introduced a mixture of customer care and total quality management programmes with a varying degree of success judged on the basis of anecdotal evidence. There have been those who claim outstanding successes, acknowledged by the award of quality prizes like the Deming Prize, Malcolm Baldrige National Quality Award and the European Quality Award. Others have been less successful for a variety of reasons and they outnumber the successful candidates. The reasons for failure vary from organisation to organisation, but perhaps they all reflect an inability to manage the change of the organisation's culture.

We are interested in the way in which service organisations formulate and implement service strategies and have worked with a number of organisations to review service delivery against intended strategies (Armistead and Clark, 1991). One of the factors which has started to emerge from this work is the importance of the link between capacity management and the ability to meet targets set for service quality and resource productivity. At the simplest level we can visualise the balancing act which service managers face day to day in attempting to match the level of demand with the available capacity as a see-saw effect.

When there is a perfect balance between the demand for the services and the resources giving the capacity to satisfy them, the services are delivered to the desired service quality standards while meeting resource productivity targets. However, as all service managers know, it is difficult to achieve this perfect balance either by controlling the level of resources or by influencing demand. Consequently service delivery is often in an unbalanced state. Either there is more resource capacity than is needed for the level of demand, or demand from customers is in excess of available capacity.

When demand from customers is greater than resource capacity, then service quality is likely to suffer. This might be because customers have to wait for long periods in queues or because the service which is given is rushed so that the service quality is lower. On the other hand, when there is insufficient demand resources cannot be used productively and also there may be effects on service quality in those instances where a certain level of utilisation of resources is part of the quality assessment. Empty restaurants, leisure parks or theatres are examples where a reduction in service quality accompanies a lower resource utilisation. The effects of these imbalances in supply and demand are often most significant for customer satisfaction over short periods of time, perhaps ranging from minutes to hours.

The influence of capacity management on service quality and customer service has been recognised by other writers (Chase and Bowen, 1991; Collier, 1987; Rhyme, 1988; Sasser, 1976). However, there has been no detailed research to investigate how service managers manage the process. This gap is important in the context of service recovery, the ability of service providers to recover from mistakes caused either by the organisation or by customers (Hart *et al*, 1990). The proposition is that service organisations which are able to manage the balance between demand and capacity are in a better position to be able to handle the recovery process well.

While we have been able to gather some anecdotal evidence of how service managers are addressing these issues of capacity management and service quality, we have not known how service managers in a range of different types of service organisations manage resource capacity and the effect this has on service quality. The findings which are reported in this chapter are the result of a survey which was conducted by Cranfield School of Management in association with *Managing Service Quality*. The aims for the survey were to find out how service managers approach the management of resource capacity to satisfy the demand for their type of business and how this process affects their ability to maintain a consistent delivery of the most important features of service quality.

THE SURVEY SAMPLE

The survey was mailed to about 3000 managers, some on a Cranfield School of Management database and others who were readers of *Managing Service Quality*. A total of 167 responses were received. While not high in percentage terms, this is about the expected level given the length and complexity of the survey.

Distribution of Respondents

The respondents came from a wide range of services, with consultancy having the greatest representation. The complete distribution is shown in Table 4.1.

Nature of the Service Business

We were also interested in the types of customer which our respondents dealt with, and the nature of the services. Table 4.2 shows a breakdown of the sample based on the nature of the primary customer and Table 4.3 shows the number of customers which the organisations deal with. Finally, Table 4.4 gives an indication of the mix of services which are delivered according to whether they are standard or customised, and the relative size of the service-product range.

Table 4.1 Distribution of respondents

Service	Percentage
Consultancy	16
Manufacturing	12
After-sales support	11
Public sector	10
Distribution	8
Professional services	7
Computer services	5
Education	3
Banking	2
Building services	2
Catering	2
Financial services	2
Insurance	2
Telecommunications	2
Transport	2
Building societies	1
Retail	1
Multiple sectors	7
Other	4

Many of the respondents are serving more than one customer group, which explains a total percentage greater than 100. The majority are delivering service 'business to business' rather than to individual members of the general public. As might have been expected, there are a few who are just serving a small number of large customers and a majority whose customer base consists of a mix of large and small customers. The nature of the services which are delivered by the respondents in the sample tends towards standard products rather than those tailored to the individual needs of customers. Consequently we see in the sample mainly service companies which are operating business to business, delivering service-products which are essentially standardised with some need for customisation at times, and with a service-product mix which is fairly constant in 90 per cent of cases.

We might surmise that for the majority of respondents the process of matching capacity and demand should be made easier by standardisation, as there will be a higher level of predictability of the capacity requirement for each service event.

Table 4.2 Primary customers

Type of customer	Percentage
Companies	63
General public	25
Local government	19
National Health Service or utilities	14
Retailers	12
Dealers	9
Others	6

Table 4.3 Customer profile

Number of customers	Percentage
Few large and many small customers	64
Few relatively large customers	21
Many relatively small customers	12
One major customer	3

Table 4.4 Mix of service-products

Type of product	Percentage
Mainly standard products with some customised	34
Largely customised with few standard products	27
Wide range of standard products	22
Limited range of standard products	17

THE IMPORTANT FEATURES OF SERVICE QUALITY

We wanted to find out which are the most important features of service quality for our respondents. We recognised that the answers we would receive would be based on a variety of assessments, from individual judgement to results of detailed customer research. The questionnaire presented respondents with a detailed list of dimensions of service quality which encompassed all those in the various classifications in the service quality literature. Respondents were asked to assess each service dimension on a scale between 1 and 5 reflecting an increasing importance, with 5 indicating a dimension which wins customers and 1 not being important to customers. Table 4.5 shows the results for the full range of respondents with the importance of each dimension measured on the 1 to 5 scale.

It may be possible to infer that those attributes with higher scores are perceived to be more important in building a positive quality image. This might be so for dimensions with a score of more than 4.0. Those between 3.0 and 4.0 could be viewed as neutral, not adding positively to the perception of quality, but capable of detracting from it if not up to expectations. Dimensions with a score below 3.0 are not perceived to be important by the organisations surveyed.

We were also interested to know if different types of service delivery were associated with specific critical dimensions of service quality. Respondents were asked to identify the extent to which their service delivery was standardised or customised. We found that there were about an equal number of respondents in each category; there is not the degree of difference between the different methods of service delivery that might have been expected. The differences in the results between the two groups are not statistically significant.

What does emerge overall is the importance of *reliability* of service (and this does seem to be more to the fore in standardised service delivery), the *attitude* of staff to their interaction with the customers, and the ability to *recover* from mistakes whether they are of customers' making or due to error on the part of the service organisation. We will see that this has implications for the way in which capacity is managed. We would expect perceived value to be given a high score as this is in effect a summary of the total service experience.

We can draw the following broad conclusions:

- Organisations must work hard to establish competence, and to deliver reliably to expectations.
- Positive staff attitudes, represented by friendliness and courtesy, are seen as attributes which enhance the quality of service.
- The time dimension, which includes the time taken to make the initial response, is a key customer measure. It is worth noting that time may be used as a surrogate for an assessment of other quality dimensions such as efficiency and responsiveness.

Table 4.5 Importance of service dimensions as winning dimensions

Quality dimension	Importance of the dimension (scale 1–5)
Competence	4.6
Perceived value of the service	4.6
Reliability	4.6
Courtesy of staff	4.5
Ability to put things right:	
– when you have failed	4.5
– when the customer is in trouble	4.5
Communication with the customers	4.5
Time to deliver total service	4.4
Staff friendliness	4.2
Availability of the service	4.2
Initial response time	4.2
How important customers feel	4.1
Accessibility to right people	4.0
Product image	3.9
Customers feeling in control	3.8
Accessibility: location	3.7
Customer view of their financial risk	3.6
Time with the front-line person	3.5
Individually designed services	3.3
Clean environment	3.3
Strength of guarantees	3.2
Supporting goods	2.9
Comfort of the environment	2.9
Customer's view of their risk:	
– personal	2.8
– physical	2.6

MANAGEMENT OF THE SERVICE DELIVERY PROCESS

We wanted to explore how service managers are managing their service delivery with particular reference to the management of capacity to balance prevailing customer demand. One important aspect of service delivery relates to where the most value is added in the course of the process. The results from our sample, Table 4.6, show that in most cases most of the added value results from direct contact with the customer. This is a little surprising given the high level of business to business activity, and probably reflects the subjective view of the respondents as much as rigorous costing.

Table 4.6 Where the value is added in service delivery

Stage in service delivery	Percentage of respondents
During direct contact with the customer	58
In a centralised processing centre	18
In the 'back room' of the individual unit	14
Other	10

MANAGING CAPACITY

When it comes to managing the balance between demand and capacity, there are two basic approaches: a 'level' strategy, in which the organisation maintains a constant output and attempts to influence demand to suit, or a 'chase' strategy, when the output is flexed to match fluctuations in customer demand. Most service organisations employ both approaches to some extent. Respondents were asked to indicate which is their predominant approach; 22 per cent indicated 'level' and 78 per cent 'chase'.

Respondents were asked what actions they took to carry out these capacity management strategies and to give each action a ranking of importance between 1 and 3, with the most important as 1. The results are shown in Table 4.7. The closer to 3 the result, the more important the action. Making customers wait in queues is the most common form of dealing with an inability to change capacity, rather than proactively doing things to influence demand before the service event. Introducing longer working hours is the most important action taken to alter capacity to chase demand.

Table 4.7 Actions for managing capacity

Level strategy	Rank (scale 1–3)	Chase strategy	Rank (scale 1–3)
Queues	2.2	Overtime	2.3
Appointments	1.1	Subcontracting	1.8
Off-peak discounts	1.1	Alternative services	1.1
Price increases	0.9		

Where service organisations were keeping customers waiting in queues, we were interested to know what they were doing to manage the process. Table 4.8 shows the responses. The closer the value to 5, the more frequently the action is used. Communicating with customers comes highest in the actions. We might have expected to see a higher score for this action given the strong relationship with service quality.

Table 4.8 Actions to manage queues

Action	Frequency of use (scale 1–5)
Informing customers of length of wait	3.8
Making sure something happens frequently to allay fears of being forgotten	3.1
Ensuring 'first come first served'	3.0
Providing entertainment or distractions	1.3

In many service operations it is the inability to deliver the service in the short term which causes the problems. We asked respondents which factors influence their ability to match resource capacity and customer demand in the short term. By short term we mean it is not possible to add another unit of capacity to a bottleneck resource which is limiting capacity. The results are shown in Table 4.9. The closer the value to 5, the greater the effect of the factor. The inability to have employees available when required may be exacerbated by the lack of forecasts and the limited use made of scheduling.

The main bottleneck resources were identified as being people (53 per cent), equipment (24 per cent), facilities (9 per cent), materials (9 per cent), and information (5 per cent).

Table 4.9 Factors which influence ability to balance demand and capacity short term

Factor	Intensity of the effect (scale 1–5)
Employee availability	4.0
Availability of demand forecasts	3.8
Capacity availability information	3.4
Not having schedules	3.2
Equipment availability	3.0
Customer availability	2.9
Flexibility of facilities	2.8
Material supply	2.7
Size of facilities	2.5
Supplier's personnel	2.1

The ability to match demand in the short-term is thought to have a great influence on service quality. Short-term is considered to be when it is not possible to add any more resources to increase the capacity at a bottleneck. The factors which affect the ability to achieve a balance in the short-term, were identified by the respondents to be those listed in Table 4.9.

The aspects of service quality which start to suffer when capacity and demand are not in balance even short term, are shown in Table 4.10.

Table 4.10 Quality factors which suffer when capacity runs out

Quality factor	Percentage of responses
Timeliness	46
• responsiveness	
• lead times for service	
• inability to supply	
Customer service	32
• service levels	
• personal attention	
• communication with customers	
Capability/consistency	17
• accuracy	
• attention to detail	
No effect	5

We also asked how respondents measured any degradation in service quality and the replies are shown in Table 4.11. They suggest a greater reliance on internal measures, made by service providers or the organisation, than on external measures which involve the customer. Moreover, most of the measurements are made after the event, by which time it would be more difficult to take corrective action.

Table 4.11 Measurement of quality degradation

Measure	Percentage of replies
Internal measurements	
• at the time	6
• after the event (eg quality audits)	66
External measurements	
• at the time (eg talking to customers)	6
• after the event (eg complaints and surveys)	16
No measurements made at all	6

If organisations are to be in a position to react when demand is exceeding capacity it is important to have 'early warning signals' which alert the service providers that something needs to be done. We asked respondents to say what were their signals. The results are shown in Table 4.12.

Table 4.12 Early warning signals that there is not enough capacity

Early warning signal	Percentage responses
Falling service standards	36
• timings missed	
• material shortages	
Customers	21
• waiting	
• complaining	
• taking business away	
Overloads	21
• backlogs	
• overtime	
Planning and monitoring	18
• forecast vs capacity	
• plans against actual	
Staff	6
• complaining	
• becoming irritable	
• walking out	

HOW WELL DO ORGANISATIONS RECOVER FROM MISTAKES?

Service organisations with any degree of customer involvement in the process must be able to recover quickly from problems which are either of their own or the customer's making. In particular there is a need for immediate solutions, the ability to respond in such a way as to satisfy the customer without resorting to layer upon layer of procedures, all of which effectively leave the problem with the customer.

Table 4.13 shows which group of people or resources has the greatest effect on customer satisfaction in the event of a mistake or failure.

Contact staff are seen to be able to influence customer satisfaction to the greatest extent, for good or ill. This should cause organisations to question the degree to which they are equipped and supported to deal with problems. Support staff and support systems are also seen to be important. It may be interesting to note that the rankings of support staff and support systems were identical. Could this mean that support staff are identified primarily as part of the system rather than as individuals? What are the implications for a flexible response to problems?

Table 4.13 Resources or people having the greatest effect on customer satisfaction in the event of failure

Resources/people	Rank (scale 1–5)
Contact staff	4.7
Support staff	3.6
Support systems	3.6
Suppliers	3.2
Information systems	3.2
Customers	2.8
Equipment	2.4
Premises/facilities	2.3

We asked respondents to tell us which strategy they have found to be most effective in dealing with a crisis which was not of the customer's making. Although 42 per cent take some form of direct action, 36 per cent believe that open and honest communication with customers is the best course. It may be right to be proactive and not hide problems, but there is a suspicion that some feel this is where the responsibility ends, with the problem in the customer's court once it has been explained. The results are summarised in Table 4.14.

Table 4.14 The most effective strategy for dealing with a crisis of the organisation's making

Strategy	Percentage of mentions
Doing something	
Action teams	18
Rapid response	10
Crisis plans	9
Teams including customers	2
Money to customers	2
	41
Talking to customers	**36**
Using systems	
BS5750, etc	6
Escalation procedures	5
Spare capacity	2
	13
No formal systems	**5**
Developing people	
Empowering staff	2
Training	2
	4

Given the amount of discussion about employee empowerment, it is interesting to note the low emphasis placed on it. We wonder if this highlights general confusion as to what empowerment means in practice. Is empowerment only another form of job expansion, giving staff wider responsibilities? Does empowerment have to be institutionalised before anything happens?

We asked about actions taken to recover from mistakes. The results, given in Table 4.15, again indicate a heavy reliance on systems rather than predominantly on people. This may be the result of the fact that many of the respondents are quality managers or quality champions.

Table 4.15 Actions taken to recover from mistakes

Action	Percentage
Analysis and preventive action	
Foolproofing, redesign	10
Feedback or analysis	17
Change procedures	8
	35
Take immediate action	
Corrective action	13
Complaints procedure	7
Firefight	2
	22
People-based actions	
Replace staff involved	2
Use high-level staff	5
No recriminations	2
Disciplining	1
	10
Compensation	
Free of charge service	7
Extend warranty	2
Provide alternative	3
	12
Customer-centred action	
Contact and review	16
Apologise	5
	21

The emphasis in Table 4.15 is on making sure that the mistake does not recur. Indeed, one respondent included the statement 'convince the customer that it was a one-off mistake'. Again, this is sound quality theory, but we would have expected there to have been more emphasis on recovering the immediate situation, making sure that the customer was satisfied with the action taken.

We were disappointed that only 5 per cent included apologies in their response. Customers are often fobbed off with money or promises that the system has been changed for the future, but are often left with the feeling that they, the customers, have basically expected too much, and any action is a goodwill gesture on the part of the service provider.

Only 22 per cent emphasised immediate action, although this includes 7 per cent who suggested that their complaints procedure is sufficient to cope with most situations. There was one respondent who reported an interesting mixture of analysis, to remove problems in systems and processes for the future, and 'vicious disciplining' of any staff found to be in serious error (edited version). We were quite pleased to see this honesty; while we agree with Deming that most quality problems are the fault of the system (which includes management), there has to be a place for dealing with people who have not performed properly.

In general this section gave the impression of a reactive approach to recovery, perhaps resulting in customers being 'mollified' rather than 'satisfied'.

MANAGEMENT OF SERVICE QUALITY

The final section of the survey investigated general approaches to quality management. Table 4.16 shows the degree to which these approaches are used and felt to be effective. The answers were on a scale from 1 to 5, where 1 was 'approach not used' and 5 was 'approach very effective'. For this report we have added together responses of 4 and 5 to produce the 'effective' column in the table.

Table 4.16 The effectiveness of approaches to service quality management

Approach	Used (%)	Effective (%)
Standard procedures	91	60
TQM	84	71
Customer care programmes	77	46
BS5750	72	45
Customer satisfaction index	65	40
Quality circles	64	24

Given the nature of respondents, likely to be quality enthusiasts, it is perhaps not surprising that TQM receives a higher rating than we might have expected given the number of programmes that are reported not to have achieved their expected results. It was not possible within the context of this questionnaire to probe this more deeply, but the figures would suggest that other approaches used in isolation are less likely to be effective.

Measurement of quality is clearly an important ingredient in quality management. Table 4.17 lists the methods of measurement used, Table 4.18 the frequency of production of such information, and Table 4.19 the people who receive the information.

Table 4.17 Methods of service quality measurement

Method	Percentage
Internal measures	81
Customer surveys	75
Employee surveys	36
Audit by customers	29
Independent surveys	27
Industry audits	25
Mystery customers	9

From previous surveys we have conducted it would appear that there has been a marked increase in the percentage of companies developing more comprehensive internal measures, and a continuing increase in organisations conducting regular customer surveys. The message of 'listening to customers' seems to have had an effect. It is also pleasing to see that a significant number of organisations also survey their employees.

Table 4.18 Frequency of quality information

Frequency of information	Percentage
Daily	20
Weekly	14
Monthly	31
Quarterly	10
Six-monthly	7
Yearly	7

Again, Table 4.18 would suggest that quality measures are now being taken seriously, with 65 per cent of organisations producing information at least monthly, 34 per cent weekly.

Table 4.19 People receiving quality measurement information

People	Percentage
Board members	51
Service managers	45
Contact staff	35
Service director	28
All company management	56

Table 4.19 suggests that service quality measurement is now receiving more attention, with 51 per cent of organisations sending information to board members. It is pleasing to see that contact staff receive this information. However, in all categories it could be said that there is room for improvement.

An open question about how successful organisations have been in improving quality was generally encouraging, with most reporting steady if slow improvement. Some specific examples are:

- Mean time between failure (MTBF) improved from 24 months to 60 months over the last three years.
- We have reached BS5750 in 4 months from start.
- Quality costs: 1988 £700k; 1989 £3200k; 1990 £100k; 1991 predicted £38k.

Table 4.20 shows the extent to which individuals or teams are rewarded for quality success.

Table 4.20 Rewards for quality success

Reward	Percentage
No reward	36
Recognition	25
Performance bonus	20
Part of appraisal	11
Job satisfaction	8

The underlying message from Table 4.20 is that organisations appear to be trying to understand the link between reward/recognition and quality success, but many would feel that they have not yet found the full answer. A large percentage of organisations which reported 'no reward' also said that this was under review. Many of those giving a performance bonus identified that they were rewarding managers but not staff for performance improvement. A small number felt that quality service was the norm, and so lack of criticism was the only reward required!

CONCLUSIONS

In carrying out the first stages of analysis, we have confirmed our belief that there are many approaches to managing service quality, no single method being appropriate for every situation.

There are two dimensions which are particularly important in determining a quality strategy. The first is the extent of standardisation or customisation of service delivery; and the second is whether the organisation is serving the general public or is a business to business service provider.

The standardised/customised dimension will determine whether quality management is based on procedures and systems, giving some but limited discretion to employees; or whether the emphasis is likely to be on recruiting and training the best people and then supporting them with relatively flexible systems.

The effect of the customer, general public or business to business, is likely to manifest itself in the number and intensity of customer contacts, many consumer services having to manage many contact points. This dimension is not as clear cut as standard versus customised, since human beings are involved in both!

The link between capacity management and quality was not as well defined as we would have liked. In a manufacturing situation, it may be very obvious that when the schedule is overloaded, response times deteriorate. When dealing with services with a significant intangible element this relationship may not be as obvious, although it exists none the less. On the other hand, we found that about 20 per cent of organisations were able to identify an average utilisation figure above which service quality begins to fall off. Together with our informal research with service organisations, this encourages us to continue to investigate this area.

Following on from this, we were relatively disappointed that there was not a greater understanding of what suffers when the organisation runs out of capacity. We believe that many informal 'coping' strategies exist to deal with short-term demand, and would like to see more work carried out here.

Finally, we would have expected to see more about flexibility or empowerment, given the generally held view that if an organisation can recover well from a mistake or crisis, customers are more likely to be satisfied.

To end on a more positive note, we were encouraged by the detailed response to our questions. Many organisations are clearly taking service quality improvement very seriously indeed, and a number are able to report significant gains.

One of our respondents reported that their product quality was excellent, but their service quality patchy. In our work with service organisations this story is often repeated, but we are encouraged that many are working hard to improve and we are looking forward to identifying more 'world class' service providers in the 1990s.

References

Armistead, C G and Clark, G R (1991) 'Improving service delivery', *Managing Service Quality*, July.

Chase, R B and Bowen, D E (1991) 'Service quality and the service delivery system' in, Brown, S W, Gummersson, E, Edvardsson, B and Gustavsson, B (eds) *Service Quality: Multidisciplinary and Multinational Perspectives,* Lexington Books, Massachusetts, Toronto.

Collier, D A (1987) 'The customer service and quality challenge', *Service Industries Journal*, Vol 7, No 1.

Hart, C W L, Heskett, J L and Sasser, W E (1990) 'The profitable art of service recovery', *Harvard Business Review*, July–August.

Rhyme, D (1988) 'The impact of demand management on the service system performance', *Service Industries Journal*, Vol 8, No 4.

Sasser, W E (1976) 'Match supply and demand in service industries', *Harvard Business Review*, November–December.

5

INTERNAL MARKETING: A NEW PERSPECTIVE FOR HRM

Brett Collins and Adrian Payne

OUTLINE

Over the past few years the term 'internal marketing' is increasingly being used to describe the applications of marketing *internally* within the organisation. Although internal marketing relates to all functions within the organisation, it is particularly concerned with the management of human resources. Many traditional personnel departments have focused on control and administration activities rather than the alignment of human resources towards achieving corporate strategies and organisational goals.

This chapter considers the importance of the internal marketing of the human resources function, illustrating how concepts used in traditional marketing can be usefully employed by human resource (HR) managers.

The chapter investigates:.

- the nature of the challenges and opportunities confronting human resource managers;
- the central task for the human resource manager and professional;
- the similarities between external marketing of products and internal marketing of the HR function;
- how marketing tools and concepts can assist HR managers in making a more effective contribution towards their organisation's objectives.

The *findings* are as follows:

- HR managers are faced with new challenges in a role which is now recognised to be of high strategic importance. An organisation's flexibility to cope with change, improve the quality of performance of people and retrain personnel is

98

a key issue for HR managers and directly affects the bottom-line performance of a company.

- HR managers have not gained widespread support from senior management, partly because of a failure to convince chief executives of the payoffs of effective human resource management (HRM). Measurement of the contribution of successful HRM to achieving corporate goals is therefore an essential task.

- HR managers have traditionally been orientated towards developing products without due attention to organisational objectives and satisfying the needs of internal markets. The long-term growth of an organisation is assisted by developing a marketing orientation towards HRM, focusing on the contribution of HRM to organisational objectives.

The following marketing principles can be usefully employed by the HR function to help in achieving organisational goals:

- Market research of internal client needs should be undertaken to help identify organisational problems. Commitment to resolve these problems is vital for the future credibility of HR managers.

- A human resources mission statement which identifies the role of HR within the organisation and helps focus HRM effort.

- Market segmentation allows efficient resource allocation for different internal client groups, emphasising the areas that are of greatest importance to achieving organisational objectives.

- Developing and implementing a marketing mix aimed at these segments which includes designing appropriate activities such as training programs and effective internal communications to achieve desired results.

In service organisations, where people are very often the main asset, internal marketing of the HR function has particular relevance:

- Concepts borrowed from marketing can usefully be employed by the HR function to manage people effectively and achieve organisational goals.

- Marketing principles can also usually be adapted for other key markets within the 'relationship marketing' framework.

- HR managers should adopt a market rather than a product orientation to their policies, focusing on the needs of internal customers and stimulating improved internal service levels.

- HR managers have a responsibility to convince chief executives of the strategic importance of HRM in achieving business success. Marketing has a central role in this.

INTERNAL MARKETING AND HRM

There are two dimensions relevant to a discussion of internal marketing. First, there is the notion that every department and every person within an organisation is both a supplier and a customer. The second aspect relates to the organisation's staff and involves ensuring that they work together in a manner supporting the company's strategy and goals. This has been recognised as especially important in service firms where there is a close relationship between production and consumption of the service. It is thus concerned with both quality management and customer service and involves coordinating people and process improvement strategies.

In this chapter we explore the marketing of a particular internal service within the organisation — the human resource function. Our purpose is to illustrate how internal marketing concepts and methods used by marketing managers can provide the basis of a new perspective on meeting the opportunities and challenges faced by human resource managers. A market-oriented human resource manager is more likely to make an impact on the success of a company, through being more effective in both demonstrating the relevance of human resource management to all management team members, and helping other managers to increase their productivity.

Our approach is first to consider the nature of the challenges and opportunities confronting human resource managers. A view of what is seen to be a central task for the HR management professional is then outlined. The congruence between marketing function activities and HR management activities is then described. Finally, we consider how the HR manager can utilise the philosophy, ideas, and tools of the marketing function to make a more effective contribution to achieving the organisation's objectives.

CHALLENGES FACING THE HR MANAGER

The managers in a company who deal with the 'people' issues are now recognised as having an increasingly strategic role in the success of many businesses. Regardless of whether the function these managers perform is called personnel, human resources, industrial relations, or training and development, it collectively now represents a business role similar in importance to the areas of finance, marketing and operations management. This trend has been driven by a more intensely competitive business environment, increased use of technology in some industries, and the shift in corporate philosophy from asset management to operations management.

A focus on operations management has forced chief executive officers (CEOs) to understand the need for skilled HR executives if they are to cope successfully with change. An organisation able to adapt to change is generally found to be more able to sustain competitive advantage in an environment of increasing uncertainty. The constant stress of corporate takeovers, new ventures, the restructuring of companies, rationalisation of existing operations, new technology introduction and staff layoffs, means that the success of basic strategic decisions increasingly depends on 'matching skills with jobs, keeping key personnel after a merger, and solving the human problems that arise from introducing new technology or closing a plant' (*Business Week*, 2 Dec 1985). The dramatic turnaround of SAS by Jan Carlzon was driven by people rather than by an expensive investment in equipment and assets (Carlzon, 1987).

Increasing attention is being focused on the area of external customer retention and the enormous potential for improved profitability (Reincheld and Sasser, 1990; Buchanan and Gillies, 1990). Top managers should also seek to obtain improved organisational performance through effective HRM strategies aimed at improving personnel retention. The base-line benefits are cost savings on retraining in a job market with rapid turnover and cutting down the equally expensive knowledge drain. Companies able to manage this issue will reap the rewards which go with a team of committed, active individuals at a time when under-training is sapping productivity among competitors.

Increased use of technology in some industries has led to the assumption that the quality of people's performance will become a less important issue as technology becomes more pervasive. However, the maintenance of reliable performance by competent employees is becoming more crucial. For example, we are now in an era when electronic banking means fewer face-to-face encounters between the bank and its customers. Consequently the importance of handling these interactions, and the 'costs' of not making the most of opportunities, are greater. In a relatively homogeneous industry such as banking, a key opportunity for banks to gain a competitive edge over competitors lies in the quality of its people. In an era of electronic fund transfer there is opportunity for a bank to position itself as one that has good people, not just good machines (Berry, 1981). Many of the key challenges facing retail banking involve the employee: the need to sell and cross-sell, unionisation, electronic banking, affirmative action, service quality management and technology management.

It has been argued that HR professionals have failed in the past to reach their full potential within the corporate framework because they devoted themselves to the creation of ever more sophisticated programmes and forgot the whole purpose of the business (Baird and Meshoulam, 1986). HR managers have had a role in organisations dealing with outside pressures such as government, unions and safety, but their active involvement and collaboration is also needed with the production, marketing and finance functions. They have been responsible for fending off interruptions, handling the reporting requirements of regulatory bodies, and dealing with social responsibility issues, but often are not involved in activities perceived by other managers to be fundamentally important to the business.

Managing a corporation is complex, and CEOs find it necessary to simplify their task by concentrating on what appear to be the most important strategic issues. Because of resource limitations, it is necessary to focus senior managers' attention and time on those aspects of the business process with the highest expected payoff. This means that some areas with extremely high potential impact, but a very low perceived probability of delivering significant results, must get less attention than one might really wish. Strategic HRM requires a significant investment of organisational resources, which directly and immediately affects profits and can thus make it unattractive to managers under pressure for short-term results. Furthermore, any real understanding of what competent HRM could contribute to the success of a business has only been popularised fairly recently (Peters and Waterman, 1982). For these reasons senior managers have often failed to grasp why HRM was relevant to business strategy, business performance and the cost management function.

Clearly the central task of HRM must be to gain the support of senior managers, secure the commitment of the CEO, and ensure HRM makes the most effective contribution possible to the organisation's objectives.

The HRM function in a company is never likely to be valued unless it convinces managers it can provide significant payoffs, and is part of the key interactions between the organisation and the environment. HRM will become established as an integral part of a business through helping other managers to increase their productivity. Managers do not require more sophisticated programmes. They require someone who understands their problems, can actively contribute to the more effective and efficient management of human resources, and who has a good understanding of the business. We will now consider how the roles of marketing managers and HR managers are linked.

THE MARKETING–HRM ANALOGY

The HRM function has three distinct client groups, or markets, with which it must deal effectively: employees within the organisation; other managers involved with senior management tasks including the CEO; and external groups such as prospective employees, government, unions and regulatory bodies. Consideration of the challenges faced by HR managers indicates that they are similar to those challenges faced by other senior managers, and requirements for success correspond to those needed by good marketing managers. The use of marketing ideas does not need to be confined narrowly to products and markets. Marketing has been defined as 'a social process by which individuals and groups obtain what they need and want through creating and exchanging products and value with others' (Kotler, 1984), and implies two voluntary parties with unsatisfied needs, an expectation of mutual benefit, a means of communication, and a medium to complete the exchange.

People who buy goods and services are involved in the same type of exchange process as people who seek employment that is satisfying, interesting and more than a well lit work space. The relationship between buyer and seller in a labour market is such that the employee must sell labour to earn an income. A company must create goods or services and exchange them in order to earn profits. Clearly there are times when one party to an exchange has much more bargaining power than the other party. The manager who seeks mutual benefit through working closely with the HRM department is involved in a similar exchange process to that which takes place between consumers and companies everywhere.

One source of interdepartmental conflict can be the need for a marketing manager to represent the interests of a customer against the needs of other managers. We do not lack examples of conflict between the marketing and accounting functions. For example, while the sales department is properly concerned with maintaining a good relationship and undisrupted supply to the customer, the accounts department is concerned with administering credit control. Accounts may seek the withholding of supply, because credit guidelines have been exceeded, at a time when sales is trying to service a sudden increase in demand, resulting in open conflict (Collins, 1985). Similarly, an HR manager can become involved in interdepartmental conflict through a need to represent the interests of an employee against the needs of another manager. Like marketing, HRM is a function where success requires close cooperation with other functions, but there can be significant potential for conflict. The coalitions of power and politics at the core of fundamental conflicts such as this can be used to maximise business performance, or detract from it. The task for the HR manager is made more difficult because the quality of management performance is difficult to quantify — there is no bottom-line responsibility. This can leave the HR manager without the defence available to managers of profitable business units who have tangible evidence of performance in their regular financial reports: bottom-line results.

Marketing performs a valuable role in that it creates utility, the capacity to satisfy needs (Murphy and Enis, 1985). The HR manager is similarly concerned with the creation of utilities. The marketing philosophy or concept states that, in serving marketplace needs, the entire organisation should be guided by thinking that centres around the consumer. For our purposes the concept has three key elements:

- The HR manager requires a thorough knowledge of the needs, wants and problems of the CEO, other managers and employees. Ideally the HR manager should start with a knowledge of client needs and work backwards to developing products and services to satisfy them.
- The second element requires that the cost, design, implementation and follow-up on HR projects should be carefully planned so that all features are consistent with project goals, and the process coordinated with other functions in the organisation.
- Finally, in our definition of marketing we recognise that individuals or groups engaging in the marketing process have diverse goals and objectives. If the organisation itself does not gain utility from an exchange then this element of the philosophy is not met. Consequently we would expect that if an HR activity did not lead to organisational gain the activity would be discontinued.

Quantification of performance plays a crucial role in the success of the marketing function, and the performance audit guides corrective action, while providing measurements essential to supporting access to resources for projects. HR managers have sometimes been characterised by a lack of willingness to work with performance measures. Marketing depends strongly on techniques developed in the behavioural sciences for quantification of the needs, wants and perceptions of consumers. These tools can be readily adapted to the requirements of the HR manager. While measures employed by marketing managers are not always of high precision, they are essential to building credibility through measurement, and performance against explicit goals. Management performance in functions other than marketing and HRM is generally more amenable to measurement.

An HR manager with a market orientation would have good knowledge of the needs and wants of the client groups served, and develop a coordinated approach to servicing those requirements consistent with organisation goals, with the expectation of achieving organisational gain from any exchange process. In contrast, a product-oriented HR manager would place primary emphasis on the products or services the HRM department offers, and how these are provided. It is instructive to consider the differences between these two opposing views. Consider training programmes, for example: the difference between a product-oriented and a market-oriented manager is shown in Table 5.1. This example is stereotypical in that the model represents two extreme positions. No one person would be expected to exhibit all the characteristics presented for a specific orientation, but an HR practitioner would be expected to possess several if they were either market or product oriented, and the distinction between two very different management philosophies is illustrated.

We have found it a useful exercise during workshops with senior managers to discuss the role of conflicting philosophies and how they affect the achievement of a marketing orientation. This can be addressed in the context of both external customers (Payne, 1988) and internal customers (Vandermerwe and Gilbert, 1989). Although it has been accepted for many years that a market orientation is essential to the success of a business, it has not been proven in all contingent situations. Monopoly or regulated markets provide examples of non-market orientation. As the difference between a market orientation and any one of many possible conflicting orientations is accepted as the difference between unstable short-term success and stable long-term growth, it becomes of considerable importance to senior managers to push a market orientation within their company. Similarly HRM has gradually gained credibility and importance, as managers have come to understand how it can contribute to the achievement of business success. There exists an increasing number of well known companies where superior HRM is believed to be a key factor in their success.

We have seen the similarity in the roles of marketing and HR managers. The marketing and HRM processes both involve the creation and exchange of utilities. A need to represent the interests of a client, against the narrow interests of another manager, may be conducive to the wellbeing of the company but a source of open interdepartmental conflict. This conflict is difficult to manage and can detract from the effectiveness of the function and the organisation. Both functions require commitment and support from the CEO to succeed, and performance measurement is seen to be an important tool for building credibility within the company. The market orientation can be applied equally to either the marketing or HR functions when it is accepted that success is achieving organisational goals through delivering customer satisfaction. We will now consider how the HR manager can harness the ideas and tools of the marketing function to contribute more effectively towards the organisation's objectives.

Table 5.1 Stereotypical differences between market-oriented and product-oriented HR managers with respect to training programmes

Attitudes and procedures	Product orientation	Market orientation
Attitudes towards clients:	They should be glad we exist. Trying to cut costs and bring out better programmes.	Client needs determine training programmes.
Programme offering:	Department provides courses that fit our skills and interests.	Schedule programmes we know the clients need.
Interest in innovation:	Focus is on technology and cost cutting.	Focus on identifying new opportunities.
Importance of costs:	A number in the budget we cannot exceed.	A critical objective.
Number of programmes scheduled for the year:	Set with the delivery requirements in mind.	Set with client needs and costs in mind.
Role of marketing research:	To determine client reaction if used at all.	To determine client needs and if they are being met.
Attendance at programmes:	Fill all available places — repeating is good revision.	Select attendees according to their needs and coordinate this with other managers.
Promotion of programmes:	Advise managers when their staff is to attend the next course.	Demonstrate need-satisfying benefits of course to clients.

THE HRM-MARKETING FUNCTION

We are concerned here with internal marketing — that form of marketing where both the 'customer' and the 'supplier' are inside the organisation. In this context we consider employees as customers or clients. These classifications are quite broad, and could be further divided into such groupings as the board, managers, supervisors, foremen, clerical staff, etc. The HRM-marketing function can be described in terms of seeing managers and employees as in-house customers, viewing the tasks and activities performed by the HRM function as in-house products or services, and offering in-house services that satisfy the needs and wants of managers and employees, while addressing the objectives of the organisation (Berry, 1981).

The reasons for believing that marketing provides a useful framework for HRM depend largely on the congruences we have demonstrated between the essential activities of the two functions. In addition to these congruences, there is a strong similarity in the constraints and difficulties facing either marketing or HR managers. Concepts and tools proved to be useful to the marketing function can also be applied for the benefit of HRM.

The HRM function provides services or programmes to employees and managers, which means that it sells performances that directly influence business productivity. Internal marketing can help an HR manager to attract and hold the type of people a company wants and get the best from in-house customers, so the HR function can upgrade the capability of a company to satisfy the needs and wants of its external customers.

Marketing management is the process of increasing the effectiveness and/or efficiency with which marketing activities are performed. Effectiveness refers to the degree to which organisational objectives are attained, while efficiency is concerned with the expenditure of resources to accomplish these objectives. This difference is eloquently expressed in the view that it is more important to do the *right things* (improve effectiveness) than to do *things right* (improve efficiency) (Drucker, 1974). An organisation that is doing the right things wrong (effective but not efficient) can outperform organisations that are doing the wrong things right. Effectiveness and efficiency are also a concern of the HR manager seeking improved performance.

MARKETING ACTIVITIES

The marketing function in any organisation is concerned with a number of related activities which include:

- understanding the market and competitive environment;
- defining the firm's mission;
- determining the target market segments to be emphasised;
- developing integrated marketing mix strategies to accomplish this mission in the selected segments;
- implementing marketing mix strategies and controlling marketing activity.

This well known model of marketing function activities is used as a basis for a discussion on internal HRM marketing.

Market and Competitive Environment

The starting point is for HR managers to gain a good knowledge of the needs and wants of the client groups served, the significant factors influencing the HR department's operations, and identify the 'publics' which interact with the company. This process is market analysis and involves combining information on the different client markets in a database.

Market research should be used to identify internal client needs, wants and attitudes just as it can be used to identify the needs, wants and attitudes of external consumers or industrial buyers. For example, 'climate surveys' concerning perceptions of remuneration packages, employment conditions and performance appraisal, and opinions of quality improvement programmes, provide direct benefits for the redesign and improvement of key policies, processes and programmes. There is also the positive effect on morale that flows from taking an interest in the views of employees.

This channel of communication provides an early means of pinpointing organisational breakdowns and problem areas. An important requirement before undertaking data collection is to adopt a commitment to face the issues uncovered, no matter how unpalatable. It is an ongoing process requiring issues to be resolved in order to maintain the credibility of the HR department at all levels within the company. To raise the expectations of client groups without delivering can generate strongly negative effects. Finally, market research can also provide a basis for monitoring the impact of programmes on employees, and check whether HR programmes are achieving what they were designed to achieve.

This market research process sometimes suffers from a condition referred to as the 'no-full-disclosure disease' (Weinshall, 1982). It manifests itself through people within the management hierarchy who fear that the things threatening them may become known to others, and then used to their personal detriment. The extent of this problem depends on survey design and content. People interviewed tend to speak freely when given a chance to express their thoughts and opinions on HRM issues. However, undertaking not to reveal the content of an interview under any circumstances, without prior approval from the person interviewed, is sometimes necessary in order to get at the real problems and issues. Whether use is made of questionnaires, personal interviews, informal meetings of managers, or group discussions, market research provides a clear means of identifying client needs and wants. It also provides the means for tracking performance.

Mission

The second step involves the development of a mission for the HR department. The corporate mission statement for an organisation is too broad to be meaningful for a specific business function, and consequently a mission statement should be specifically developed for the HRM function. It involves asking the questions: 'what is our role within the organisation?' and 'what should our role be within the organisation?' Figure 5.1 provides an example of an HR mission statement based on one developed with a leading British service organisation.

At the HRM level the definition of mission does not have to be complex. It should provide a framework for explaining the HR department's role and how it can help the different levels and units of an organisation to coordinate their efforts to achieve the organisation's overall objectives.

Once the mission statement has been adopted, objectives need to be formalised. Because objectives are not equally important, a hierarchy of potential services, programmes and projects should be put together. If possible these objectives should be operationalised — stated in terms that are specific, and which will lead to measurable end results. It is important to understand what needs to be accomplished, when the task should be completed, and how it will be decided that the task is completed. This process links very closely with the market research function which can be used to demonstrate performance against specific objectives. A function which provides a service, and deals predominantly in intangibles, requires tangible evidence of success in order to demonstrate competent performance and help build credibility.

To develop and promote the highest quality human resource practices and initiatives in an ethical, cost-effective and timely manner to support the current and future business objectives of the organisation and to enable line managers to maximise the calibre, effectiveness and development of their human resources.

This will be achieved through working with managers and staff to:

- develop an integrated human resource policy and implement its consistent use throughout the organisation;
- enhance managers' efficient use of human resources through the provision of responsive and adaptable services;
- be the preferred source of core strategic HR services;
- provide high-quality tailored HR consultancy;
- introduce methods to plan for the provision of the required calibre and quantity of staff;
- ensure consistent line accountability throughout all areas of the organisation;
- assist the organisation in becoming more customer aware and responsive to changing needs;
- define and encourage implementation of an improved communications culture throughout the organisation;
- maintain an innovative and affordable profile for HRM.

Figure 5.1 Human resource mission statement

Market Segmentation

The third step is deciding which market groups should be emphasised. Market segmentation is a process by which we divide the total, heterogeneous group of clients into smaller, more homogeneous groups with similar needs and wants that the HR function can satisfy successfully. By developing specific services we can generally improve the effectiveness of our performance in satisfying clients. It may cost more to serve smaller groups, or to handle problems requiring customised solutions. Because of this, there is sometimes a need to balance the level of customisation required to solve a problem adequately against the benefits which might accrue to the organisation. This is very much a cost–benefit exercise. The characterisation shown in Figure 5.2 can be helpful for sorting problems into classes, each of which require different capabilities.

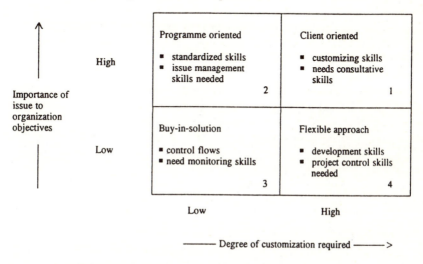

Figure 5.2 Characterising HR marketing problems

At a high degree of customisation, there is increased demand for resources from the HR function. The HR cost to the organisation increases with an increase in the level of customisation. Programmes or projects undertaken by HR typically involve long-term benefits with short-term costs, and given limited resources, this has a direct impact on the HR department's effectiveness.

Quadrant 1 in Figure 5.2 represents the situation where there is need to fit a key programme to the specialised needs of a client group. A major company wishing to run an in-house strategic management seminar, enabling senior managers to review and discuss current management thinking and practice, is an example. The CEO would perceive this to be of high value to the organisation, while requiring this process to fit closely with the business context.

The programme-oriented task found in quadrant 2 is characterised by the opportunity for a high quality but standardised approach to be taken. For example, consider a betting agency involved in the conversion of operations from a manual to a computerised telephone betting system. There is a need to develop and implement a programme at low cost which will enable a smooth transition to the new system. Due to the large group of operators requiring new skills there is an opportunity to seek savings through standardisation. The importance of this issue means that effective performance by the HR department is more critical.

In quadrant 3 the degree of customisation required for a task is low — for example when factory staff are being given first-aid training. The content of a first-aid training programme will be fairly standard across a range of industries. Such a programme is not central to achievement of organisational objectives, and represents a situation where service delivery can readily be obtained from outside the organisation. Once the training programme was in place, knowing who had attended the course and monitoring the training process would be the key tasks.

An increase in the degree of customisation required corresponds to an increase in the level of organisation-specific content, as shown in quadrant 4. Consider a retail tyre organisation which needs to train shop-floor staff in the testing and servicing of car batteries. This more specialised course requires company-specific input, and an in-house programme is the best solution. In this quadrant the need is for course development skills, a flexible approach and the ability to manage the development process. Other examples are custom-designed employee retire-ment programmes, or surveys of work group satisfaction where there is a need to design and implement a project with the specific needs of a client group in mind.

Obviously most impact can be made by HRM focusing efforts in those quadrants involving problems of high importance to the organisation, but not involving significant short-term investment. This type of problem area, identified because the issues involved are considered central to the achievement of business objectives, will often be more able to attract support and adequate funding. Working in areas requiring a high level of customisation, which are also critical to business success, is the challenge facing HR. This is the direction in which HR requirements have moved due to the increased complexity of business, changing technology, and the shift from an asset management to operations management philosophy.

Segmentation of employees on the basis of their needs and wants, as opposed to the segmentation of management clients, recognises the need to accommodate individual differences. This is the basis for concepts such as negotiable remuneration packages, employment contracts, flexible working hours and job sharing. The techniques used for consumer segmentation by marketers can be applied directly here. It provides opportunity for companies to 'lessen the influence of unions by placing greater emphasis on direct employee communica-tion, in addition to, or instead of, industrial relations conducted in the traditional representative way' (Cupper, 1987).

Developing and Implementing the Marketing Mix

Once the tasks of determining the mission of the HR department and the target market segments to be emphasised have been undertaken, a marketing-oriented HR function will focus on the 'marketing mix'. The marketing programme is developed based on a decision about marketing mix variables over which the HR manager has some control: designing the product or service, costing it, setting up a service delivery system, promotion of the product to clients, and gaining commitment for proposals from management. Table 5.2 illustrates the four elements of the marketing mix which need to be addressed. While all elements need to be considered, two key variables — the design of the 'product' (ie courses or services) and communications — are especially important. These two key variables and their relevance for the HR manager are now reviewed.

Table 5.2 The four elements of the marketing mix

Elements of the marketing mix for a company	Equivalent elements for the HRM function
1. Products or services.	1. 'Products' (services, courses, etc).
2. Place (distribution).	2. The location and delivery means of services and courses.
3. Promotion (mainly through advertising and personal selling).	3. Communications with client groups (primarily through discussion and documentation).
4. Pricing.	4. Transfer pricing and expense allocation.

Designing the 'product'

It has been pointed out that the process of a marketing department introducing a new product and the resolution of a complex longstanding problem by the HR function are very similar. Figure 5.3 illustrates this, and is based on Desatnick (1983) who argues that 'as the contribution of HRM is less tangible and more difficult to measure in terms of end results, it is even more important to market it effectively. This implies taking the time to reflect, to position, to package, to merchandise, and to sell.' Thus the HR manager must get the maximum impact from each situation through careful management of those elements that can be controlled. Developing a product or service for a client group is an activity over which the HR manager has a great deal of control, and consequently provides an area where management attention can be rewarded with maximum impact.

Communication

Communication represents promotional activity in the form of advertising, indirect publicity and face-to-face selling, which is employed by marketers to influence potential or existing customers to behave in desired ways, such as to

Introducing the new product (1 to 3 year cycle)	Resolving a complex HR issue (1 to 3 year cycle)
DETERMINE NEED FOR NEW PRODUCT	**DETERMINE NEED FOR NEW PROJECT PROGRAMME**
Who will buy it and why? How much will they spend on it? What needs will it satisfy?	What is the cost of not resolving this issue? What will be its impact on norms and values? What is cost/benefit value to internal clients?
SCREEN NEW PRODUCT IDEA	**EVALUATE POSSIBLE SOLUTIONS FOR CLIENTS**
What impact will it have? Will it be profitable? Is it compatible with existing products?	What impact will it have on operations? Who will manage and use the project? How does it fit with current projects/priorities?
TEST MARKET THE PRODUCT	**CONDUCT A PILOT PROJECT**
How do prospects view the product? What needs does it satisfy? Have we designed the right product?	Do internal clients find it useful? Will they support/pay? To what extent? Who will oppose it? Why?
EXPAND TO OTHER TEST MARKETS	**ADVANCE TO OTHER POTENTIAL USERS**
Are findings consistent? Are there logistic/quality problems? Did promotions result in expected sales?	Is the project valid/reliable? Does it meet the needs of all company locations? Have the benefits been properly communicated?
ANALYSE, MEASURE, PROJECT	**ASSESS OUTCOME IN ADVANCE**
What impact on other functions? Detailed budget and plans. Have all implications been considered?	Which functions are affected and how? Will it cause confusion? Have times, resources and costs been detailed?
EXPAND TO A NATIONAL LAUNCH	**IMPLEMENT COMPANY WIDE**
Does the potential outweigh risks? Are promotions and follow-up planned? Are logistics and supply lines ready? Have we means for identifying service problems and dissatisfactions?	Does project add to HR's credibility? Who will train whom to do what, where, when? Have we an effective audit/evaluation system? Will the issue really be resolved?

Figure 5.3 Comparing product development to resolving a complex HR issue

undertake the trial purchase of a product the firm has just launched on to the market. Promotion can also be used to influence employees to reconsider attitudes, to inform managers, or to alter the way in which a particular programme is perceived by the clients to whom it is directed. The use of 'publicity' through internal publications and other documentation can provide feedback to employees on current issues, as well as enhance and reinforce the credibility of the research process. A well conceived internal promotional programme can have very positive effects on employees. It can motivate, educate or help provide a sense of belonging. The famous Avis Rent-a-Car slogan suggesting that Avis employees 'try harder' was as effective for their employees as it was for the public image of Avis. This type of corporate advertisement primarily seeks to influence the perceptions of external publics, but managers tend to forget that these campaigns are also critically viewed by employees at all levels within the organisation. A campaign which lacks credibility with employees is not consistent with the development of a positive organisational culture. Managers should develop corporate communications which are consistent with the HRM objectives of the organisation. Simpler, less ambitious projects can also produce a significant impact for the HR function.

Personal interaction with other functional areas can contribute significantly to HR marketing efforts. In situations where a service or programme is either partly or fully dependent for success on the performance of employees, the communications and promotional activity should be concerned not only with encouraging clients to buy, but with encouraging employees to perform. Success in business requires the commitment of both employees and managers.

The implementation and control processes represent the final step, which involves measuring effectiveness and efficiency, taking corrective action, and iteration through the marketing planning processes. The well established marketing planning literature (McDonald, 1989) provides a framework to follow in undertaking this task.

CONCLUSIONS

The 1980s saw the start of a new emphasis on the HRM function. It has been pointed out that the reality is that a firm adopting 'HRM' may simply involve a retitling of the old personnel department with no obvious change in its functional role, or it may be 'strategic HRM' which represents a fundamental reconceptualisation and reorganisation of personnel roles and departments (Guest, 1987, 1989). The focus of strategic HRM encompasses all those decisions and actions which concern the management of employees at all levels within the organisation and which are directed towards creating and sustaining competitive advantage (Miller, 1989), but recent European research suggests that 'strategic HRM' is still not widespread. Findings from the Price Waterhouse/Cranfield HR research project show that in many European organisations HR strategies follow behind corporate strategy rather than making a positive contribution to it; and although HR representation at board level is becoming more common, this does not necessarily bring with it involvement in key decisions (Brewster and Smith, 1990; Burack, 1986). Some firms have been able to integrate HR and strategy but to achieve this usually requires a concentrated and multidimensional effort (Buller, 1988).

The scope of marketing has traditionally been limited to the exchanges that take place between organisations and their customers. More recently this scope has been expanded to encompass the field of 'relationship marketing' (Christopher *et al*, 1991) which suggests that marketing principles can be applied to a number of other key markets, including internal markets within the firm. We argue that there exist compelling reasons for bringing the internal marketing concept to bear on problems faced by all HR managers, but the greatest value will be obtained in these firms adopting 'strategic HRM'.

The shift in organisational philosophy from asset management to operations management, the introduction of new technologies to some industries, and the increased strategic importance of managing human resources effectively and efficiently, have meant that the role performed by HR managers demands a much higher level of competence and professional skills. Marketing provides an action framework and a practical approach by which the HR manager can provide effective solutions to key corporate problems. This fresh perspective will bring market-oriented HR managers significant benefits.

In spite of the emphasis in this chapter on the need for HR managers to deal effectively with the challenges they face, it must be recognised that much opportunity for the future status of HRM lies with CEOs. Their task is to provide organisational vision, and many have still failed to recognise the value of strategic HRM in the present business environment. In spite of this, the HR manager must share the responsibility through not having convinced top managers that HRM is strategically relevant to business success. Adopting a market orientation requires the HR manager to focus on the needs and wants of internal customer groups and to stimulate internal service. An investment in the marketing approach is an investment in people.

References

Baird, L and Meshoulam, I (1986) 'A second chance for HR to make the grade', *Personnel*, Vol 63, No 4, April.

Berry, L L (1981) 'The employee as customer', *Journal of Retail Banking*, Vol 3, No 1, March.

Brewster, C and Smith, C (1990) 'Corporate strategy: a no-go area for personnel?', *Personnel Management*, July.

Buchanan, R W J and Gillies, C S (1990) 'Value managed relationships: the key to customer retention and profitability', *European Management Journal*, Vol 8, No 4, December.

Buller, P F (1988) 'Successful partnerships: HR and strategic planning at eight top firms', *Organizational Dynamics*, Vol 17, No 2, Autumn.

Burack, E H (1986) 'Corporate business and human resource planning practices: strategic issues and concerns', *Organizational Dynamics*, Vol 15, No 1, Summer.

Carlzon, J (1987) *Moments of Truth*, Ballinger Publishing Company, Cambridge, Mass.

Christopher, M, Payne, A F T and Ballantyne, D (1991) *Relationship Marketing: Bringing Quality, Customer Service and Marketing Together*, Heinemann, Oxford.

Collins, B A (1985) 'The friction between marketing and finance', *The Australian Accountant*, Vol 55, No 4, May.

Cupper, L G (1987) 'An employee's viewpoint on the use of dialogue in industrial and employee relations', *Melbourne University Business School Association Journal*, Vol 10, No 1.

Desatnick, R L (1983) 'Marketing HRD: the credibility gap that's got to go', *Training*, Vol 20, No 6, June.

Drucker, P F (1974) *Management: Tasks, Responsibilities, Practices*, Harper & Row, New York.

Guest, D E (1987) 'Human resource management and industrial relations', *Journal of Management Studies*, Vol 24, No 5.

Guest, D E (1989) 'Personnel and HRM: can you tell the difference?', *Personnel Management*, Vol 13, No 1, January.

Kotler, P (1984) *Marketing Management* (5th edn), Prentice Hall, Englewood Cliffs, NJ.

McDonald, M (1989) *Marketing Plans: How to Prepare Them; How to Use Them* (2nd edn), Heinemann, Oxford.

Miller, P (1989) 'Strategic HRM: what it is and what it isn't', *Personnel Management*, February.

Murphy, P E and Enis, B M (1985) *Marketing*, Scott, Foresman & Co, New York.

Payne, A F T (1988) 'Developing a marketing oriented organisation', *Business Horizons*, Vol 31, No 3, May–June.

Peters, T J and Waterman, R H Jr (1982) *In Search of Excellence: Lessons from America's Best Run Companies*, Harper & Row, New York.

Reincheld, F F and Sasser, W E Jr (1990) 'Zero defections: quality comes to services', *Harvard Business Review*, September–October.

Vandermerwe, S and Gilbert, D (1989) 'Making internal service market driven', *Business Horizons*, Vol 32, No 6, November–December.

Weinshall, T D (1982) 'Help for chief executives: the outside consultant', *California Management Review*, Vol 24, No 4, Summer.

6

THE VALUE OF TRUST IN SERVICE SECTOR MARKETING

Haider Ali

OUTLINE

Models of marketing which have been developed to serve the needs of large businesses may be inappropriate for the small business or the self-employed professional in the service sector. For these groups of people an alternative paradigm may be needed, one which acknowledges the intangible nature of what is being sold and which is based on interpersonal relations or the network of the principals of the business. The key aspect of the management of a business based on network relations is the reliance on trust between the parties to the transaction. This chapter reports the result of a survey conducted among service sector self-employed about the methods they use to acquire customers in order to gain market entry. The principal issues considered in this chapter are.

- the importance of customer-perceived risk for service providers;
- the role of interpersonal relations (eg the network) and communication (eg by word of mouth) as a means of overcoming customer-perceived risk.

The findings discussed in this chapter are as follows:

- For the self-employed traditional marketing concepts can be effective where tangible goods/services are being sold; where intangibles are being sold, alternative concepts may be necessary and in particular networking may play an important role.
- Networking can be a planned strategic activity, in particular the use of value chains and gatekeepers is important. Through the gatekeepers (another business or organisation which can provide the marketer with personal access to the customer) the marketer can initiate a commercial relationship. Gatekeepers are, therefore, different from traditional distribution channels.

- The importance of interpersonal trust may mean that a homogeneous service can be exploited to provide greater added value once trust develops on the part of the customer. The creation of trust means that the customer will be willing to undertake more risk, ie purchase services of higher value.

The implications are that:

- Customer-perceived risk is an important issue in the provision of some services. The antidote to risk is trust. Where risk can be identified it is important to consider how any existing trust between buyer and seller may be used and also how trust may be developed.
- For some businesses requiring trusting customers, large numbers of such customers may be needed. In these situations consideration may be given to the gatekeeper.
- It is possible to develop trust in risk-free services. Where this happens, it may be possible to exploit the existence of trust by offering added value.

INTRODUCTION

Over the past 50 years, while the number of firms in production industries has risen by 28.8 per cent, the corresponding rise for the finance and business sector has been 86.4 per cent and for other services 100 per cent (Daly, 1990). Furthermore it is small businesses which dominate the service sector. Those regions of the UK which could support a service sector saw numbers of small businesses rise by up to 40 per cent, as was the case in the south-east. However, the marketplace is no soft option for those leaving the labour market. Over a third of start-up small businesses fail in the first year and it is marketing that they cite as being their most acute problem.

This chapter considers the use of personal networks in the market entry activities of the self-employed in the service sector. Existing marketing orthodoxy is based on a model of the marketing mix known as the 4 Ps. The marketer has four tools with which he can compete; the price, the product characteristics, the promotional activity and the place where the product is to be sold. However, this model does not adequately address the marketing of intangibles. The latter involve greater perceived risk on the part of the customer. When faced with perceived risk, customers buy from suppliers they can trust and/or acquire information about their intended purchase from trustworthy sources, for example by word of mouth.

On this basis, the chapter draws a dichotomy between businesses which can sell to the network 'network marketing',[1] and those businesses which can sell to people with whom the business owner has no existing relationship, 'stranger marketing'. The latter businesses can, for example, sell on the features and benefits of the product. In contrast, 'network marketing' businesses cannot sell on the basis of features and benefits and it is the strength of interpersonal relationships which will matter.[2]

Risk and Intangibility

The very act of purchasing involves risk, in the sense that the purchase will lead to consequences which the customer cannot anticipate with anything approximating certainty, and some of these consequences are likely to be unpleasant. Such customer-perceived risk can be divided into two components: the amount that would be lost (ie that which is at stake) if the consequences were not favourable, and secondly the individual's subjective feeling or degree of certainty that the consequences will be unfavourable.

If it is the amount[3] that is at stake and the certainty with which consumers can regard the outcome of the purchase as an unfavourable one, which contribute to perceived risk, then it ought to be possible to evaluate different products and services by these criteria. Purchases which are tangible, which can be seen, felt, even used before purchase, ought to have limited outcome risk.[4] On the other hand, with a purchase which is intangible customers do not know what they will get until they have bought it and the degree of outcome risk is therefore high. With tangible products/services, therefore, there is little need for there to be trust between the seller and the buyer. With intangibles, however, the customer is vulnerable to the quality of promises made by the seller and so trust does need to exist to facilitate exchange.[5]

Just as risk can be considered in terms of the certainty of an unfavourable outcome for an event, so trust can be considered in terms of an individual's confidence that a positive event rather than a negative one will occur. If you are a

---

[1] This use of the term has no relationship with any notions of multilevel marketing or new developments on pyramid-selling schemes.

[2] This terminology has corollaries in the field of marketing, with relationship marketing being analogous to network marketing and transactions marketing being analogous to stranger marketing.

[3] The certainty that the consequences will be favourable is 'outcome risk' and can be reduced by the acquisition of information; in contrast the amount that is at stake is consequent risk and that can be reduced by reducing how much is at stake. In the marketplace the types of risk to which consumers are exposed are social consequences; financial loss; physical danger; loss of time and performance.

[4] It should be noted that the traditional dichotomy between products (tangible) and services (intangible) has not been repeated here. Surveys of consumer attitudes have found that they regard some services to be more tangible than some products.

[5] It has been argued that professional services are regarded as entailing more perceived customer risk than generic services for the following reasons: problem recognition; search process; evaluation of alternatives; choice and post-purchase evaluation. In the case of problem recognition the effect on consumer risk perception is as follows. In the purchase of generic services it is the purchaser who defines the problem and does not rely on the seller for advice; in contrast, with professional services the buyer is dependent on the professional to identify the problem. In the latter case, therefore, the customer will perceive greater risk. The other three factors also lead to greater perceived risk on the part of the buyer of professional services.

customer the factors which affect your confidence are: your past experiences in similar situations; the past experiences of others; the opinions held by others whom you respect; your personal assumptions about the benevolence/malevolence of the reality you are in; your confidence about being able to influence the occurrence of a positive outcome through your own action or through available help. These factors can be categorised into three major areas: past personal experience; information from a variety of formal and informal sources; manipulation of interpersonal relationships. In terms of the marketplace the services of an architect are inherently risky, there is a large amount at stake (the cost of a building) and a great deal can go wrong. In this risky purchase the customer can nevertheless proceed if the chosen architect is one the customer has successfully used before or if the architect has been recommended by someone the customer trusts.

So customer-perceived risk can be counterpoised by the existence of trust that the customer may have in the service provider or the sources of information which are recommending a service provider. In the case of trusting a service provider, it is important to note that trust in exchange parties is not likely to appear early in a relationship because there would be little basis in past experience for its existence and trust is the product of individuals sequentially reacting to each other's behavioural displays.[6] This latter consideration of trust relies on a dynamic process with trust developing within an ongoing relationship. This notion is discussed below.

Mechanisms which produce trust are of three types: process based; character based; institution based. Process-based trust is founded on past and expected future exchanges between buyer and seller. Norms of reciprocity build up over time among the small number of participants and these serve as common expectations on which exchange is based. This form of trust is characterised by strong constitutive expectations. Goodwill develops in recurring exchanges, repeated economic relations become overlaid with social content which carries a strong expectation of trust and abstention from opportunism.

Character-based trust is said to arise out of such characteristics as ethnicity, gender and age. These serve as indicators of membership in a common cultural system and shared background expectations. The mere occurrence of social interaction has the effect of building faithfulness, because the more people participate in a social system, the more they acquire an affective bond with others.

By their nature process-based and character-based trust depend on a small number of relatively homogeneous exchange participants. However, as the social

---

[6] The latter notions are vividly illustrated in the commentary provided by respondents to questions posed by Larson (1988) in a study of small business networks and in a survey of production networks in Silicon Valley by Saxenian (1991).

order breaks down (perhaps due to demographic changes) so there may be a greater reliance on institution-based trust. This is also more likely to be associated with stranger marketing, where people undertaking transactions do not know each other and character-based trust and process-based trust are not likely to arise.

It should be noted that institution-based trust is not founded on the individuals to a transaction, but rather on institutional practices. The factors which contribute to the production of institution-based trust are individual and firm-specific actions, eg the gaining of an MBA, membership of trade associations. It should be noted, however, that in such transactions the social network between participants is likely to be less dense and people are more likely to be influenced by economic criteria, intermediaries or regulations. In the extreme it could be argued that no trust is needed in the exchange partner, since people will wholly rely on the law for the fulfilment of obligations.

The above discussion produces a continuum of trust, which is differentiated on the basis of personal to impersonal relations. Each trust mechanism is said to exhibit a different level of impersonality and therefore expectation. Personal relations are correlated with stronger expectations and levels of trust. Indeed, when high levels of trust are present, the introduction of formal mechanisms such as contracts may displace human linkages and thereby break down trust.

In summary, risk is likely to exist in the purchase of intangibles. In order to overcome risk consumers will rely on information they can trust or buy from those suppliers they can trust. In both instances this is likely to be with people they already know, members of the network rather than strangers. The implication for marketers is that if they are selling intangibles it is the more personalised, network-oriented marketing methods which are likely to be successful.

Trust and Relationship Marketing

Thus far the emphasis has been on showing the relationship between intangibility, risk and the need for trust. This argument is now considered in terms of 'transactions marketing', which it is argued here applies to the marketing of tangibles, and 'relationship marketing', which is suited to the marketing of intangibles.

Marketing was originally developed as a tool within a wider conceptualisation which regarded trade as consisting of the exchange of various types of values. This is encapsulated in the 1985 American Marketing Association definition of marketing: 'Marketing is the process of planning and executing the conception, pricing, promotion, distribution of ideas, goods and services to create exchange and satisfy individual and organisational objectives.'

Underlying this definition is the notion that firms should base their activities on customers' needs and wants in selected target markets. It has been argued (Grönroos, 1990), that this notion and the marketing mix concepts which grew out of it were developed in a particular environment, namely the US in the 1960s, which represented a large domestic market, unique media structure and a competitive distribution system. Furthermore the paradigm was developed to deal with the marketing of consumer goods in the mass market. It was never intended to serve the needs of, for example, the marketing of services.

Indeed the existing notion of marketing is grounded in the framework of exchange which represents a static and discrete view of how firms conduct business. Within this framework there is no acknowledgement of a dynamic or ongoing development of long-term relationships between buyer and seller; instead the focus has been on single transactions between buyers and sellers. Customers have been considered to be members of an anonymous mass, who could be easily and cheaply replaced if they left. Their replacement could be achieved through advertising, for example.

The desirability or profitability for the supplier of maintaining such a revolving door policy in such markets as industrial products and professional services has been questioned. According to the Nordic School of Marketing the important factors in marketing are customer relationships. The aim of the marketing activity of a business ought to be the establishment, strengthening and development of customer relationships. Such evolution of relationships can be achieved through the exchange of information, goods, services and social contacts. In line with this new emphasis on relationships, an alternative definition of marketing can be construed which considers the purpose of marketing to be the establishment, maintenance and enhancement of relationships with customers and other parties at a profit. This would be achieved by mutual exchange and fulfilment of promises.

Grönroos (1991) provides some explanation as to the role of promise fulfilment in a business relationship. According to Grönroos, establishing relationships means giving promises, maintaining relationships is based on fulfilling promises. This conceptualisation of promise fulfilment can be viewed in terms of the concept of trust discussed above — an individual will trust those who have kept their promises in the past.

The economic basis of relationship marketing rests with the notion that it is cheaper to have a long-term, stable customer relationship than to spend money continuously generating new relationships. This argument, according to Grönroos, applies in certain situations. There will be circumstances where the transaction marketing approach will actually be optimal. Jackson (1985) has defined the conditions when transactions marketing will be preferred by marketers. Her typology of marketing situations comprises an 'always-a-share model' where the customer faces low costs for switching between different suppliers and where it is economic to use transactions marketing. The second model is 'lost-for-good' where the customer faces high switching costs and changes suppliers only reluctantly. Grönroos views relationship marketing and transactions marketing as being at opposite ends of a continuum.

The transaction approach to marketing, epitomised by the Borden 4P model (Christopher *et al*, 1991), works where the seller is addressing a mass market, there is no contact with ultimate customers and the price sensitivity of customers is high. At the opposite end of the continuum a company may be providing a service where there is a high degree of interaction with the customer and the customer is not so price sensitive. It is in these latter situations that relationship marketing may play a role. Relationship marketing is characterised by the seller going for long-term goals rather than immediate returns, the focus is on customer retention, and there is a high degree of customer contact (Christopher *et al*, 1991).

In summary, there are two types of marketing. Transactions marketing covers those transactions which are short-term, bargaining relationships and where the seller's debt of performance and the buyer's debt of payment are unambiguous. In this form of exchange the benefits to be exchanged are clearly specified, so no trust is required, there is no room for bargaining, negotiation or mutual adjustment and the operators who contract together need not enter into a recurrent or continuing relationship. Between two individual parties, these transactions are characterised by being on a one-off basis, with little likelihood that the transaction will be repeated.

Price is only one of the factors which play a role in the coordination of economic exchange between agents within network exchange relationships; reciprocity norms, personal relationships and reputation are all important factors. The network medium of exchange is by definition informal, and is characterised by the lack of written contracts. Within network exchange input markets and output markets are held to be heterogeneous in character.

The preceding discussion has served to provide a framework for the survey of self-employed marketing practices. It is expected that marketing activities will be split into those which have relationship marketing characteristics and those which have transactions marketing characteristics. The former marketing activities will be considered in more detail since that is a facet of marketing which has attracted limited attention. Since this study deals specifically with the self-employed, a change of vocabulary will be preferred. Instead of relationship marketing, which applies to larger businesses, the study used the term network marketing to emphasise the idea that it is the relationships of one person, the business owner, that are being considered. Secondly, rather than the term transactions marketing the term 'stranger marketing' was used instead, once more to emphasise that small businesses which conduct short-term transactions will be doing so with people who are strangers to the business owner.

The study dealt with the start-up self-employed, specifically those who are on the Enterprise Allowance Scheme, a subsidy started in 1983 by the Department of Employment to encourage people to start their own businesses. The types of businesses studied were all in the service sector. However, unlike the typical business set up on the scheme, the business owners tended to be well qualified with businesses being set up in design, consultancy, teaching and alternative medicine. Some respondents were moving into areas such as catering from unrelated backgrounds, owing to the ease of market entry into such businesses. The study was carried out with businesses which were generally in their first year of trading, which means that the marketing activities being considered dealt with market entry. Where possible attention is drawn to marketing activities the individuals intend to use in the future.

STRANGER MARKETING AND NETWORK MARKETING

Stranger Marketing

The key characteristic of stranger marketing is that the sale is made to someone with whom the business owner has no prior relationship. There are some marketing activities which by their nature are associated with selling to strangers, eg telesales, direct mail, cold calling at potential customers' premises. Secondly, there is little likelihood of repeat sales to the same party or if they are made this is done on a strict quid pro quo basis. In contrast, network marketing involves sales being made to people with whom the business owner is already acquainted or through word of mouth or referral. Furthermore there is a likelihood that a long-term relationship will develop between the two parties based on reciprocity and diffuse relations.

In terms of personal characteristics, the people running businesses in the 'stranger marketing' category did not have or indeed appear to need specialist skills or qualifications. What these people did cite was the existence of general skills: personnel management, sales skills, logistics management, dealing with people. Where individuals in this category do have some sector-specific skills, for example the fudge sales business makes a special type of fudge, such skill lends itself to a product which either has tangible features and benefits, or as in the case of the fudge can be sold on a basis which involves little risk for either consumer or retailer. However, within stranger marketing there was a difference between businesses which were '*buying market share*' and '*shoe-leather marketing*' businesses. The former relied principally on attracting customers through money spent on advertising or the location of premises. In contrast, the 'shoe-leather marketing' group was characterised by people who relied on their selling skills to win customers.

Stranger marketing businesses charged relatively low prices and needed high numbers of customers. They sell directly to consumer markets, or in the case of the fudge sales business the sale is made via a retail intermediary. In all instances the products being offered were commodities in terms of the ease of substitution and their services could easily be replaced by the customer without any perceived loss. Indeed, this is how the businesses had gained customers in the first place. The sandwich delivery business owner talked of the sandwich wars which take place in her business. This happens when she realises that there is a competitor for a particular client and therefore calls earlier in the morning than usual in order to beat the competitor. The customers appear to be ambivalent as to who they buy from.

It should be noted that the tour operator is selling expensive niche market holidays which do not match the price pattern of the other businesses. However, he overcomes the perceived risk through the mass media advertising he uses and his ATOL (Air Travel Organisers Licence) bonding, which is issued by the Civil Aviation Authority. The brochure also helps provide some tangibility as to what people can expect. Therefore while businesses in this category could have high added value, this is overcome by adding tangibility to what is being offered.

Previous writers have said that homogeneous input/output factors are characteristic of the market-mediated exchange (stranger marketing) and heterogeneous inputs and outputs are characteristic of the network types of contract. This notion may need to be refined. The window cleaner is providing a very homogeneous service, however once he develops a relationship based on trust with a customer, the service becomes heterogeneous. The actual work has remained the same, the window cleaning is still homogeneous. The difference is that the customer trusts this particular supplier, hence the heterogeneity arises from the introduction of 'interpersonal trust' between buyer and seller.

One way of showing this trust may be to offer more work to the same window cleaner. It is therefore argued here that otherwise homogeneous/tangible services can be made heterogeneous/intangible through the introduction of other factors, mainly interpersonal factors rather than those associated with the trade. This finding therefore qualifies the idea that the inputs/outputs will be heterogeneous when the network is being used for making the sales. The input/output factors themselves can in fact be homogeneous; it is the interpersonal relationship between buyer and seller which can cause the heterogeneity to arise. The service supplier can exploit this to bring greater added value to the service being offered; in this scenario the increase in added value was through cleaning the windows of the properties managed by an estate agent as well as the offices.

Having gained market entry selling to strangers using media advertising, the tour operator is in addition now seeking to make use of some word of mouth and the existence of previous customers by selling to the latter and encouraging customers to recommend the package to others. He anticipates holding seminars and events where people who came on holiday this year can show their photographs to people who may be interested in coming in future. Such word-of-mouth and evidential marketing is aimed at overcoming perceived risk. Therefore while customers were originally attracted purely through stranger marketing, it is anticipated that more network-oriented methods will be used in future to take advantage of the goodwill which has developed. The relatively high cost of the holidays makes it economic to pay this amount of attention to get individual customers. It should be emphasised that the tour operator only considers repeat business to be a likelihood in his fifth year of trading, when people who came a few years earlier come again. This example shows how network marketing can be used once customers have been attracted using stranger marketing.

Finally it should be said that pure stranger marketing is an extreme situation. All the businesses cited above had some elements of relationship marketing which tinged their association with their customers. While the second-hand shop owner is fairly tough with her customers, she suffers from shoplifting in a rough area of north London; however, even here she has 'regular customers' who are telephoned when she receives some good stock.

Mixed Marketing

In the 'mixed marketing' category there were three separate subdivisions: '*all sorts*', '*split markets*' and '*cooperative alliances*'. The businesses with '*split markets*' were those which served two separate markets and used stranger marketing to sell to one market and network marketing to serve the other. With the first group, '*all sorts*', elements of both types of marketing were well integrated in attracting similar types of customers. The feature of the 'cooperative alliances' group was that the services had the intangibility associated with the network marketing category but the respondents formed cooperative alliances with strangers, who served the purpose of providing the gateway to a stream of customers. The actual customers tended to be people who needed the service being provided for relatively short periods of time and as such the respondents in the sample needed a steady stream of customers — the gatekeepers with whom the alliances were made served this purpose.

In the '*split markets*' category are businesses which sell to two types of customer, one through stranger marketing and the other through network means. One respondent sells software and undertakes consultancy. The proprietary item of software is sold through magazine advertising, the computer consultancy is undertaken for customers who had been clients of their previous employer (ie the latter customers were obtained through network means of marketing). Future customers in the consultancy activity have also originated through the network. Another example of a split market is the magazine publisher. He had obtained advertisers through word of mouth and a personal presence at the right exhibitions. In addition, subscribers had been obtained through direct mail and the magazine's presence in specialist shops. Having such split markets can be useful, as the software developers found, since failure in one market can be compensated by the other — their consultancy provided income at a time when the software was not selling.

'*All sorts*' are the businesses which do not appear to use a predominant method of marketing. Aspects of both relationship and network marketing are used together with reliance on stranger marketing. After 15 months of trading the bridalwear shop was attracting customers both due to its location (market mediated) and referrals (network). However, it should be said that market entry was gained predominantly through stranger marketing, ie passing trade. Now that the business is more mature it can take advantage of the goodwill it has developed on the part of previous customers.

The dresses are highly priced, £300 to £900, and involve a high degree of creativity and skill. Moreover the higher-priced dresses are bespoke and therefore the customer does need to have some trust in the ability of the designer. In this instance the social background of the owners of the business did not match that of their target market, so reliance on friends and family for custom was not viable. In addition the nature of the business means that they can only serve a person once and therefore a long-term relationship based on repeated custom becomes impossible. The use of a shop has, to an extent, overcome this problem. Its high street presence has meant that there are a steady stream of customers who do in fact drop in to buy, or who pick up cards for people who they think may be interested. In terms of the network terminology it could be said that the shop has served to bring them in touch with a far more diverse network (ie that represented by their customers) and this is important when dealing with a product which needs new customers all the time.

A good example of the difference between the effectiveness of network marketing compared to stranger marketing is shown by the example of the ex-editor at Thames TV who now has his own editing suite at home. He initially spent £2000 on brochures which were sent to names taken from a trade directory. This mailshot resulted in no trade at all. Customers have subsequently come from his brother, word of mouth and referrals. An HIV/Aids trainer started by getting business from her ex-employer. However, the goodwill this has generated has meant that she can also gain customers through both cold calling and using referrals. The start given by the network has been an important means of leveraging marketing legitimacy with people unknown to her. This is an interesting example of a business starting using the network, due to the existence of trust. Once the legitimacy has been acquired within the marketplace more formal means can then be used for marketing to strangers. This process of moving from predominantly network marketing to incorporating features of stranger marketing is in contrast to the activity observed above, for example the tour operator who moves from stranger marketing to incorporating features of network marketing. These results therefore refine the polar opposites of transactions and relationship marketing discussed above. It is in fact possible for businesses to combine aspects of both. What is being considered is a continuum rather than a straightforward dichotomy.

The '*cooperative alliance*' businesses were trying to overcome the lack of a network or indeed the exhaustion of a network where the businesses appear to need a relatively large number of clients. A successful homoeopath cited the importance of delivering classes, lectures and workshops on the subject and talking to friends and acquaintances about it whenever the opportunity arises. Through associations with women's groups and others she has been able to get customers and mothers of the friends of her three young children are also good prospects.

Relationships with such groups enables her to use them as gatekeepers to her target audience. A gatekeeper is different from a distribution channel in so far as the former enables the marketer to meet the potential customer with whom a relationship can be developed, outside the realm of the gatekeeper. For this reason this type of relationship is considered to be relationship marketing while using a shop as a retail outlet is considered to be stranger marketing. A distribution channel does not enable the marketer and the end-user to develop an interpersonal, albeit commercial relationship. Furthermore the gatekeeper need not necessarily receive financial remuneration, which is always the case with a distribution channel. So while word of mouth and referrals are adequate for businesses selling high-value services, gatekeepers will be needed where the service is intangible and the marketer also needs customers in volume.

Network Marketing

Within the network marketing group were two major subsets. One group of businesses had predominantly 'ex-employers' as customers, the second predominantly served 'friends and family'. The ex-employer businesses provided business to business services; the nature of the service provided and the charges made meant that they could rely on a relatively small number of customer relationships to survive. Within the ex-employer subset there were further subdivisions, '*scavengers*', who took customers from ex-employers who had gone out of business; '*predators*', who took customers from employers who were still in existence and were able to do this poaching due to a close relationship that they had developed with the customer; '*alliance*' refers to respondents who had a working relationship with an ex-employer to the extent that the ex-employer passed on customers; finally the respondents grouped under '*generic*' used the contacts and knowledge they had gained in their previous employment and used it to get customers — they were not competing in any way with their ex-employer.

The people serving friends and family were providing consumer services. Business failure in this group was due to the respondent being unable to move beyond the social network of friends and family for customers when this mine was exhausted. This problem was particularly acute for a homoeopath in the sample, whose business was of the type which needed a steady stream of customers. Businesses such as hers which appear to have done rather better have developed cooperative alliances with other businesses which have served as gatekeepers, as discussed above.

The product or service being offered by firms in the network category depends on the sector-specific skill possessed by the individual concerned, for example a sound recording engineer with a degree in music. The products/services being offered in this category were uniformly of high added value, high absolute value and involved business sector-specific skills.

The existence of customers in these businesses depended on the quality of the existing network of contacts. If the network was rich in potential customers then the business appears to have been doing well. Thus, for example, while architects generally have been badly hit by the downturn in the construction trade, the two architects considered by this study have both been able to undertake substantial amounts of work due to the existence of a network. While a perfectly flexible labour market (like any totally flexible market) would mean that prices would fall uniformly if demand fell and supply remained constant, this appears to be happening to only a limited extent in the architectural trade and the film industry. As well as any institutional factors affecting prices, a barrier to entry appears to be the existence of personal relationships which impose costs on the customer. For example, one architect has been able to continue working for the clients of his now liquidated employer since his employer's customers would have found it expensive to hire someone else and begin from scratch.

In the subset headed '*alliance*' the sound recording engineer did not steal customers from the initial employer, rather the latter appeared to be the gateway to future potential customers. In businesses such as this it ought to be emphasised that not only are such intangibles as creativity important, but also the personality of the individual which can also be used to impose barriers to entry. The film cameraman describes film sets as very tense and charged places, where the demonstration of the right sort of temperament can be a good recommendation for future work.

It is therefore important to note the experiential nature of such businesses. Customers only know what they have received once the service has been provided. This imposes perceived risk and therefore people prefer to deal with those they know or who have been recommended. Where such a trade depends on relatively high charges per customer, networking can be perfectly valid, indeed the exclusive marketing activity. However, some businesses are caught in situations where they need not only a high level of charges but also relatively large numbers of customers due to natural rates of customer turnover, eg personal training and homoeopathy. In such cases the marketing needs to combine networking and word of mouth with methods which bring a steady stream of customers to the business.

Where the businesses needed to deal with a small number of customers and there was a high degree of customer-perceived risk, the existence of other clients was an important factor. It added to the legitimacy of the business (Venkataraman *et al*, 1990) and new clients were interested in the 'track record' of the business, ie the record of the business owner. The quality of the show reel in film making, or the last design project in architecture, or the portfolio for designers is important to develop confidence in future customers. In such businesses, while the initial customers can come from immediate contacts, future customers may well come from referrals and word of mouth.

It should be noted that in these business to business services one large client can continue to supply enough trade for a small business to survive in the medium term. Hence the presence of some contacts in such an area is enough to guarantee survival. However, where personal services are concerned each client can only be served for a relatively short period of time, after which someone else has to be sought. In that regard it is important to note that people supplying personal services have entered into cooperative alliances with others — these alliances enable them to be on the receiving end of a stream of customers.

The group entitled 'generic' in this category are interesting from the perspective that their ex-employer did not necessarily serve the customers that they are serving. However, experience in particular trades has given them not only contacts but also the perception of an opportunity. In the case of the artist, he used to be working as a musician and used the contacts in that trade to set up as a graphic designer.

The use of a 'network' by a number of people shows the implicit use of a value chain pertinent to their particular trade. Developing links with other businesses in the value chain appears to offer such people as architects and sound recording engineers the opportunity to diversify their network and come into contact with groups of potential customers.

While networking is an increasingly fashionable phrase, the notion of value chains offers some strategic method to the networking madness of the businesses studied. Some respondents are making judicious use of the value chains applicable to their business sectors. Such use allows them to be in a relatively powerful position *vis-à-vis* other businesses and again the use of network concepts (as developed in sociology) is useful to understand observed behaviour. An architect within the sample gets work from quantity surveyors, interior designers, builders and so on. In turn he reciprocates by telling useful members of the network about projects to which they can contribute. The sound engineer started work with a particular studio, where he works with bands which may use him when they subsequently record at another studio. Furthermore the manager of a particular band may use him with another band, as may the record label itself. These groups represent the value chain of the sound recording engineer, use of which enables him to diversify his network of potential customers.

CONCLUSION

This chapter has looked specifically at the market entry methods of the self-employed in the service sector. What has been seen is the value of considering the marketing activity in terms of risk and trust. These notions may add to the concepts of transactions and relationship marketing. Regardless of the size of the business, service marketers may find value in looking specifically at the notion of customer trust and how its existence may be used in the marketing of intangibles. Moreover, even where the service entails low risk, once trust develops that may present an opportunity to offer services with greater added value. For the small business in particular, gatekeepers may serve a useful role for those service providers who need to develop personal contact with their target customers. Furthermore the notion of value chains may be useful when considering networking activity by the self-employed.

References

Christopher, M, Payne, A, Ballatyne, D (1991) *Relationship Marketing: Bringing Quality, Customer Service and Marketing Together*, Butterworth Heinemann, Oxford.

Daly, M (1990) 'The 1980s: a decade of growth in enterprise', *Employment Gazette*, November.

Grönroos, C (1990) 'Marketing redefined', *Management Decision*, Vol 28, No 8.

Grönroos, C (1991) 'The marketing strategy continuum', *Management Decision*, Vol 29, No 1.

Jackson, B B (1985) Build customer relationships that last', *Harvard Business Review*, November–December.

Larson, A L (1988) *Co-operative Alliances. A Study of Entrepreneurship* PhD Dissertation, Harvard University.

Saxenian, A (1991) 'The origins and dynamics of production networks in Silicon Valley', *Research Policy*, Vol 20, pp 423–437.

Venkataraman, S, Van de ven, A H, Buckeye, J, Hudson, R (1990) 'Starting up in a turbulent environment: a process model of failure among firms with high customer dependence', *Journal of Business Venturing*, Vol 5, pp 277–295.

Williamson, O (1985) 'The economics of organisation: the transaction cost approach', *American Journal of Sociology*, Vol 87, No 3.

7

THE FUTURE RESOURCING OF THE SERVICE SECTOR

James Arrowsmith and Ann McGoldrick

OUTLINE

Labour market conditions in the fast-growing service sector industries have recently led to initiatives to attract and recruit older workers as a relatively cheap and flexible human resource. This addresses previous discriminatory practices which have generally tended to marginalise older employees, resulting in a withdrawal of labour force potential from the workforce. More significantly for the sector, it has been found to be a strategic response to resourcing, improving efficiency and quality in service to provide increased competitive advantage for many employers.

This chapter reports on a current investigation of service sector resourcing which is designed to examine:

- the disadvantaged nature of older workers' experience of employment;
- the challenge towards more strategic human resourcing for the sector;
- positive benefits from the employment of older workers.

The following lessons are evident from this research:

- The older employee has been a neglected human resource.
- Service sector industries can effectively respond to their utilisation.
- Stereotypes regarding older workers should be avoided.
- Mature employees can contribute to the labour force in respect of commitment, flexibility and performance.
- Balance in the labour force is a key issue.

INTRODUCTION

For many employers older workers are a 'forgotten resource' for whom opportunities in recruitment, promotion, training and development are restricted on no other grounds than age. In recent years conditions of sustained economic growth together with geographically specific demographic pressures led many organisations, particularly those in the fast-growing service industries which had traditionally relied on younger labour, to begin to revise past attitudes and practices towards workers in the older age groups. Initially developed as a temporary reaction to specific labour market conditions, the success of these mainly service sector initiatives implies that the development of a more proactive and integrated approach to the older worker can contribute a relatively cheap and effective solution to many of the quantitative and qualitative issues relating to human resourcing in the service industries.

The categorisation and definition of the group 'older workers' can be a difficult and potentially arbitrary exercise. In the first place, although advancing age can generally be associated with decreasing opportunities in recruitment and training and with increasing exposure to redundancy and long-term unemployment, the effect is variable since the process is mediated by factors such as gender, occupation and skill. At an individual level the application of chronological age as a classificatory device can also be problematic, in that heterogeneity within the group can limit the elaboration or usefulness of group-specific characteristics. As a result, any discussion of the older worker must take into account differential experiences of the labour market and recognise the diversity of indiviual circumstances and characteristics within the group.

The disadvantaged position of older workers in the labour market, structured by age-specific barriers to occupational entry and reinforced by increased liability to exit, bears close similarities to the situation of women who may seek to leave the labour force temporarily for domestic reasons. Indeed for many purposes these 'women returners' may be considered within the older worker category, although here attention will be paid mainly to those further up the age spectrum where disadvantage and discrimination are at least more explicitly institutionalised in organisational practice. Certainly employers have on the whole been slow to address the potential of the older worker resource, and this chapter is concerned with an examination of developments within the service sector which have encouraged employers to consider the older worker more actively in their human resourcing strategies.

'MARGINALISATION' OF OLDER WORKERS

The effects of industrial rationalisation and restructuring in the 1980s fell heavily on the older age cohorts as compulsory and 'voluntary' service-related redundancy packages and early retirement schemes were used to manage the downsizing process (Trinder, 1989, 1991). Many of these workers faced severe difficulties in finding re-employment and became long-term unemployed or effectively prematurely retired (Standing, 1986; Laczko and Phillipson, 1991), while others experienced occupational downgrading into less well paid and less secure employment (Evans, 1990; Casey and Laczko, 1992). The contrast between this process of widespread labour force exclusion, encouraged and facilitated by the State and trade unions, and previous exhortations in conditions of full employment to recognise and utilise the older worker resource, lends credence to a characterisation of older workers as a 'secondary labour force' or 'buffer group' in the labour market (Casey and Wood, 1990; Harris, 1991); although much of this analysis relates primarily to the position of older men, since the female concentration in the expanding service industries afforded some protection from many of the upheavals faced by manufacturing industry in the last decade (Casey *et al*, 1991).

Nevertheless, age-related barriers to occupational entry continued to be particularly resilient in service sector industries. Discrimination on the basis of age in recruitment and selection decision making is central to the marginalisation process. The most rigid and explicit form of age discrimination here is the use of age bars in job advertisements, which continue to be widely deployed despite the potential cost in precluding many experienced, able and well qualified individuals from participation in the recruitment and selection process (Jolly *et al*, 1980; Nicholls and Haskel, 1988). A recent study of age discrimination in recruitment advertising discovered that upper age limits were most often used for managerial positions and especially in the finance and insurance, retailing and business service sectors (McGoldrick and Arrowsmith, 1992). Although the use of such explicit age bars was beginning to decline, the evidence suggested that their use continued to be more popular in service industries and any decline may indeed have been accompanied by a shift into more indirect or hidden forms of discrimination.

The operation of age bias may be more disguised in the selection process where it is less easy to observe how certain negative age-related assumptions come to be used as a device to filter candidates (Singer and Sewell, 1989). For most employers the interview remains the most important stage in the selection procedure, despite doubts relating to its reliability and validity (House of Commons, 1991). Here the possibility arises of subjectively formulated stereotypes and acceptability criteria being applied, even to the extent of 'crowding out' more concrete job-related criteria based on individual suitability (Kinicki and Lockwood, 1985; Brown and Scase, 1991).

Research evidence indicates that employers have a well developed package of stereotypical assumptions relating to older workers' abilities, performance and potential for development (Rosen and Jerdee, 1976a, 1976b; Metcalf and Thompson, 1990). Within this the more positive supposed characteristics relating, for example, to reliability, integrity and maturity, are overwhelmed by negative assumptions regarding flexibility, productivity, trainability, energy and dynamism (Singer, 1986; Walker, 1990). These stereotypes, which become more pronounced when selection choices have to be made between older and younger candidates (Lee and Clemens, 1985), are fed and reinforced by a relative lack of formal qualifications and up-to-date skills within the older cohorts which many employers claim to be one of the biggest constraints on their employment (Thompson, 1991). This does not explain, however, why employers seem to be unwilling to develop training solutions to these supply-side problems (Rosen and Jerdee, 1977; Clarke, 1991). Again this may be due more to simple and misplaced assumptions as to older workers' trainability and longevity in employment, than a result of any particular problems inherent in older workers themselves (Employment Department, 1991; WNC, 1991).

As with most stereotypical generalisations, any usefulness in application as a convenient standard for measuring or filtering information is lost in the inaccuracy of the assumptions. Most of the available research evidence indicates that chronological age alone is a poor test or predictor of performance; indeed if anything job performance, productivity, motivation and satisfaction may actually be positively related to age (Waldman and Arolio, 1986; Humm and Sharp, 1991; Snyder and Dietrich, 1992). Similarly, although some techniques may have to be modified to take into account the needs of those unaccustomed, for example, to a formal learning situation, the evidence indicates that older workers are not necessarily any more difficult to train. Furthermore, given the often relatively lower turnover rates of the older age groups, employers are likely to recover a greater return on their initial training investment (Plett, 1990). This depends of course on successful management methods which recognise and value the older worker as a positive resource and avoid an environment in which some of the more negative assumptions come to be self-fulfilling (Luthans and Thomas, 1989).

SERVICE SECTOR HUMAN RESOURCE MANAGEMENT AND THE OLDER WORKER

Quality, Efficiency and Strategic Labour Management

The emergence of a more strategic approach to human resource management within the service sector has been associated with a requirement to secure continued improvements in quality and efficiency in service provision in increasingly competitive conditions and frequently within the constraints of relatively tight labour markets. This process was often further facilitated by trends towards concentration and the application of new technology within many service industries.

The service sector may be characterised as a diverse range of consumer, producer and social service industries which nevertheless share certain characteristics both in terms of product (intangibility, simultaneous production and consumption, non-standardisation, etc) and employment patterns (relatively labour intensive, significantly female and part time). The nature of the service-product ensures a particular importance is given to the 'people dimension' in delivering quality — the degree of closeness to the customer, by which both management and front-line staff are involved in a direct and immediate relationship with the consumers of their product, implies that staff motivation, loyalty and commitment can be fundamental in contributing to continuously high standards of service provision. This in turn suggests that the human resource management function can make a crucial contribution to organisational success in recruiting, retaining and training staff with the necessary motivation, product knowledge and interpersonal skills (Willman, 1989).

In recent years tendencies within the service sector towards greater rationalisation and concentration have been partly facilitated by the introduction of new technology, which has had the effect of simultaneously lowering operating costs while creating new economies of scale and consequently raising new barriers to entry (Segal-Horn, 1989). The application of new technology has also enabled many firms to adopt a more complete approach to the management and utilisation of labour, particularly as within each industry competitive pressures continue to intensify. In finance and banking, for example, deregulation and the introduction of office-based information technology and self-service automated teller machines have contributed to large-scale rationalisation programmes and enabled greater flexibility in working practices (Fifield, 1989; O'Reilly, 1992). In food retailing the expansion of the multiples has been associated with greater centralisation in management, which together with the introduction of, for example, laser scanning and electronic point of sale (EPOS) technology at the checkout, has enabled a more sophisticated deployment of labour to correspond more closely with customer flow. These gains in efficiency have been translated into a more effective response to the challenge raised by the discounters (Sparks, 1989). In the public sector the compulsion to address issues of efficiency in labour utilisation has been imposed centrally with pressures, for example, to introduce greater competition through competitive tendering and decentralisation in order to improve standards of 'customer' service (Flynn, 1989).

Taken together these developments contributed to the emergence of an increasingly sophisticated human resource function within service industries. Furthermore, the continued expansion of the sector and the possibility of constraints arising from changing conditions in the labour market enabled the function to develop an increasingly proactive approach to resourcing issues. In particular, a response had to be made in recent years to emerging recruitment difficulties, which together with high rates of labour turnover had the effect of raising recruitment costs and also brought negative implications for quality and customer service. The relatively labour-intensive nature of much of the service sector largely precluded a response to the twin problems of recruitment and turnover based on improving pay or developing channels of career progression. In these circumstances one successful solution to the quantitative and qualitative problems of staffing which were intensified by the labour market conditions was found to be to target non-traditional sources of labour, and in particular the older worker.

Labour Market and Demographic Change: The Service Sector Response

For much of industry the response to the employment challenges raised by the implications of demographic change for the labour market were slow to come and limited in nature. Even in a context of tightening labour markets and developing skills shortages, employers chose on the whole to make a more short-term set of responses based primarily on increasing competition for traditional sources of labour (NEDO, 1989; Thompson, 1991). Whether this was a result of a lamentable short-termism and complacency within UK industry (Nicholls and Haskel, 1988; Fielder *et al*, 1991), or due to a more rational analysis that labour market change represented either no immediate or no long-term danger to current resourcing policies and plans (Casey and Wood, 1990), it was certainly the case that the more innovative responses were generally confined to the service sector where a relatively high dependence on young labour and sustained levels of growth added a greater sense of urgency to the demographic issue. These firms were also well placed to draw successfully on such groups as women returners and older workers, given the degree of flexibility prevalent in working time arrangements which could allow for a smoother combination of work with domestic or leisure commitments.

One of the best known examples of such an initiative is that of B&Q, the largest D-I-Y chain in the UK. Problems in securing an adequate supply of young people and concerns relating to standards of customer service and product knowledge encouraged the company to experiment with an over-50s store in Macclesfield as a test of older workers' ability. The company found that the older workers brought positive gains in terms of sales, productivity, shrinkage, turnover, absenteeism and customer service, cost no more to employ and were no more difficult to train (Barth *et al*, 1991; Hogarth and Barth, 1991). The exercise was also deemed a success in terms of breaking down line management scepticism and resistance, and the company plans to increase the numbers of over-50s employed throughout its stores as an integral and long-term element of its human resourcing strategy.

The supermarket chain Tesco, acting in response to geographically specific recruitment problems in the late 1980s, similarly undertook a range of initiatives aimed on the one hand at improving the competitive position of the company in the market for young labour while simultaneously targeting the over-55s. Gains were again reported in terms of absenteeism, turnover rates and improved standards of customer service. Additionally it was discovered that older workers could work well alongside younger age groups and could have a positive effect on the latter's stability and job performance (House of Commons, 1989; Lennon, 1989, 1990). Similar longer-standing experiments in the US, at for example Days Inns of America and the Travellers' Corporation, have also illustrated that the purposeful employment of older workers can produce positive results in recruitment, retention, flexibility and employee motivation (McNaught and Barth, 1992).

Although these initiatives were largely specified by geography and time, being in the main a response to tightening labour markets in the growth conditions of the later 1980s, they remain of more significance in countering some of the negative stereotypes relating to older workers and illustrate how this group can be successfully utilised to address some of the quantitative and qualitative labour issues relating to recruitment, retention, employee motivation and standards of customer service within the service sector. The extensive utilisation of older labour may not necessarily be a relevant or complete response for all service firms or occupations. Barriers may be raised, for example, where it is perceived to be important to match staff with customer type (as in some areas of clothes retailing), while supply-side frictions may exist as a result, for instance, of the gender-stereotypical nature of much service sector work (Harrop, 1990; Fielder *et al*, 1991). These and other examples, however, do illustrate how the older worker resource can be an important medium to long-term possibility, particularly in meeting three of the functional requirements which characterise much of routine service sector labour, described below.

Part-time and Flexible Working Arrangements

Part-time and other flexible forms of labour are an essential requirement in service industries where demand is variable and labour is relatively intensive, making total labour costs relatively high (Walsh, 1990). Most older workers prefer to work part-time (Casey and Wood, 1990).

Need to Contain Labour Costs

The labour-intensive nature of service industries, together with often tight margins, has contributed to relatively lower rates of pay in the service sector. Many older workers seek employment for social as much as instrumental reasons and may already be in receipt of pension or investment income.

Commitment and Quality in Service

A lack of opportunities for career advancement may not demotivate older workers as much as younger employees. Many firms have also observed that the older worker can have a strong work ethic and bring a greater commitment to high standards of service.

While we are wary of the risk of generalisation concerning older worker motivation and ability, it becomes clear that it is in the interest of service sector employers to address the older worker resource more positively, particularly as the, albeit delayed, effects of demographic change may yet bring into further question any continuing overdependence on younger labour. Case examples clearly illustrate how a range of different service sector employers are beginning to recognise the older worker resource in their present and future planning.

RECOGNISING THE OLDER WORKER RESOURCE: SOME CASE EXAMPLES

Case investigations from research among service sector employers indicate how and why different organisations have begun to develop or re-evaluate past employment practice towards the older worker, highlighting some of the differences and common factors underlying their approach.

Public Sector

Manchester City Council

Local authorities constitute a significant sector of the UK economy, employing nearly two million people and managing some 11–12 per cent of gross national product (Storey and Fenwick, 1990). In recent years central government reforms, such as the introduction of compulsory competitive tendering, have been directed at the authorities as part of an attempt to improve local accountability through the introduction of a more competitive and efficient operating environment. The reform process, which can be traced back to the 1974 local government reforms and which has been sustained under the auspices of the Audit Commission, has increasingly facilitated the emergence of a more managerial and performance-oriented culture within the local government sector, moving away from the traditionally prevailing administrative and professional ethos (Flynn, 1989; Rothwell, 1990). Ever tighter financial constraints have served to reinforce the impetus towards improving efficiency in service provision, often for example through a reorganisation on business lines. This has accelerated the professionalism of local government management in general and of human resource management in particular within the sector. Increasingly the personnel function has adopted a more strategic role in providing a general advisory and support service input into human resource planning and policy making, in addition to their more traditional administrative and O and M (Organisation and Methods) services. In Manchester this is most noticeable in the area of equal opportunities, where added local political pressure to address the issues of race, ethnicity and gender discrimination also contributed to an overhaul of existing recruitment and selection procedures. This was designed to improve efficiency, objectivity and hence effectiveness, both in terms of fulfilling the requirements of the equal opportunities programme and in better meeting current and future human resourcing needs.

The Manchester equal opportunity initiative advanced considerably in 1985 with the formation of an equal opportunity committee, race and equal opportunity units and the establishment of departmental equality working parties. The following year, an 11-page policy statement was produced. By 1989 a comprehensive 41-page code of practice was completed, which set out very detailed procedures for each stage of the recruitment and selection process. The purpose of this exercise was to complete the break from traditional, informal patterns of recruitment by imposing a systematic, step by step recruitment and selection procedure. This was to be based solely on objective and job-related criteria, on which could be superimposed an active equal opportunity programme, involving target setting and monitoring. Initial line resistance to what was perceived to be an unjustified and time-consuming interference in line managerial prerogatives was countered by explanation and justification on business as well as ethical and legal grounds. There was in addition a three-day equal opportunities training programme, supported by the targeting and monitoring process itself, which helped to structure the equal opportunities agenda into the managerial function. Line misgivings concerning the revised recruitment and selection procedure and the new equal opportunities programme are felt to have diminished over time. It is unclear as yet whether this is a positive case of attitudes following and adjusting to new standards of legislated behaviour, or a more resigned accommodation to the new forms of standard practice over time.

Older workers are clearly recognised as a disadvantaged group by the equal opportunities programme and many of their needs are beginning to be addressed by the initiative. The policy of the Authority is that there should be no discrimination on the basis of age (up to age 65) in recruitment, selection, training or promotion opportunities. This commitment is stated in all job advertisements and is translated into practice at various stages of the recruitment and selection procedure. The application form, for example, is standardised and does not require applicants to indicate their age either directly or indirectly through dates of previous employment or of qualifications obtained. The personnel department also scrutinises the crucial person specification on which the process is based, challenging anything other than minimum and essential requirements. These include, for example, descriptions of personal characteristics which could be interpreted as age biased by potential applicants. Here further progress will depend on the interest and commitment of council members as well as officers towards addressing age as an equal opportunities issue.

This process has been delayed, however, by the current downsizing programme within the Authority. The commitment to a policy of awarding compulsory redundancies has necessitated the introduction of a large-scale early retirement/redeployment programme and a freeze on external recruitment. This has been interpreted as having negative implications for the implementation of the Authority's wider equal opportunities programme, in that the existing workforce is given priority in meeting resourcing needs (Corby, 1992). In the longer term, however, the implications for older workers may be more positive: already there is some evidence that the redeployment of older staff, particularly into relatively 'young' areas (eg the 'homelessness' project), has encouraged managers to revise upward their perceptions of older worker abilities.

New developments for the near future are likely to include, for example, a scheme whereby retired and other experienced older workers could be offered part-time and temporary contracts as the Authority completes its review of 'alternative' working arrangements. Previous political objections to part-time and other flexible forms of work have receded in the face of Audit Commission criticisms, combined with a growing realisation that flexible working patterns could be a positive and mutually beneficial means of controlling costs while improving standards of recruitment and retention. It is expected that such initiatives will continue to be developed as a contribution to meeting the obligations of the equal opportunities programme and as a response to the resourcing implications of an ageing workforce. That the Authority is aware of and developing contingency plans for the potential effects of demographic change is illustrated by its commitment to METRA (Metropolitan Authorities' Recruitment

Agency) and its campaign 'Age No Barrier', which seeks to raise awareness of age discrimination and to develop employment policies and practices relevant to an ageing workforce within the local authority sector.

The National Health Service

Parallels with local government can be found in the development of human resource management in the NHS, which has also contributed to greater attention being paid to equal opportunity and older worker issues. Here again, central government reforms designed to extend choice and improve efficiency, primarily by effecting an internal reorganisation based on decentralist and more market-oriented lines, have acted to stimulate the personnel function into a more proactive and developmental role. At the same time, labour market conditions have also contributed to a more sophisticated approach to, for example, equal opportunity issues, in order to meet resourcing needs in a labour-intensive and financially circumscribed organisation.

The origins of the present reform process can be identified as the introduction of competitive tendering in the mid-1980s, together with the 1989 programme designed to introduce the techniques of Total Quality Management into the NHS. Both of which were aimed at cost reduction as much as improving quality of service (Brooks, 1992). The main plank of the reforms was introduced in 1991, however, when the purchasing and providing functions of the health authorities were separated. District health authorities were now obliged to set standards, targets and priorities for health care, while the operational responsibility for meeting these requirements was to be invested in the service providers, most of whom were envisaged to become autonomous, self-governing trusts with independent responsibility not only in marketing their services but in staff planning and profiling, setting terms and conditions of employment, recruitment and retention, equal opportunities and industrial relations (Corby, 1991). This decentralisation process carries with it potentially revolutionary implications for the personnel function within the NHS, as increasing local flexibility both necessitates and enables local personnel managers to adopt a more strategic approach to planning for their own current and future employment needs (Hodges, 1991).

In addition to the internal reforms, pressure on the traditional personnel role was raised by changing conditions under which the NHS had operated in the labour market. Increasing awareness of the nature and potential effect of demographic changes for resourcing the NHS was heightened by tightening labour markets. This contributed to an emerging revision of past practice, by which high rates of labour turnover were tacitly accepted, as well as to a challenge on mainstream business grounds to what was generally recognised to be a poor record on equal opportunity issues (Parkyn, 1991). The key to improving performance in recruitment and retention increasingly came to be the provision of greater flexibility as a device to attract and keep staff: flexibility in employment practices and working patterns in order to meet the needs of staff with domestic and other commitments; and flexibility in patterns of recruitment in order to widen the employment pool to other non-traditional sources of labour (Selkirk, 1991). As part of this process came a belated recognition of the potential of more mature staff. In nursing, for example, recruitment efforts have been targeted in part at older workers, and more access courses, together with part-time training facilities, have been introduced to accommodate their progression (Martin, 1990).

These trends and developments have been noticeable in the two hospitals examined in the Manchester region. Both Withington and the Manchester Royal Infirmary (MRI) are large teaching hospitals and, although only the latter has trust status, both institutions have had to adapt to the new requirements demanded as a result of large-scale organisational change. The development of the personnel function in both these hospitals illustrates how the personnel role has been transformed from an essentially administrative one, which ensures the uniform application of centrally determined rules and procedures, to a more forward-looking and advisory role. This involves the independent planning and management of institutional human resources at both a strategic and day-to-day level, working closely with line management to formulate and implement particular policies and practices according to local circumstances. Of course, the accommodation of the personnel function to the wider opportunities and responsibilities resulting from decentralisation has by no means been an easy or complete process. Particular problems are raised by the peculiar history and nature of the NHS, not least the status, authority and strong professional ethos of senior groups of staff, as well as the sheer variety of occupations and grades which has to be dealt with. Nonetheless, in both institutions independent planning for local employment needs is now well developed and several initiatives have been taken which have had the desired effect of providing greater opportunity, including for the older worker.

In both hospitals greater emphasis is being placed on flexibility in employment practice as a means of maintaining and improving performance in recruitment and retention. Although in large teaching hospitals any difficulties in recruitment for many grades are expected to continue to be less severe than for other comparable hospitals, it is recognised that greater flexibility in working practices will be necessary to accommodate the needs of women and increasingly of older employees. The proportion of student nurse entrants aged over 25 in the region has, for example, more than doubled between 1989 and 1990 to 11 per cent of the total. Where previously initiatives may have been *ad hoc* and pragmatic, they have been formalised and established as good practice. In the MRI, for example, in addition to introducing a universal flexibility package covering term-time working, flexible hours and career break schemes, arrangements have also been made where practical to extend homeworking for staff in areas such as routine laboratory work. In Withington new shift patterns have been gradually introduced, including a twilight (or 'dinner party') shift of 7.30–11.00 pm in nursing. In both hospitals the introduction of the new grades of health care assistants, medical laboratory assistants and support workers in the professional and technical group are also expected to have the effect of opening more accessible positions for older workers and the unemployed. It is intended that in these positions workers will be able to accumulate NVQ (national vocational qualification) credits and link into the qualified staff grading structure.

The case of the NHS illustrates how the effects of internal organisational change, when added to the external pressures of a changing labour market, can stimulate improvement in equal opportunities practice as a means of improving operational efficiency. Recognition of the potential of the older worker resource has been formally acknowledged at district level by an extension of the equal opportunity policy to incorporate provisions on age. Already on the ground successful approaches have been made to the older worker, most notably an initiative within Withington Hospital to target mature workers for the mobile breast-screening units. These service a client group of predominantly 50–64 year old women, requiring particular sensitivity and well developed interpersonal skills on the part of the radiography staff. Jobs were offered on a part-time basis in order to match the requirements of potential applicants, as well as ensuring consistently high standards of work in a pressurised and stressful job requiring sustained periods of concentration, while also increasing operational flexibility in, for example, covering for absence. A conscious effort was made to target recruitment on the over-40 population in an attempt to secure both a high stability rate among recruits and a high degree of quality-assured work in relating to the client group. This strategy is felt to have been proved a success on both fronts, in that turnover rates have been very low and it has been perceived that the older staff have brought more well developed life skills to the jobs. A similar approach is now being developed for the recruitment of clerical staff. One caveat should be entered here, however, in that relatively few applications came from those aged in their 50s. One might speculate that this could indicate a potential supply-side limit to the recruitment of older workers due to 'self-deselection', which might have arisen out of a belief that the challenge of new technology and of relearning may have been too much, or that the pressure of work, particularly in a mobile role, may have been too great. However, further work needs to be done before any conclusions can be reached.

Finance and Banking

The present recession has had a particularly adverse effect on employment in an industry already adjusting to an increasingly competitive post-deregulatory environment, where pressures towards downsizing had been developing out of the wider introduction of new technology and various profitability, productivity and organisational change initiatives. In general terms the downsizing process has been managed largely by a combination of sharply reduced recruitment activity, together with early retirement and voluntary redundancy incentives which, based on long service, have tended to focus exit initiatives on the upper age and particularly the over-50 population.

However, in spite of this context, attention is being paid within the sector to resourcing issues relating to older workers. A survey of banking and insurance institutions conducted in 1993 found that several were in the process of developing a more active policy on age. In part this derives from a recognition that the demographic challenge is likely at present only to be suspended temporarily, although in the main it has developed out of the success of various initiatives in recent years aimed at reintroducing women in their 30s and 40s into the banking and finance industry. The benefits resulting from these programmes in terms of improved recruitment and retention performance, as well as in the adaptability and skills which the mature workers have brought or kept with the company, have helped to encourage many organisations to move from a formally 'age neutral' approach and to begin to address the issue of age in their resourcing plans.

Midland Bank

Increasing competition and greater opportunities for choice in the marketplace have, particularly in a context of recession and retrenchment, encouraged Midland to place greater emphasis on the service element of banking as part of an attempt to become more actively responsive to market demands. Within a re-evaluation of the company's organisation and culture the importance of equal opportunities as an integral business issue has also been stressed, in order to maximise the potential of the bank's existing and future workforce. As part of this process, equal opportunities issues relating to age discrimination are beginning to be addressed and the bank is currently further developing its policy in this area.

The recognition of age as an important equal opportunities and business issue has developed from a combination of concerns relating to labour recruitment and skills retention. First, in terms of recruitment the experience of targeting 'women returners' with experience in the banking industry has helped to convince Midland of the merits of widening the potential pool for labour. This applies particularly as the demographic issue continues to be recognised as a potential medium to long-term problem. Adjustments are already being made to the recruitment procedure by, for example, putting an end to the practice of stipulating or indicating preferred age ranges in job advertisements. Secondly, older staff are increasingly perceived as important in terms of the retention of valued banking skills and experience. Although the bank has, in common with most of its competitors, managed its downsizing programme by introducing an early exit for its older staff, it is now recognised that this has gone too far. Encouraging expectations of retirement in the early 50s may bring with it negative implications for staff motivation and commitment. More importantly, the bank is losing too many people with well developed and irreplaceable skills accumulated over a working lifetime of banking experience. The renewed emphasis within Midland on the practice of 'traditional banking' requires abilities which it is felt cannot readily be developed in less experienced staff. This is particularly relevant at managerial levels, where branch managers have to assess entrepreneurial talent and business potential, while making well balanced decisions as to how best to approach and support business needs from a banking perspective. At other grades too the expansion of an increasingly wealthy over-50 population in society as a whole represents a very important potential client group for the bank.

Although older workers may or may not be any better in terms of general standards of customer service, it is felt that they may possess possible advantages in relating to the personal banking needs of this older group, particularly with regard to more sensitive issues such as making provisions for wills.

In support of the bank's change process, renewed emphasis has been placed on equal opportunities as a fundamental and characteristic element in the definition of the bank's ethos and culture. Action and initiatives in this area have been directed at line managers, whose day-to-day responsibilities for both customers and staff ensure that it is here where the success or otherwise of the venture will be decided, and efforts have been concentrated initially on securing behavioural compliance to the programme in an acknowledgement that normative commitment is much more difficult to obtain, and in the belief that attitudes will begin to adapt and follow from the assurance of compatible standards of behaviour.

The core of the programme is a ten-year plan to create and sustain a set of values and behaviours defined as 'The Midland Way'. Through this equal opportunities will be routinely established as part of good management practice and as an integral part of company culture. Overseen by a steering committee made up of senior line managers, a series of affirmative action plans is envisaged in which local-level initiatives will be taken to maintain improvements in equality ratios. General progress will be continually monitored, initially focusing on the areas of race, gender and disability, resulting in a biennial management action report. The whole exercise will be supported by a rolling equal opportunities training programme, which will continue to stress the importance of discrimination only on the basis of objective criteria relating to individual ability, and which will aim to raise awareness of the potential of previously under-recognised and under-utilised groups. Taken together, the assertion of a more traditional banking approach and the development of a wider and more active equal opportunities culture are expected to raise the profile of older workers within the organisation, even irrespective of developments in the labour market. The bank is currently in the process of defining and elaborating its stance and approach to the older worker.

Retailing

J Sainsbury plc

J Sainsbury is one of the UK's leading food retailers with over 320 stores and leads the way in terms of efficiency and profitability. The company has managed to continue to grow throughout the present recession through ongoing investment in new logistical systems, although the rate of increase of sales and profits has slowed (EIU, 1991; Sainsbury, 1992). The company also aims to be at the forefront of new developments in personnel practice and began to produce plans to meet the demographic challenge as early as 1986/87. The principal target groups identified were women returners and older workers. It was felt that the opportunities for flexibility in working time arrangements offered by the operational requirements of long opening hours and the need to deploy labour according to patterns of trade would appeal to both these groups. Immediate labour market pressures, particularly in the south-east of England, also encouraged the company to revise its past policies towards older workers. In the stores the practice of compulsory retirement at normal pensionable age was removed, enabling older staff to be retained. Store managers were also encouraged to experiment with the recruitment of older workers of any age subject to reasonable standards of health and fitness.

The programme of targeting the older worker had a cautious beginning. At first older people tended only to be recruited to very basic packing duties at the checkout and often line managers had to be convinced of their abilities even at this level. However, the store personnel managers who had routine responsibility for recruitment helped to facilitate the introduction of older workers and the proven success of the programme ensured the expansion of the scheme. All jobs in the stores up to managerial levels were opened up to older workers on permanent contracts and on equal terms and conditions of service, save for ineligibility for the company pension scheme and for medical severance coverage for the over 65s. The increasing targeting of the older worker soon resulted in a workforce of over 2000 people older than State retirement age, in addition to the many thousands of other older workers employed by the company.

A longstanding policy aim within Sainsbury's has been to secure a stable, loyal and committed workforce. The company's family-firm traditions and its ability to offer competitive terms and conditions and security of employment have helped contribute to successful retention rates, with the result that a significant proportion of staff are in their 40s and 50s. The company has also recruited in these age groups since it recognises the advantages which a mixed age profile can deliver, particularly in terms of team commitment and service. In this sense the company's active targeting of older workers was not so much a 'discovery' of the older worker but a revision and extension of its previous recognition and approach.

Nevertheless the specific programme of recruiting and retaining staff in their 50s, 60s and beyond had cautious beginnings. The development and growth of the initiative arose out of the very success of the older workers in the stores which helped to overcome line scepticism towards the programme. Internal company studies found that the positive experience of employing older workers helped to counter widespread assumptions regarding their ability and suitability for employment in the company (Sainsbury, 1991). Older workers were found to be well motivated, with a strong work ethic and placing a high value on the social aspects of working for the company; mature, with a stabilising effect on younger staff; flexible in matching their working hours to company needs; and consistently displaying a commitment to high standards of customer service. In addition, early doubts concerning absenteeism, ill-health and trainability were proved to be unfounded: rates of absenteeism, particularly of short-term absence, were if anything lower than for younger age groups, and although older workers tended to require a little more time in completing the training process, the content and methods of the programme did not have to be amended in any significant way.

The older worker initiative in Sainsbury had its origins and development in a context of continued company growth and tightening labour markets which was beginning to introduce recruitment and retention difficulties for shopfloor staff. Although at first the programme was only selectively applied and only out of necessity, the initiative grew as a result of its own success. Much of the momentum has therefore been maintained, despite the transformation in labour market conditions, and the company has now established the older worker groups as a valuable resource and as a definite part of its future workforce mix.

Littlewoods (Retail Division)

Littlewoods is the UK's largest private company, with over 30,000 employees and ownership shared 32 members of the Moores family. Private ownership has granted the company two defining characteristics: an ability to take a longer-term business view and a paternalistic family-firm ethos, which, although diminishing in a commercial sense, remains important in its approach to employee relations with a strong emphasis on recognising the value of employees and in building their trust and loyalty. Within the company a strong commitment to equal opportunities has been developed under the personal and enthusiastic interest of John Moores, son of the late founder Sir John Moores, since the late 1960s, although the company's equal opportunities programme only became more sophisticated and institutionalised throughout the organisation in the 1980s. This followed incidences of racial tension in the areas surrounding the company's headquarters and, equally as important, as a corollary to the further commercialisation of the organisation.

The development of the equal opportunities programme came increasingly to be recognised as an important business and resourcing issue, both externally in terms of introducing the company to a wider pool of potential recruits and in reinforcing the company's good reputation among customers and staff alike. Internally it enabled the maximum utilisation and development of staff to their full potential and operated as a contribution to maintaining staff motivation, loyalty and even good employee relations in a context of rapid organisational change. In this sense the programme of equal opportunities gained a renewed status in helping to manage cultural integration within a change process of rationalisation, decentralisation and redundancies by maintaining the link to the firm's paternalistic past. This also acted to reinforce the cumulative and routinised nature of the policy. The commitment of senior managers to the equal opportunities programme similarly ensures that the issue is a live and dynamic one within the company (Straw, 1989; Rajan and van Eupen, 1990). Equal opportunity policies and practices are continually and actively re-examined and revised, while the equal opportunities committee, under the chairmanship of John Moores, is particularly concerned to draw on the experience and best practice of other organisations. At one level this has contributed to a process of developing and extending the policy, for example to incorporate issues of sexual and racial harassment, paternity leave, 'eldercare' leave and leave for adoptive parents. More fundamentally the purpose is to go beyond a formal institutionalisation of equal opportunity policy or a general awareness of equal opportunities issues, so that ultimately a corporate culture is sustained in which wider equal opportunity attitudes and practice are routinely incorporated into good management practice.

Consequently, although age has not as yet been addressed as a separate and specific issue, a positive approach has been developed which fits with the stated aim of avoiding disadvantage 'by conditions or requirements which cannot be shown to be relevant to performance'. In recruitment and selection the stress placed on objectivity in matching individual abilities, experience and qualifications only to job-related criteria has prompted an end to the practice of using age restrictions in recruitment advertising. Indirect suggestions or other references to age are also challenged wherever possible and the company no longer refers, for example, to 'young' graduate trainees for its graduate entry programme. A previous age limit of 49 for recruitment to managerial positions, in operation out of a concern that the recruitment of older managers could place a burden on the pension scheme as a result of fewer contributing years, relatively high benefits and a possibility of early retirement on ill health grounds, was dropped ten years ago and currently managers are recruited even over the age of 55. The company also targeted older workers towards the end of the 1980s, approaching organisations such as the Women's Institute in order to tap the mature labour pool, although a recent decline in recruitment activity now means that such initiatives continue only at a local level. Training and education opportunities are open to individuals of all ages and the company supports a further education programme open to all employees. Finally, the company's retirement age has been equalised and raised for women to 65 (although employees may retire from age 60 with no actuarial reduction to pension entitlement) enabling the further retention of older staff.

The Littlewoods case indicates how within a wider equal opportunities culture a recognition of the potential contribution of the older worker can progressively develop without necessarily being introduced with the accompanying fanfare as an 'older worker policy'.

McDonald's Restaurants

In the UK McDonald's has followed its parent company in actively developing a targeted approach to the older worker in order to meet its staffing needs. Jobs within the company have always been open to older workers and as a keen equal opportunities employer age has been incorporated into the company equal opportunity policy. In particular the company has identified two groups as important to its resourcing plans — women with school-age children and the retired. The ability to offer flexibility in employment has been used to attract both these groups. Recruitment is mainly to front-line counter roles, where high standards of customer service and skills in dealing with the public are particularly necessary.

Several years ago, in response to specific recruitment and retention problems and in anticipation of further pressures resulting from the changing demography of the labour market, the company developed its campaign 'Over Fifty but not Over the Hill'. Restaurants facing resourcing difficulties were able to put out promotional literature and advertisements aimed at the over-50s. This exercise was particularly successful in the stores, where literature could be directly received by older people who may not have been actively considering employment or were not aware of opportunities at McDonalds's, bypassing Job Centres which older people may not visit or where they may feel or experience discouragement.

The operation of the scheme was a success and illustrated that not only young people could work in a time-pressured environment. One couple were employed, for example, on the breakfast shift in a London restaurant and managed equally well despite their both being over 70 years of age. Managers also felt that the introduction of older workers could bring stability to a work team and that older people certainly fit in with groups of other ages. Despite the company message that older workers are a valued potential resource, however, it may be that this policy has not yet been developed or emphasised to the extent that its restaurant managers, who have direct responsibility for staff recruitment and whose average age is 26, can overcome a reluctance to identify older workers as anything more than a short-term response to specific labour market conditions.

CONCLUSION

The nature and characteristics of employment in the service industries imply that a recognition of the potential of older employees can be a competitive advantage for many service sector employers. Increasingly many service sector organisations may indeed have a greater need to address the older worker resource as the effects of demographic changes on a relatively youth-oriented sector become more readily apparent. Many of these service sector firms, however, will be more able to respond through an effective approach to the older worker given the capacity for flexibility in working time arrangements. Many organisations will find that they are well placed to benefit from a number of quantitative and qualitative gains resulting from an increased utilisation of the older worker resource.

The evidence from those firms which have adopted an integrated and targeted approach to the older worker is that a series of positive results can be derived relating to recruitment, retention, absenteeism, turnover, employee motivation and standards of customer service. These are of particular importance in a competitive and cost-conscious sector, in which the attitudes and behaviour of staff can be crucial in ensuring consistently high standards in service provision. The case examples outlined above illustrate that a range of service sector organisations are beginning to address the older worker resource. For many a useful point of departure in approaching what may have been a previously neglected resource has been through the development of a more active equal opportunities programme, which elaborates and incorporates specific action on age. For these and other organisations, however, the issue is not merely one of 'updating' an equal opportunities policy or even rectifying past unfair discriminatory practice. For them, addressing the older worker resource has come to be a mainstream business issue and a significant element in a human resources strategy designed to improve operational efficiency in an increasingly competitive environment.

References

Barth, M C, Hogarth, T and McNaught, W (1991) 'Employing Older Workers in the USA and the UK', Paper presented to Conference on Strategic Issues and Planning for Insurance, London, October.

Brooks, T (1992) 'Total Quality Management in the NHS', *Health Services Management*, April.

Brown, P and Scase, R (1991) 'Social change and economic disadvantage in Britain', in Brown, P and Scase, R (eds) *Poor Work: Disadvantage and the Division of Labour*, Open University Press, Milton Keynes.

Casey, B and Laczko, F (1992) 'Older worker employment: change and continuity in the 1980s' in Gilbert, N, Burrows, R and Pollert, A (eds) *Fordism and Flexibility*, Macmillan, London.

Casey, B, Lakey, J and Fogarty, M (1991) *The Experience and Attitudes of Older People to Work and Retirement*, Carnegie Trust (UK), London.

Casey, B and Wood, S (1990) 'Firm Policy, State Policy and the Recruitment and Retention of Older Workers in Britain', Paper prepared for Conference 'The Firm, the State and the Older Worker', Berlin, September.

Clarke, K (1991) *Women and Training: A Review*, Equal Opportunities Commission, Manchester.

Corby, S (1991) 'Prospects for industrial relations in NHS Trusts', *Industrial Relations Journal*, Vol 22, pp 170–180.

Corby, S (1992) 'Equality on a tight budget', *Personnel Management Plus*, March.

Economist Intelligence Unit (EIU) (1991) 'Company Profile no 3: J Sainsbury', *EIU Retail Quarterly Trade Reviews*, No 20, December.

Employment Department (1991) *Equal Opportunities: Training for Older Workers*, Employment Department, Sheffield.

Evans, L (1990) 'The demographic dip: a golden opportunity for women in the labour market', *National Westminster Bank Quarterly Review*, February.

Fielder, S, Rees, G and Rees, T (1991) *Employers' Recruitment and Training Strategies*, University of Wales, Cardiff.

Fifield, P C (1989) 'Consumer financial services', in Jones, P (ed) *Management in Service Industries*, Pitman, London.

Flynn, N (1989) 'Pubic sector services', in Jones, P (ed) *Management in Service Industries*, Pitman, London.

Harris, C C (1991) 'Recession, redundancy and age', in Brown, P and Scase, R (eds) *Poor Work: Disadvantage and the Division of Labour,* Open University Press, Milton Keynes.

Harrop, A (1990) *The Employment Position of Older Workers in Europe: A Demographic Profile*, Age Concern Institute of Gerontology, London.

Hodges, C (1991) 'Metamorphosis in the NHS: the personnel implications of Trust status', *Personnel Management*, April.

Hogarth, T and Barth, M C (1991) 'Costs and benefits of hiring older workers: a case study of B&Q', *International Journal of Manpower*, Vol 12, No 8.

House of Commons Employment Committee (1989) *The Employment Patterns of the Over-50s Vol II*, HMSO, London.

House of Commons Employment Committee (1991) *Recruitment Practices Vol I: Report*, HMSO, London.

Humm, J and Sharp, N (1991) *Age Discrimination: An Empirical Study*, Campaign for Work, London.

Jolly, J, Creigh, S and Mingay, A (1980) *Age as a Factor in Employment*, Department of Employment, London.

Kinicki, A J and Lockwood, C A (1985) 'The interview process: an examination of factors recruiters use in evaluating job applicants', *Journal of Vocational Behaviour*, Vol 26, pp 117–125.

Laczko, F and Phillipson, C (1991) *Changing Work and Retirement: Social Policy and the Older Worker*, Open University Press, Milton Keynes.

Lee, J A and Clemens, T (1985) 'Factors affecting employment decisions about older workers', *Journal of Applied Psychology*, Vol 70, No 4.

Lennon, P (1989) 'Demographic Change and its Implications for Employment', Paper given at IPM Conference, October.

Lennon, P (1990) 'Facing the demographic challenge', *Employment Gazette*, Vol 98, No 1, January.

Luthans, F and Thomas, L T (1989) 'The relationship between age and job satisfaction: curvilinear results from an empirical study — a research note', *Personnel Review*, Vol 18, No 1.

Martin, L (1990) 'Nursing skills: is there a shortage?', in Bosforth, D L and Dutton P A, (eds) 'Skill shortages in the 1990s', *International Journal of Manpower*, Vol 11, No 2/3.

McGoldrick, A E and Arrowsmith, J (1992) 'Age Discrimination in Recruitment: An Analysis of Age Bias in Job Advertisements', Paper presented at ESRC Workshop, 'The Employment of Older Workers in the 1990s', April

McNaught, W and Barth, M C (1992) 'Are older workers "good buys"? — a case study of Days Inns of America', *Sloan Management Review*, Spring.

Metcalf, H and Thompson, M (1990) *Older Workers: Employers' Attitudes and Practices*, IMS (Institute of Manpower Studies), Brighton.

NEDO (1989) *Defusing the Demographic Timebomb*, National Economic Development Office, London.

Nicholls, E and Haskel, C (1988) *Survey of Employer Attitudes Towards the Recruitment and Employability of Older Graduates*, AGCAS (Association of Graduate Careers Advisor Services), London.

O'Reilly, J (1992) 'Banking on flexibility: a comparison of the use of flexible employment strategies in the retail banking sector in Britain and France', *The International Journal of Human Resource Management*, Vol 3, No 1, May.

Parkyn, A (1991) 'Operating equal opportunities in the Health Service', *Personnel Management*, August.

Plett, P (1990) 'Developing education and training for an agency society: a European dimension: older people — appreciating assets', *Journal of Educational Gerontology*, Vol 5, No 2.

Rajan, A and van Eupen, P (1990) *Good Practices in the Employment of Women Returners*, IMS (Institute of Manpower Studies), Brighton.

Rosen, B and Jerdee, T H (1976a) 'The nature of job-related age stereotypes', *Journal of Applied Psychology*, Vol 61, No 2.

Rosen, B and Jerdee, T H (1976b) 'The influence of age stereotypes on managerial decisions', *Journal of Applied Psychology*, Vol 61, No 4.

Rosen, B and Jerdee, T H (1977) 'Too old or not too old?', *Harvard Business Review*, Nov–Dec.

Rothwell, S (1990) 'Planning for a changing labour market', *Manager Update*, Vol 1, No 4.

Sainsbury, (1991) *Employing the Over-50S — The Sainsbury Experience*, J Sainsbury plc, London.

Sainsbury, (1992) *Press Release: Preliminary Results 1991/92*, J Sainsbury plc, London.

Segal-Horn, S (1989) 'The globalisation of service firms', in Jones, P (ed) *Management in Service Industries*, Pitman, London.

Selkirk, A (1991) 'Wessex plans for change', *Personnel Management*, January.

Singer, M S (1986) 'Age stereotypes as a function of profession', *Journal of Social Psychology*, Vol 126, No 5.

Singer, M S and Sewell, C (1989) 'Applicant age and selection interview decisions: effect of information exposure on age discrimination in personnel selection', *Personnel Psychology*, Vol 42, pp 135–154.

Snyder, R A and Dietrich, F H (1992) 'Age/job satisfaction: assessment of the shape of the relationship from a systems perspective', *Personnel Review*, Vol 21, No 2.

Sparks, L (1989) 'The retail sector', in Jones, P (ed) *Management in Service Industries*, Pitman, London.

Standing, G (1986) 'Labour flexibility and older worker marginalisation: the need for a new strategy', *International Labour Review*, Vol 126, No 3, May–June.

Storey, J and Fenwick, N (1990) 'The changing face of employment management in local government', *Journal of General Management*, Vol 16, No 1.

Straw, J (1989) *Equal Opportunities: The Way Ahead*, Institute of Personnel Management, London.

Thompson, M (1991) *Last in the Queue? Corporate Employment Policies and the Older Worker*, IMS, Brighton.

Trinder, C (1989) *Employment Over Fifty-five*, NIESR (National Institute for Economic and Social Research), London.

Trinder, C (1991) *Older Workers and the Recession*, Employment Institute, London.

Waldman, D A and Arolio, B J (1986) 'A meta-analysis of age differences in job performance', *Journal of Applied Psychology*, Vol 71, No 1.

Walker, A (1990) 'The benefits of old age? Age discrimination and social security', in McEwan, E (ed) *Age: The Unrecognised Discrimination*, Age Concern, London.

Walsh, T J (1990) 'Flexible labour utilisation in the private service sector', *Work, Employment and Society*, Vol 4, No 4, December.

Willman, P (1989) 'Human resource management in the service sector', in Jones, P (ed) *Management in Service Industries*, Pitman, London.

Women's National Commission (WNC) (1991) *Women Returners: Employment Potential*, WNC, London.

Part Two

SERVICE SECTOR SPECIFIC MANAGEMENT ISSUES

8

GROCERY RETAILING IN THE SINGLE EUROPEAN MARKET: DEVELOPMENTS IN STRUCTURE, STRATEGY AND SHARE

Simon Knox and Keith Thompson

OUTLINE

As the prospect of a Single European Market (SEM) grows closer, the strategic intent of both manufacturers and retailers in the unified grocery market has become clearer. To survive and prosper in the enlarged market, acquisition, merger and strategic alliances have become commonplace among manufacturers. For instance, in the UK, Nestlé bought Rowntree for its national confectionery brands in 1988 and the French Perrier Company for its international mineral water brand in 1992. PepsiCo, on the other hand, combined acquisition with merger. During 1991, it created Snack Ventures Europe by the merger of its continental European snack food companies with General Mills to form the largest snacks manufacturer in Europe with sales of £350m. Many manufacturers are now looking to produce from a limited number of fixed points and are tending to market on a pan-European basis. Although there are still relatively few true pan-European grocery brands, it is not necessary to get to the point where there are no differences between brands in various national markets before scale effects can be achieved. This position will be optimal, however, when differences occur as a matter of deliberate policy rather than by accident.

At a recent retailing conference in the US, Richard Piper of Europanel Database (UK) commented

> The SEM and its creation of common standards and regulations offer multinational manufacturers and producers considerable opportunities for increased efficiencies

155

and economies of scale, not to mention negotiating strength with the retail trade if they [the retailers] fail to get their act together.

The purpose of this chapter is to focus attention on recent developments in European grocery retailing in order to explore emerging market structures, strategy and share implications. In particular, the myopic approach adopted by leading UK retailers receives special attention since, by most evaluation criteria, they are world-class operators yet they all show a marked reluctance to expand into mainland Europe. While their domestic performance (return on sales and market share) remains first class, their sphere of influence on the larger European stage is significantly reduced.

Through a structural analysis, we argue that UK retailers have adopted a defensive strategy towards new competition from within the single market in order to hold domestic market share, while their European competitors seem intent on penetrating the broader market, primarily through organic growth. Should the penetration of the UK market by mainland European retailers such as Aldi and Netto in the discount segment be replicated by players that are competing more directly in the mass market, then the major UK retailers will be forced to reconsider their strategy. This penetration strategy could be orchestrated in the short term by the acquisition of a UK retailer or, in the longer term, by the sustained organic growth of a European retailer. In the concluding comments, future growth options for UK retailers in Europe are discussed and both organic and acquisition strategies are considered in the context of appropriate geographic territories.

INTRODUCTION

According to the thesis proposed by Levitt (1983), 'companies that do not adapt to the new global realities will become the victims of those which do'. While Levitt may be overstating the case for globalisation, the enactment of some 300 articles to remove all non-tariff trade barriers to create a Single European Market (SEM) makes 'Europeanisation' a reality for British industry during the 1990s.

The European market is even bigger in population than the two leading world commercial powers, the US and Japan. However, the economy of Europe has been held back by the historical fragmentation of the market into smaller national markets (Figure 8.1). The purpose of the SEM is to encourage firms to take advantage of the enlarged market of 325 million people so that improved economies of scale can drive up productivity and reduce costs. As the benefits of the SEM become clearer for manufacturing industry, the question arises as to whether the same opportunity exists for service industries, such as retailing. Van der Ster (1989) argues that food choice is simply too nationalistic in character for the export or import of store concepts to be successful in the short term. He concludes that it may be the twenty-first century before we can anticipate the emergence of a 'Euro-lifestyle' leading eventually to the development of pan-European store concepts. Although van der Ster's view may seem appealing and logical to marketing theorists, the reality of the marketplace is somewhat different.

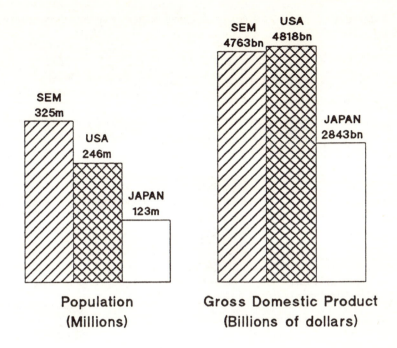

Source: OECD

Figure 8.1 GDP and population of the world's leading commercial powers, 1988

Many large grocery retailers from France, Germany and the Benelux countries already have an impressive record of cross-border operations within Europe (Table 8.1). These continental retailers, driven by saturation in their national market and static (or declining) population levels, are planning further expansion within the SEM. Aldi, Europe's largest retailer, has already set up operations in the UK. This privately owned, German discount grocer has managed to undercut almost every competitor in every European country it has entered (*Marketing*, 1 March 1990). On balance, Britain offers a more tempting prospect for grocery retailers from mainland Europe than the European markets do for British retailers (see Davies, 1989).

While Marks & Spencer does sell some food items in a number of its overseas stores and Iceland has recently opened for business, it would seem that none of the top five British grocery retailers has any shops in continental Europe. Furthermore, Killen and Lees (1988b) found that none of the large UK food retailers seems to have any intention of expanding into Europe in the foreseeable future. For instance, Tesco's managing director, David Malpas, affirmed this policy in a speech to the Food and Drink Federation: 'there are opportunities abroad and an eye must be kept on the wider horizon but you must realize that we are very busy at present with our programme of expansion in the United Kingdom' (Malpas, 1989). More recently, in denying rumours of a European takeover bid by Tesco (for French grocers Genty

Table 8.1 European representation of major EC grocery retailers

	Benelux	France	Italy	Spain/ Portugal	West Germany	UK
Benelux						
Delhalze	■			▨		
GB – Inno – BM	■	▨	▨			
France						
Auchan		■	▨			
Carrefour		■		▨		▨
Casino	▨	■				
Docks de France		■				
Euromarche		■		▨		
Promodes		■	▨	▨	▨	
West Germany						
Aldi	▨	▨			■	▨
Tengelmann	▨				■	
UK						
Marks & Spencer	▨	▨		▨		■
Iceland		▨				■

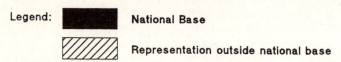

Legend:　■　**National Base**

　　　　▨　**Representation outside national base**

Cathiard) chairman Sir Ian MacLaurin stated, (*The Times*, 3 Jan 1990), 'Our research shows that there are still enormous opportunities for growth within the United Kingdom and we intend to continue our development here with the greatest vigour.' Sainsbury, the largest UK grocery retailer, has only one overseas subsidiary and that is in the US. In a recent letter to us, the company stated, 'We have chosen the USA for overseas expansion rather than extending our operations into other European countries. We have no plans to alter this policy.' Thus the major British grocery retailers reject the idea of expansion into Europe. Their preferred choice for overseas growth remains the US; a difficult market in which many British retailers have failed to succeed (Ogbanna, 1989).

Grocery retailing in Europe is about to undergo more dramatic changes than at any time in the last 25 years. At the very least, the balance of power between grocery buyers and food manufacturers must again be brought into question, particularly if manufacturers are quick to take advantage of the SEM to create pan-

European firms. At the same time, UK grocery retailers are likely to be challenged on their home ground by their European peers.

The purpose of this chapter is to explore the possible effects of changes on UK retailing which stem from the SEM. Our analysis has been limited primarily to prospects within the UK, although in our concluding comments we do look at opportunities within Europe.

UK GROCERY MULTIPLES AND EUROPE

The response by UK grocery multiples to the domestic and European threat has been mainly defensive. First, they have attempted to occupy the high ground in the UK with the best sites and, secondly, they are exploring the possibilities of forming buying groups in Europe to balance an increase in supplier size and bargaining power. This hardly seems an adequate response to the prospect of a market which is expanding sixfold in population and which means, in European terms, that their market shares will effectively be reduced to one-sixth the level they currently enjoy under trading conditions in the UK.

It was Porter (1980) who suggested that a U-shaped relationship exists between market share and return on investment (ROI) in many markets. He argues that very

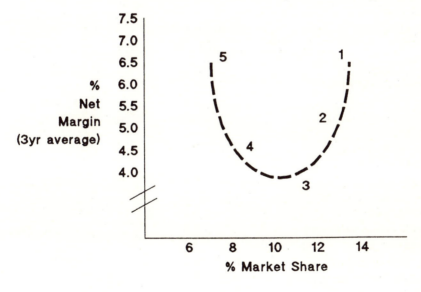

Legend: 1 : Sainsbury   2 : Tesco
3 : Gateway   4 : Argyll   5 : Asda

Source: Company reports and Economist Intelligence Unit, 1989.

Figure 8.2 Structure of UK grocery retailing, 1989

large firms in an industry tend to be profitable through economies of scale, experience curve effects and wide market coverage. The small firms in that industry also tend to be profitable by developing specialized approaches to focus on a particular niche. In the trough of the curve, medium-sized companies with no distinct competitive advantage tend to be the poorest performers. Viewed in isolation from Europe the major UK grocery multiples currently conform to Porter's view of market structures (Figure 8.2); they display a U-shaped relationship between net margin and market share. As part of a much larger European market structure, the UK's biggest grocery retailers may become only middle ranking players, since they are considerably smaller in turnover than several of their continental rivals (Table 8.2). Thus, by confining themselves to only one-sixth of the total market, the possibility of UK grocers becoming major players in Europe is simply unrealistic. As the new order emerges and the established competitive structures disintegrate, UK grocery retailers could become 'stuck in the middle' or, at best, niche marketers relying on a defence of their geographical segment within the European market to bring the rewards of a focused strategy. However, given the evident internationalism of some of their European rivals and the progressive convergence of lifestyles across Europe, perhaps even this defence is a forlorn hope (see Salmon, 1989; Mintel, 1989).

Table 8.2 Turnover of the major European grocery retailers, 1987/88

Organization	Turnover £1000m 1987/88	Country
Tengelmann	10.0	Germany
Spar Internationale	9.0	
Rewe Buying Group	8.4	Germany
Edeka Buying Group	7.1	Germany
Leclerc	6.6	France
Albrecht (Aldi)	6.4	Germany
Carrefour	5.7	France
Rewe-Liebrand	5.0	Germany
Dee Corp (Gateway)	4.8	UK
Sainsbury	4.8	UK
Marks & Spencer	4.6	UK
Tesco	4.1	UK
Intermarché	3.8	France
Promodes	3.5	France
Ahold	3.5	Netherlands
Casino	3.5	France
Argyll	3.2	UK
Asko	3.1	Germany

Source: Dawson and Burt, 1988.

The SEM will facilitate a greater European retail presence in the UK and will ultimately result in a European retail grocery market in which British retailers will have no choice but to compete. But when this happens, will the UK's major grocers be looking the other way . . . across the Atlantic?

In the next section, we analyse the changes in market structure which are likely to occur in UK grocery retailing as a result of the SEM.

THE FRAMEWORK OF ANALYSIS

Porter's structural framework (shown in Figure 8.3) offers a suitable vehicle for the analysis of change as the UK becomes part of a unified European market. In carrying out such an analysis, we believe that two structural changes emerge as being particularly important in the grocery market: the threat of new entrants into the UK and an intensification of rivalry. Consequently, these factors are considered first.

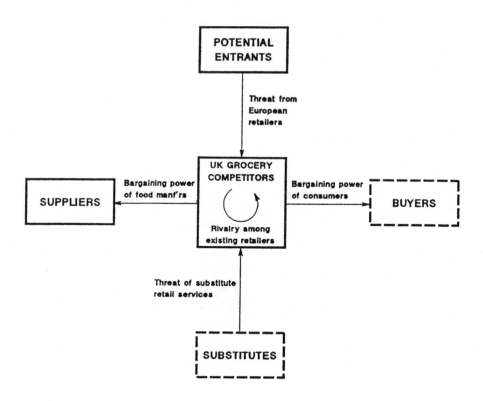

Source: Adapted from Porter, 1980.

Figure 8.3 Porter's structural framework

THE THREAT OF NEW ENTRANTS

Government Policy

As this chapter is concerned with the consequences of the SEM for what might be termed the UK segment of the European food retail market, it is government policy (aimed specifically at removing entry barriers across European markets) which is the principal change agent. The SEM has opened up UK grocery retailing to experienced, aggressive market entrants from continental Europe. These retailers are large enough not only to overcome the barriers of scale but, because they exhibit a diversity in objectives and style, they also threaten to change significantly the 'rules of the game' in the UK.

The fact that foreign investment is welcomed by the British government is in marked contrast to the protective attitudes displayed by other European countries, such as Germany. Foreign takeovers are much easier to orchestrate in the UK than in many other EC countries, rendering UK grocery retailers much more vulnerable than their European counterparts. At the local government level, the attitude towards planning controls is much freer in the UK in comparison with procedures in many continental countries (Foyil and Seward, 1988).

Despite these enabling factors, it is important to recognise the fact that UK retailers have already established themselves in the best locations, leaving only secondary sites available to newcomers looking for growth in the UK market.

Economies of Scale

While acknowledging that entry barriers for aspiring grocery retailers are generally low, Duke (1989) points out that scale barriers are implicit in the need for new entrants to attain competitiveness by acquiring a degree of monopsonistic power similar to that enjoyed by incumbent rivals. The buying power of major multiples enables them to obtain favourable prices which their smaller rivals have no chance of obtaining. This advantage enables the largest grocery retailers to increase their customer base by offering lower prices, leading to a cycle of concentration at the exclusion of small-scale competitors (Figure 8.4).

Therefore, to gain enough bargaining power to be competitive in the UK, European entrants will need to acquire a large number of scarce, expensive sites. Furthermore, they must achieve it in a short time span in competition with existing UK retailers who are already reporting major difficulties in finding suitable large-store sites (Key Note Publications, 1988). Possibly, the only way for a newcomer with adequate capital to acquire a sufficient number of good sites is to take over an existing retailer. However, those companies which are vulnerable to acquisition are often so only because they are flawed. Gateway, which ranked number three in the market during 1986, is a case in point. Unable to integrate the disparate assortment of acquired sites and stores efficiently, the company's

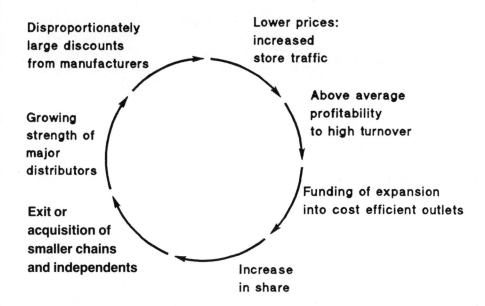

Source: McKinsey and Co, 1987.

Figure 8.4 The cycle of retail concentration

performance remained so far below par that eventually it was acquired by Isosceles in 1989.

An alternative strategy for retailers, in their drive to attain economies of scale and monopsonistic power, is the formation of European buying groups. The founding of the European Retail Association by Argyll of the UK, Casino of France and Ahold of the Netherlands is a good example of this. The combined turnover of the three members of this association is even greater than the established buying groups which are an important feature of European markets (Table 8.3).

Table 8.3 Comparison of the turnover of European grocery buying groups with the European Retail Association

		Turnover 1987/88 (£'000m)	
European Retail Association:			
	Ahold	3.5	
	Argyll	3.2	
	Casino	3.5	
	ERA total		10.2
Spar Internationale			9.0
Rewe buying group			8.4
Edeka buying group			7.1

Source: Dawson and Burt, 1988.

If the SEM makes it easier for producers to move goods across frontiers, it will also be easier for retailers to buy the goods and then move them across frontiers. Thus there is significant scope for retailers to develop scale economies in this way.

It is likely that buying groups across Europe can operate within the same pan-European market and still not be in direct competition with one another. In such cases it would be feasible for buying groups to cooperate with similar groups in 'paralleling' their sources of supply, whereby one buying group (A) buys, say, muesli not only for its own group members but also on behalf of a second buying group (B) (Figure 8.5). Scale economies would not then be confined to the crude use of buying power but would be sufficient to tempt producers into partnerships, possibly as dual suppliers, through the prospect of greater volumes as well as entry into new geographic markets.

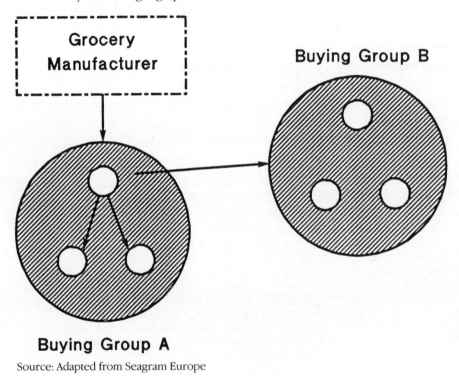

Source: Adapted from Seagram Europe

Figure 8.5 Paralleling

Access to Distribution Channels

Continental retailers looking at the UK market may be discouraged to see that their UK rivals have achieved a very high degree of control over the distribution network. Some 70 per cent of the sales volume of the UK's top seven grocery multiples passes through consolidation warehouses and distribution services under their direct control, frequently through the use of captive subcontractors using vehicles painted in the grocer's livery. By comparison, the contract fleet's share in France and Germany is 14 per cent and in Spain only 3 per cent (*Marketing*, 1989). However, deregulation in transport and the completion of the Channel tunnel may render the notion of domestic captive-warehousing obsolete for pan-European retailers and, therefore, no longer a barrier to entry into the UK market.

INTENSITY OF RIVALRY

Self-service grocery retailing in the UK is a mature industry with a relatively high degree of concentration. The pecking order of major competitors is well established so that even though competition is often intense, it is also orderly. This has resulted in a confident and profitable industry by any international standard.

Slow Industry Growth

The major UK food retailers have achieved considerable growth in recent years but, since expenditure on food has been static, this growth has been at the expense of smaller rivals (Table 8.4).

Table 8.4 UK food sales by sector, 1980–1988
(unit % value analysis)

	1980	1982	1984	1986	1988
Large grocers	40.8	46.5	51.3	55.1	59.0
Small grocers	18.2	16.1	12.6	11.4	10.5
Cooperatives	16.9	14.9	13.9	12.9	11.8
Others	24.1	22.5	22.2	20.6	18.7
Total	100.0	100.0	100.0	100.0	100.0

Source: adapted from Euromonitor, 1987b and Mintel, 1989.

Growth is currently based on the development of superstores mainly on out-of-town sites. Industry experts believe that the limit to superstore growth will be reached by 1994/96 (Killen and Lees, 1988a). However, a more recent survey by Verdict Research (1990) concludes that this saturation date may be rather optimistic if the current downturn in UK retail spend continues. In a static food market, this will mean that the only way for major grocery retailers to grow will be to take market share from each other. UK supermarket operators will become much more vulnerable, not just through this increased rivalry but also because of the entry threat of large, foreign rivals. These new entrants are already experienced in operating outside their domestic markets and are fully conversant with the critical success factors necessary for international operations (Treadgold, 1989).

Shifting Rivalry

Since continental retailers are accustomed to margins which are only a fraction of those in the UK (Table 8.5), they are unlikely to be deterred by the threat to margins facing UK retailers as a result of intensified competition. As mentioned earlier, Aldi has already opened its first 50 stores in Britain. More may follow very soon. After all, the purpose of opening up European markets is to increase competition and the UK market appears to offer considerable benefits to French, German, and Benelux retailers (Davies, 1989). According to research conducted by MORI (1989), nearly half (46 per cent) of the estate agents in the UK were negotiating with European retailers for high street sites.

Table 8.5 Net profit as a % of sales of selected European grocery retailers

	1985–86
Carrefour France	1.3
Ahold Netherlands	1.2
Casino France	1.1
GB-Inno-BM Belgium	1.0
Delhaize Belgium	0.8
UK supermarkets	6.3

Source: Adapted from Euromonitor, 1988; and ICC, 1989.

Diverse Competitors

As Porter (1980) points out: 'Foreign competitors often add a great deal of diversity to industries because of their differing circumstances and often differing goals.' For instance, Aldi and Tengelmann of Germany and Vendex International of the Netherlands are privately owned companies not answerable to share-holders. They may, therefore, be prepared to accept a subnormal return on investment to facilitate cut-throat entry strategies. In the diverse competitive environment thus created, players may find it difficult to read each other's intentions accurately and so fail to agree a set of 'rules of the game', thereby leading to uncertainty and suboptimal performance for all concerned.

Lack of Product Differentiation

UK consumers seem to regard retail services as a near-commodity, switching loyalties easily if the retail offer or service becomes deficient (Euromonitor, 1987a). We would argue that the product differentiation which would normally provide layers of defence against new competitors is simply not there. With the increasing fragmentation of mass consumer markets (as a consequence of consumers adopting more individualistic and experiential attitudes), UK retailers must begin to adapt to the specialist requirements of their consumer groups. Despite many claims by UK retailers to be pursuing differentiation strategies; there seems very little real difference between the market offerings of the main contenders. The fact is that the single most important criterion in determining the choice of shop is proximity; quite simply, shoppers go to the nearest store. The question remains whether this lack of differentiation is due to the absence of any real differences between consumer groups, or whether it is due to the lack of a genuine competitive drive for differentiation. Until now, the major multiples have been able to build their market share in the UK at the expense of smaller competitors (see Table 8.4 above). This has cushioned them from the full impact of having to compete with each other while adapting to changing market conditions. In an industry that is characterised by openness to stakeholders and little protection from patents or technological edge, it has been all too easy to imitate the successful strategies of peer organisations.

It is our belief that this scenario is changing; the arrival of major continental competitors in a market reaching saturation point means intensified competition. Consequently, multiple grocery retailers may find it prudent to develop more distinctive identities by seriously endeavouring to relate their market offering to particular customer groups. New entrants from the continent are likely to hasten the process of differentiation by injecting their own characteristic styles of operation and by seeking out niche markets as a way of gaining a toe-hold in the UK.

BARGAINING POWER OF SUPPLIERS

Despite the very large size of food manufacturers operating in the UK, their relative power has been diminished due to the fact that the six largest grocery retailers now account for over 70 per cent of the market. (Corporate Intelligence Unit, 1988). In recent years, the balance of power has rested with the food retailers who have used their power to oblige manufacturers to cut prices, share promotional costs or supply own-label products (de Chernatony, 1986). The food manufacturers' defence against this has been years of heavy promotional spending to build consumer loyalty through product differentiation (Whitaker, 1983). By comparison, retailers' attempts to establish store loyalty have met with little success (Denison and Knox, 1992).

Given the relative ease of moving tangible goods across frontiers compared to the difficulty of moving retailing services (which must be consistently produced and consumed at the point of sale), it is generally agreed that the SEM will benefit manufacturers more than retailers. Fletcher (1989) has expressed the concern that, if manufacturers choose to develop competitive advantage by forming pan-European organisations, the balance of power could be shifted back towards suppliers.

167

UK grocery multiples are showing no real inclination to move into Europe as an offensive measure. However, as a defensive strategy, some are banding together to form European buying groups. This may be sufficient to maintain the *status quo*, since a manufacturer would have to be vast indeed to gain the upper hand should these buying groups really choose to bare their teeth.

THE THREAT OF SUBSTITUTE SERVICES

Although it is easy to dismiss any idea of substitutes for grocery retailers, no doubt the same level of confidence was also felt by businesses in the coal, railway and mechanical cash register industries a few decades ago. Even now there are straws in the wind such as the return in popularity of neighbourhood shopping (Key Note, 1988). A number of trends are combining throughout Europe which suggest that the needs of a significant proportion of consumers may be more effectively satisfied by alternative retail methods:

- An ageing population which is likely to be less mobile may show a distinct preference for smaller-scale shopping.
- 'Green' consumers may reject processed, packaged 'supermarket' products as ecologically unsound.
- The view that cars and roads destroy the social and natural environment may lead to higher taxes and contribute to a general reduction in mobility.
- The trend towards more working women is increasing demand for extended opening hours and fast, convenient shopping. (This should also lead to more men participating in shopping!)
- A 'cash rich, time poor' society may be prepared to pay premium prices for the convenience of teleshopping and specialogues. Although teleshopping and other means of direct marketing may not seem the most appropriate medium for food shopping, they do account for 15 per cent of all household sales of frozen food in Germany (*Marketing*, 1989).

BARGAINING POWER OF CONSUMERS

The entry by continental retailers into the near-saturated UK grocery market will offer people more choice and greater variety, effectively shifting the balance of power further towards consumers.

Although Porter (1980) suggests that knowledge is power for industrial buyers, by analogy it can be the very lack of knowledge in an increasingly complex world which may cause consumers to withdraw their custom from a store group in the face of the latest food scare in one of their retail outlets. With some 21 million households in the UK, it must be said that retail customers represent a very fragmented force with little individual power. However, it is their lack of loyalty to a service which they have come to regard as a near-commodity, combined with low switching costs and a ready acceptance of imports, which makes simple fickleness a threat to UK retailers (Euromonitor, 1987a).

It is unlikely that a new market entrant would rely solely on a low level of loyalty as a basis for growth. It is to be expected that continental competitors will build on their existing strengths (such as German staff training and service techniques and French skills in decentralising international store management) to segment the UK market effectively. Their task is being made easier by a convergence of consumers' requirements throughout Europe; Dawson *et al* (1988) have already identified broad trends in shopping behaviour which they perceive as common to all European countries.

CONCLUDING COMMENTS: OPPORTUNITIES IN EUROPE FOR UK GROCERY MULTIPLES

We have argued in this chapter that the combination of retailing saturation and the imminent arrival of European competitors, together with the current slowdown in consumer spending, signals an intensification of competition in UK grocery retailing in the 1990s.

We suggested earlier that one effect of the SEM will be to reduce the market shares of UK retailers to only one-sixth of their current levels. However, that calculation is based on population size and, since British per capita expenditure on food is relatively low, the UK really only accounts for about one-tenth of the EC food market (Table 8.6).

Table 8.6 European Community food market by country, 1985

	Market size[a]
West Germany	96,155
France	89,136
Italy	86,986
United Kingdom	44,232
Spain	41,471
Netherlands	15,837
Belgium	13,537
Greece	7,897
Portugal	7,872
Denmark	7,392
Ireland	4,792
Luxembourg	474
EC total	415,781

[a.] $m @ 1986 exchange rates, some figures include VAT
Source: Adapted from Euromonitor, 1987a.

Clearly, the scale economies available to a national grocery retailer in any one of the big three markets are substantially greater than those available to those in the

169

UK or any of the remaining markets. The UK is not, therefore, the ideal market from which to base an international food retailing strategy. The slow start in Europe by UK food retailers can be attributed in part to the favourable trading conditions in the UK during the 1980s. By comparison, grocery multiples in several Northern European countries have been faced both with tougher competitors, in the shape of buying groups and cooperatives, and with legal restrictions on the acquisition of sites (for instance the German Land Use Act *Baunutzungsverordnungen* and the French *Loi Royer*). These factors have obliged large grocery multiples in France, Germany and the Benelux countries to look outside their domestic markets for growth, giving them a head start over their UK rivals.

For UK retailers wishing to stay competitive in the enlarged 'home' market there seem to be two main growth options: organic growth in the larger markets of Southern Europe or a takeover strategy in Northern Europe.

Organic Growth Strategy in Southern Europe: Spain

For French grocery multiples, Spain has been a profitable market for expansion abroad. While the population may be relatively small, the food market is as large as the UK (see Table 8.6) and, with one of the more dynamic economies in Europe, consumer prosperity is set to grow. Furthermore, the Spanish government has given strong, practical encouragement to inward investment which has provided the opportunity to open up their very traditional and underdeveloped retail system to modern retail methods. There are, however, two main problems. The first is that the internationally minded French grocery multiples have got there already. Carrefour, Auchan, Promodes and Docks de France all have a strong presence. The second barrier is the complicated system of product licences which will persist well into the 1990s as Spain is still receiving preferential treatment in the SEM harmonisation process. Taken together, these factors may reduce the attractiveness of the Spanish market for UK retailers.

Organic Growth Strategy in Southern Europe: Italy

With a strong private industrial sector generating a GDP which equals the UK's and a food market which ranks in size with Germany, Italy looks a promising prospect for overseas expansion. However, distribution remains fragmented in Italy because of legislation dating back to the 1930s which is strengthened by the powerful lobby of small shopkeepers. As a result, large-scale food retailers' share of the market is still less than 18 per cent growing very slowly (Jones, 1992). However, organic growth may be an option if a long-term view is taken.

Takeover Strategy in Northern Europe: Germany

Of the more developed retail environments of Northern Europe, Germany would seem a prime candidate for overseas expansion by UK grocery multiples. The highly protected nature of public companies in Germany and the capital structure of its major food retailers have resulted in a sluggish and cautious outlook in German retailing (Treadgold, 1989). However, the protective cocoon of regulatory mechanisms used to block hostile takeovers has been suppressed as part of the harmonisation process for the SEM. It is difficult to see how leading companies in the biggest consumer market in Europe can then remain immune from aggressive takeover bids.

Despite unification, Germany has a stable, low-growth economy that is the largest in Europe and a number of grocery retailers which will become vulnerable to takeover. The opportunity exists for UK multiples to pursue an acquisition strategy in Germany and to exploit their significant competitive advantages in operating EPOS systems, in-store credit cards, merchandising, stock control and promotional methods (Sljivic, 1990).

References

Corporate Intelligence Unit (1988) *Retailing and 1992 — The Impact and the Opportunities*, Corporate Intelligence Unit,

Davies, R L (1989) 'A checklist of development opportunities and constraints — Britain versus the continent' in *Responding to 1992: Key Factors for Retailers*, Oxford Institute of Retail Management, Templeton College, Oxford.

Dawson, J A and Burt, S (1988) *The Evolution of European Retailing*, Vol II, University of Stirling Institute for Retail Studies.

Dawson, J A, Shaw, S A and Rana, J (1988) 'Future trends in food retailing: results of a survey of retailers', *British Food Journal*, Vol 90 No. 2.

de Chernatony, L (1986) 'Consumer perceptions of the competitive tiers available within specified product fields' in *Managing Marketing*, Cowell, D and Collis, J (eds) Proceedings of MEG, Plymouth, UK.

Denison, T J and Knox, S D (1992) *Profiling the Promiscuous Shopper*, AIR MILES Travel Promotions Ltd, Crawley, West Sussex.

Duke, R C (1989) 'A structural analysis of the UK grocery retail market', *British Food Journal*, Vol 91 No 5, July–August.

Economist Intelligence Unit (1989) *Retail Business: Quarterly Trade Reviews, No 12, Grocers and Supermarkets*, Economist Intelligence Unit, London.

Euromonitor (1987a) *Grocery Distribution in Western Europe*, Euromonitor Publications Ltd, London.

Euromonitor (1987b) *Retail Trade UK 1987/88*, Euromonitor Publications Ltd, London.

Euromonitor (1988) *Europe's Major Retailers*, Euromonitor Publications Ltd, London.

Fletcher, J (1989) 'UK retailers will be bound for Europe', *The Grocer*, 15 April.

Foyil, D and Seward, B (eds) (1988) *Europe 1992: Breaking Down the Barriers*, UBS-Phillips and Drew, London.

ICC Information Group (1989) *Industrial Performance Analysis*, ICC Information Group Ltd, London.

Jones, M (1992) 'Sizing up Europe', *Super Marketing*, 16 October.

Key Note (1988) *New Trends in Retailing*, Key Note Publications Ltd, London, pp 4-8.

Killen, V and Lees, R (1988a) 'The future of grocery retailing in the UK, part 1', *Retail and Distribution Management*, July–Aug.

Killen, V and Lees, R (1988b), 'The future of grocery retailing in the UK, part 2', *Retail and Distribution Management*, Nov–Dec.

Levitt, T (1983) 'The globalization of markets', *Harvard Business Review*, Vol 61, No 3, May–June.

Malpas, D (1989) '1992: Consumers have no voice', *The Grocer*, 4 March.

Marketing (1989), Special Report 'Consumer Marketing in Europe', 4 May.

McKinsey and Company (1987), in *The European Food Marketing Directory*, Euromonitor Publications Ltd, London.

Mintel (1989) *Retail Intelligence*, Vol 1, Economist Intelligence Unit, London.

MORI (1989) *The Retail Property Market*, (a study on behalf of Argos Distributors Ltd, MORI, London.

Ogbanna, E (1989) 'Strategic changes in UK grocery retailing', *Management Decision*, Vol 27, No 6.

Porter, M E (1980) *Competitive Strategy*, The Free Press, New York.

Salmon, W J (1989) 'Multinational food retailing in the nineties', *Proceedings of the Albert Heijn Conference*, Noordwijk, Koninklijke Ahold nv. Zaandam, Netherlands.

Sljivic, N (1990) 'The German retail property market', *International Journal of Retail & Distribution Management*, Vol 18, No 1.

Treadgold, A (1989) 'Retail Internationalization — 1992 in context', in *Responding to 1992: Key Factors for Retailers*, Oxford Institute of Retail Management, Templeton College, Oxford.

van der Ster, W (1989) 'Food retailing in the 1990s, a Dutch View', *Proceedings of the Albert Heijn Conference*, Noordwijk, Koninklijke Ahold nv. Zaandam, Netherlands.

Verdict (1990) *The Space Report*, Verdict Research, London.

Whitaker, J (1983) 'To spend or not to spend?', *Nielsen Researcher*, Vol 2, pp. 1–14.

9

THE CHANGING ROLE OF BUILDING SOCIETIES IN THE 1990S

Joseph Nellis

OUTLINE

As a result of extensive government deregulation during the 1980s the UK financial services sector has seen the erosion of many of the traditional barriers between the market segments for different financial services. A new framework for the financial services environment is evolving to the extent that, for example, banks and building societies are now direct competitors across a wide range of financial products and services, particularly in terms of mortgage lending and retail savings. Not surprisingly, the speed of change within the sector has posed considerable adjustment problems for all players.

This chapter examines the challenge of change facing the building societies in the UK, drawing on the experience of the past few years. In particular, it analyses the following:

- the nature of the new competitive environment and the opportunities offered to building societies for new business activities;
- the impact of change in terms of developments involving the structure of the building society industry as merger activity increases;
- the challenge of change presented by the new environment in terms of the impact at the building society branch level.

The findings discussed in this chapter are as follows:

- Deregulation throughout, the 1980s has substantially changed the way in which building societies in the UK now operate. At the centre of the new legal framework surrounding them lie particular capital adequacy rules which bring the prudential requirements for societies more into line with those that apply to commercial banks.

- A major impact of the implementation of the new capital adequacy rules is that the societies have become increasingly conscious of the need for greater profitability, since this not only ensures the maintenance of adequate reserves but also provides societies with the opportunities to expand their business activities.
- During the past few years societies have demonstrated great enthusiasm to take advantage of the more relaxed environment by developing a full range of many transmission services, placing them in direct competition with the retail banking system.
- The impact of change stimulated by this new environment has been particularly prominent at branch level. As a consequence, branch staff performance and appraisal now receive much greater attention with appropriate reward systems now high on staff development agendas. The focus on profitability has at the same time brought about a dramatic cultural transformation within building societies in terms of staff attitudes, management practices and business expectations. One particular consequence has been a quickening in the pace of branch rationalisation.
- Many building societies are now experiencing severe difficulties in the recruitment and retention of well qualified staff. Pressure is building up concerning the question of competitive rates of pay and performance-related bonus payments.
- Branch managers have experienced a sharp reversal of their traditional role as administrators to one where they are being given more direct managerial responsibility for staff motivation and training. They have also been given some increased flexibility regarding lending limits that they can sanction, a move that is welcome by branch managers in general.

The following lessons are drawn:

- Research presented in this chapter highlights a number of key issues which will have to be addressed by building societies in the UK if they are to maintain their position in a dynamic financial services environment.
- While building societies have demonstrated that they have the ability and confidence to compete in an aggressively competitive environment, they must not be complacent — much greater attention will have to be given to staff training and development with reward more closely linked to performance.
- While profitability has become a focal performance measurement, building societies should not forget the need to maintain a high quality service — they have a competitive edge over many of the other players in the financial services sector in terms of public perception, but they must be careful to balance financial targets with the need to maintain their strong links with their customer bases.
- As the cultural environment continues to change within the societies, there will be a need to manage staff expectations, particularly as staff loyalty cannot be taken for granted as in the past.

- Given the plethora of changes that are taking place, building societies must ensure that communications between head office and branches are satisfactory — in many societies there is currently an impression that head office management is not in tune with branch needs and aspirations.

INTRODUCTION

During the past decade, the UK financial services sector has been subjected to an unprecedented scale of deregulation. As a consequence, banks and building societies have attacked each other's traditional business sectors as they have sought to take advantage of new-found freedoms. Consequently, banks and building societies are now direct competitors across a wide range of financial products and services, with banks competing aggressively for the traditional core mortgage and retail savings markets of building societies while the societies now have the powers to provide, for example, an extensive range of money transmission services which had previously been monopolised by the commercial banks. Adjustment to this new environment has been a daunting challenge for the societies but, based on the evidence so far, they have demonstrated that they are capable of making the necessary transformation. This chapter examines the challenge of change facing the societies, drawing on the experience of the past few years. In particular, it focuses on:

- the nature of the new environment and the opportunities it offers for new business activities;
- the changing structure of the building society industry as merger activity accelerates in the new environment;
- the challenge of change at building society branch level.

The future for the societies is highly complex and, despite their success to date, they will still face considerable challenges in the years ahead both nationally and increasingly internationally as the Single Market in Europe develops. The purpose of the analysis reported in this chapter is to create a platform for continued debate among the societies in terms of future strategies concerning their changing objectives, merger activity, branch networks, new product development, diversification and marketing.

THE ORIGINS AND GROWTH OF THE BUILDING SOCIETY MOVEMENT

The foundations of the UK building society movement, with its status of mutuality, were laid in the late eighteenth century when groups of people banded together to build houses. The group members would pay a weekly contribution to a fund which was used to buy land and then to finance the building of houses. When all the members had been housed the society was disbanded. By the middle of the nineteenth century, societies had largely ceased to build homes but were changing to become permanent institutions which supplemented their funds by borrowing from people who did not want to buy houses and lending to other people who wished to buy existing dwellings or finance the building of new properties.

Building societies operate under their own specific legislation, rather than the more general company or banking laws in the UK. The first Building Society Act was passed in 1874, establishing the societies at that time as a distinct legal form operating under specific, though restricted, objectives. There were three additional Building Society Acts in 1884, 1939 and 1960 and a further Act in 1962 which was mainly a consolidating statute. There was thereafter no major legislative change to affect how building societies operated until the implementation of a new Act in 1986 (see below).

In the years since its origin, the building society movement has been transformed from a very large number of small, individual societies, to a smaller number of larger societies with branches which in many cases are spread right across the country. Although the number of societies has decreased year by year, the number of members — investors and borrowers — has dramatically increased, particularly since World War II. The building societies have established themselves as major specialised financial institutions in the UK for personal sector savings and have consistently been the principal providers of finance for private sector house purchase. As shown in Figure 9.1, the number of societies still in operation at the end of 1992 was 105. It can be seen that by the end of 1992 the number of building societies had fallen to just over 4 per cent of the number in existence at the start of the century. Table 9.1 shows how this rate of decline has varied decade by decade. Between 1900 and 1930 the decline in the number of societies was fairly steady, while between 1930 and 1960 the rate of decline fell. However, between 1960 and 1990 there was a sharp increase in the rate of decline, with the 1980–90 decade showing the peak at an annual rate of decline of over 8 per cent. This was a decade of extensive deregulation in the financial services sector (see below).

Table 9.1 Rate of decline in number of building societies, 1990–1992

Decade	Annual rate of decline %	Decade	Annual rate of decline %
1900–10	2.8	1950–60	1.2
1910–20	3.0	1960–70	4.0
1920–30	2.1	1970–80	5.5
1930–40	0.7	1980–90	8.1
1940–50	1.5	1990–92	5.3

Source: Coles, 1992.

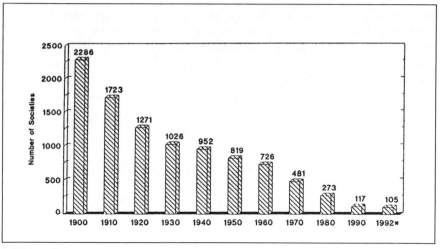

* BSA estimates

Source: Annual Reports of the Chief Registrar of Friendly Societies and of the Building Societies Commission

Figure 9.1 Number of building societies in UK, 1900–1992

The decline in the number of societies has been accompanied, not surprisingly, by an increasing share of building society assets being accounted for by the larger societies (for further details see Coles, 1992). Table 9.2 shows trends in the degree of concentration of the building society industry over the period 1930–1991. It will be seen that the largest five societies gradually increased their share of total assets until 1988, although since then this share has declined by almost 2 per cent (partly because the former Abbey National Building Society converted to plc status in 1989.[1] The share of the next group of five societies grew steadily until 1985, falling away in the late 1980s, but has since grown again. Overall, the share of the largest 20 societies has grown steadily year by year, from 65 per cent in 1930 to 92.5 per cent by the end of 1991. In total, the number of borrowers in the UK today with building society mortgages is now in excess of seven million (in 1970, the number was less than four million).

DEREGULATION IN THE UK FINANCIAL SERVICES SECTOR

Since the arrival of a Conservative government in 1979, the UK financial services sector has been subject to an unprecedented scale of deregulation. Relaxation of the interventionist policies which had dominated business during the preceding decade began with the abolition of foreign exchange controls, followed by the

---

1. It should also be noted that there was a particularly sharp jump in the market share of the top five societies following the merger of the Nationwide and Anglia Building Societies in 1987.

removal of restrictions on domestic bank lending (via the ending of the Supplementary Special Deposits Scheme — the so-called 'corset'). This relaxation on lending by the commercial banks was the signal that the banking community had been waiting for to move into new areas of business activity, especially the then lucrative UK mortgage market (which had previously been dominated by the building society movement through an effective cartel arrangement). In 1981, the

Table 9.2 Growth of concentration in the building society industry based on share of total assets

Year	Largest 5	Next 5	Largest 10	Largest 20	All societies
	Share of total %	Share of total %	Share of total %	Share of total %	Total assets £m
1930	39.1	14.4	53.4	65.0	371
1940	38.0	12.3	50.3	60.7	756
1950	37.3	11.5	48.9	62.5	1,256
1960	45.3	11.6	56.9	68.6	3,166
1970	50.1	14.2	64.3	77.4	10,819
1980	55.4	15.7	71.0	84.3	53,793
1981	55.1	15.6	70.7	84.8	61,815
1982	55.7	17.3	73.0	86.3	73,033
1983	55.7	17.6	73.2	87.0	85,868
1984	56.3	17.2	73.6	87.7	102,688
1985	56.6	19.9	76.4	88.6	120,764
1986	56.9	19.8	76.7	89.2	140,603
1987	60.8	18.5	79.3	89.9	160,097
1988	62.5	18.2	80.7	90.8	188,844
1989	61.0	18.1	79.1	89.9	187,012
1990	59.9	19.8	79.7	91.2	216,848
1991	59.2	21.8	81.0	92.5	243,980

Note: The Halifax Building Society makes up its balance sheet as at 31 January and the Leeds Permanent on 30 September. Until 1989 the Woolwich also had a year end of 30 September. Since 1988 Nationwide has had a year end of 4 April. The table is not, therefore, comparing like with like, but the error is minor and thus the trends are a realistic reflection of what has been happening.

Source: Amended version of Table 9 in Coles (1992), based on individual societies' balance sheets, either directly or as published in the Building Societies Year Book. The figures are an aggregation of societies' financial years ending between 1 February of the year in question and 31 January of the following year.

authorities also relaxed their controls on interest rates by ending the formal announcement of the Minimum Lending Rate as well as the abolition of a reserve asset ratio requirement on banks' balance sheets.

These changes were in parallel with the ending of the Building Societies Association (BSA) mortgage rate cartel, followed by further relaxation of controls over building societies in 1983 which opened up access to wholesale funds and the sterling Eurobond market. The effect was to increase competitive pressures still further in the financial services sector by giving the societies access to a cheaper source of funds compared with their traditional (though still dominant)

Table 9.3 Summary of UK financial deregulation measures, 1979–1991

Year	Deregulatory measures
1979	• Abolition of foreign exchange controls.
	• Relaxation of government controls over BSA mortgage rates.
1980	• Abolition of Supplementary Special Deposits Scheme (the 'Corset').
	• Abolition of formal announcement of Minimum Lending Rate.
	• Abolition of banks' reserve asset ratio.
	• Reductions in banks' cash ratio (from 1.5% to 0.5%).
	• Greater freedom for building societies to compete for retail deposits.
	• Ending of BSA mortgage rate cartel.
1982	• Abolition of remaining hire purchase controls.
1983	• Further relaxation of controls over building societies (opening up access to wholesale funds and the sterling Eurobond market).
	• Banks' cash ratio reduced further to 0.45%.
1987	• Financial Services Act (1986).
	• Building Societies Act (1986).
	• Banking Act (1987).
1988	• Further relaxation of controls over building societies in terms of access to wholesale funds, the issue of subordinated debt and the provision of banking, investment and insurance services.
1989	• Banks and building societies permitted to issue sterling commercial paper.
	• Abbey National Building Society converts to plc status.
	• Building societies allowed to provide a wider range of money transmission services.
1991	• Banks' cash ratio reduced to 0.4%.
	• Building societies permitted to issue permanent interest-bearing shares.

Source: HM Treasury, 1991.

source of retail deposit taking via the branch networks. At the same time, the commercial banks saw a gradual reduction in the legal requirements for their cash deposit ratios (from 1.5 per cent in 1981 to 0.4 per cent by 1991). The Financial Services Act (1986), the Building Societies Act (1986) and the new Banking Act (1987) gave still more momentum to the process of liberalisation in the UK financial services sector (for further details see Johnson, 1991 and Ennew *et al*, 1990).

Table 9.3 provides a summary of the key UK financial deregulation measures and their timing over the period from 1979–1991. These measures have coincided with other factors beyond regulatory developments, particularly the internationalisation of financial markets and the development of information technology, all of which have contributed to a dramatic increase in competitive pressures both in the UK and overseas.

The effect of deregulation and increased competition has meant that during the 1980s the UK financial services industry (including business services such as those relating to investment advice) achieved the highest rate of growth compared with any other sector of the economy in terms of output. According to official statistics, the real output of financial services doubled during the period 1979–1989 (with an average annual growth rate of over 7 per cent), while real output for the economy as a whole rose by a quarter. During the same period, the average annual rise in employment in the financial services sector was just over 5 per cent with roughly a 2 per cent increment in labour productivity.

Apart from the impact of deregulation, the impressive performance of the financial services sector can also be attributed to a general rise in living standards during the 1980s. As the general level of economic welfare has increased, so the consumption of financial services has tended to increase, but at an even faster rate. This phenomenon is not new, nor is it unique to the UK, and highlights the fact that as consumers become wealthier they tend to save and borrow more and generally become more sophisticated as consumers of financial products. The effect of this has been that the scale and range of financial investments on offer have become greater, with a coincident expansion in the provision of business-related services concerning, for example, legal advice about investment and house purchase. This is reflected in the marked increase in owner occupation and wider share ownership in the UK during the 1980s.

An important consequence of the deregulatory measures shown in Table 9.3 above is that banks, building societies and other financial institutions are now in direct competition across a wide range of financial services and products. For example, banks now compete aggressively for the traditional core mortgage business of building societies, while the societies have exploited their new freedom to provide an extensive range of money transmission services, many of which were previously exclusive to the commercial banking sector. In general, competition across the various types of institutions has focused on five key areas of business activity. These areas and the key players involved are listed in Table 9.4.

It is against this background of deregulation and the increased competitive environment that we shall examine the changing role and structure of the building society movement in the UK and, specifically, explore the ways in which these developments have affected operations at the branch level. First, however, we set the scene by analysing in some detail the nature of the new environment in which the societies find themselves, setting out the extent to which they now have greater freedom to expand their activities.

Table 9.4 Key areas of business activity

Business activity	Key players
Mortgages	Banks, building societies, insurance companies and specialist suppliers such as the centralised lenders
Money transmission services	Banks and building societies
Higher interest accounts	Banks and building societies
Longer-term investments	Insurance companies, unit trusts, stockbrokers (and, more recently, some of the major building societies)
Attraction of young investors	Banks and building societies

THE NEW ENVIRONMENT FOR BUILDING SOCIETIES

On 1 January 1987 the UK building society industry was presented with a new regulatory framework enshrined within the Building Societies Act (1986). As noted above, the building societies had previously been facing increasing competitive pressures from other financial institutions, primarily the high street banks and new players in the mortgage market (namely centralised lenders). The removal of artificial controls from their balance sheets by 1980 gave commercial banks the freedom they needed to compete for both savings and mortgage business. At the same time, technological developments throughout the 1980s increasingly broke down competitive barriers between financial institutions generally and the building societies quickly found themselves coming under increasing pressures as they struggled to match their competitors' services.

As a consequence, building societies began to experience significant encroachment on their traditional business of mortgage lending for house purchase. In particular, the banks became the predominant providers of mortgage finance at the more expensive end of the UK housing market, which gave them an opportunity to cross-sell other high value-added products (such as house insurance and personal pensions). In 1980, bank mortgage lending totalled £600 million, but had risen to £5000 million by 1982. In market share terms, this represented a change from 8 per cent to 36 per cent of new lending in just three years. This success had largely been achieved by offering discounts on the standard mortgage rate for larger loans. The societies, through necessity rather than choice, were forced to examine their mortgage lending procedures and terms so that many reacted by shifting their lending down market. The effect, however, was a general lowering of the quality of their mortgage business compared to that which had prevailed in the past. Many societies also reacted by abolishing the practice of charging higher interest rates for larger loans.

In just a few years, therefore, the building societies moved from an environment in which they faced little competition to one in which competitive pressures were rapidly intensifying on both sides of their balance sheets (the savings side was also being encroached on from the early 1980s as a direct result of the government's decision to fund a larger share of its budget deficit through a range of tax-free and/or index-linked financial instruments such as National Savings). Retaliatory measures by the societies were, however, limited because of the restrictions at that time enshrined within their legal framework which generally prevented societies from substantially altering the pattern of their business activities.

It is not surprising, therefore, that the pressure for change in their regulatory framework to allow greater freedom for activity came from the building societies themselves. It is fortunate that this pressure for change happened to coincide with the then government's own objectives of deregulation and competition, particularly in the case of the financial services sector. At the centre of the new legal framework surrounding building societies lie the capital adequacy rules enshrined in the 1986 Building Societies Act. Essentially, these rules provide a more sophisticated system for measuring the capital adequacy of building societies and also bring the prudential requirements for their operations more into line with those which apply to commercial banks. The societies are compelled to comply with these rules in order to be able to take advantage of new areas of business. The most important consequence of the implementation of these capital adequacy rules is that the societies now have become increasingly conscious of the need for greater profitability. Meeting traditional reserve and liquidity requirements is no longer sufficient, since higher profitability in their activities not only ensures the maintenance of adequate capital reserves but also provides societies with the opportunity to take advantage of the new regulations which permit them to expand their business activities. In particular, Schedule 8 of the 1986 Act (as well as amendments to the Schedule implemented by the government in August 1988) gives societies the power to operate in the following new areas (for full details see BSA, 1988 and Nellis and Litt, 1990):

- Money transmission services.
- Foreign exchange services.
- Making or receiving payments as agents.
- Management, as agents, of mortgage investments.
- Provision of services relating to the acquisition or disposal of investments.
- Establishment and management of personal equity plans.

- Arranging for the provision of credit to individuals and unincorporated businesses.
- Administration of pension schemes.
- Arranging for the provision of insurance of any description, including life insurance.
- The power to establish or take over existing estate agencies.
- The power to undertake fund management, including offering their own unit trusts.

Thus from January 1987 building societies in the UK have had the power not only to offer a full range of money transmission services with cheque books, cheque guarantee cards, overdraft and foreign exchange facilities, but also to conduct business across a wide range of other activities that hitherto had been monopolised primarily by banks, insurance companies, fund managers, etc. In many cases, full service cheque book accounts are available with interest paid on credit balances, with the consequence that all the large banks have been forced to offer similar accounts. Inevitably this has put pressure on margins and has focused attention on profitability and performance. This greater consciousness of profit, however, has opened up many related and, in some cases, sensitive issues. Staff performance and appraisal now receive much greater attention with appropriate reward systems high on staff development agendas. In addition, the societies (as well as banks) face an even more fundamental question: how can profitability be measured accurately? The societies have been accustomed to the concepts of 'adequate' reserves and liquidity, but now questions are being asked concerning the difference in profit margins on different products, such as a mortgage versus a particular type of savings account. Furthermore, profitability as a target and key performance measure highlights the problems associated with making comparisons between branches in different locations, facing very different competitive environments. Such questions have acted as the catalyst for driving change within the building society industry. The effect has been a dramatic cultural transformation within building societies generally, in terms of staff attitudes, management practices and business expectations (discussed further below).

While new strategies within a new business environment are being formulated at head offices, implementation is ultimately the responsibility of branch managers who, in general, are required to perform without the complete information which they consider necessary for them to be fully effective.[2] Thus perhaps the greatest challenge facing building societies today relates to the development of new policies which address the strategic importance of the role of the branch managers and, ultimately, the branch network.

As the speed of merger activity between building societies has increased in recent years, so branch rationalisation has become a major feature of current business strategies. This rationalisation is not unique to the building society

---

2. For further details of how corporate strategies are changing in response to the new challenges see Balmer and Wilkinson (1991).

sector — banks in general have seen a reduction in the total number of their branches year by year during the past decade. Table 9.5 shows the pace of the branch rationalisation programme being carried out by building societies and banks in recent years. It will be noted that, apart from in 1989 when the banks' figures first included the branches of Abbey National, there has been a steady decline in the bank branch network throughout the whole period. This decline was especially marked in 1991 when there was nearly an 18 per cent fall in the number of bank branches, reflecting the weak financial position of almost all banks in the UK in the wake of an unprecedented scale of business bankruptcies and personal sector debt problems as the economic recession deepened. In contrast, the number of building society branches increased steadily from 1980 up to and including 1987. The fall of nearly 10 per cent in 1989 was largely due to the exclusion in that year of Abbey National branches. It is notable, however, that branch rationalisation in the building society sector has continued since then up to the end of 1991 (latest figures available). This raises the question as to whether or not this rationalisation will continue still further in the 1990s (for further analysis of the prospects for branch rationalisation see Fleming and Nellis, 1992).

Table 9.5 UK branch network — building societies and banks

	Building societies[a]		Banks[b]	
	Number[c]	Annual % change	Number	Annual % change
1980	5,684	-	14,756	-
1981	6,162	8.4	14,738	−0.1
1982	6,480	5.2	14,669	−0.5
1983	6,643	2.5	14,487	−1.2
1984	6,816	2.6	14,359	−0.9
1985	6,926	1.6	14,294	−0.5
1986	6,954	0.4	14,013	−2.0
1987	6,962	0.1	13,828	−1.3
1988	6,912	−0.7	13,722	−0.8
1989	6,236	−9.8	14,110	2.8
1990	6,051	−3.0	13,526	−4.3
1991	5,921[d]	−2.1	11,110	−17.9

Notes

a. Abbey National figures are included in those for building societies only up to and including 1988; after 1988 they are included in those for banks.
b. Girobank branches are not included in the figures.
c. Total number of offices (including one-office societies).
d. Provisional figures provided by the BSA.

Source: Annual Abstracts of Banking Statistics, Vols 8 and 9, Statistical Unit, British Bankers' Association, London.

We return below to the issue of branch management and the impact of the new business environment on the various aspects of branch activity. First, however, we examine more closely the cultural transformation (noted above) that has been achieved within the building society movement. This provides a useful overview of the extent and impact of the challenges of change which are being faced at the branch level.

CULTURAL SHIFTS IN THE BUILDING SOCIETY INDUSTRY

In the new environment of competition described above, the need for change within the building society movement across all aspects of business has never been more daunting. The greatest challenge facing the societies, apart from the necessity to change their physical operational structures in terms of management, branch networks, products etc, is the need to reassess their culture. Coming from a 'safe' background in which the speed of change was barely perceptible, the societies now find themselves thrust into an altogether more dynamic environment with competitive pressures increasing day by day. These pressures are consequently forcing managers to react speedily in their attempt to bring about a change in attitude among staff from an emphasis on social aspects (which dominated business objectives in the past) to the hard cold commercialism which is the dominant feature of their business environment today. For many staff, particularly those appointed before the mid-1980s, the transformation demanded of them must, in the words of Tom Peters, present an impression of the 'world turned upside down', with even the sacred status of 'mutuality' now being questioned following Abbey National's successful conversion to plc status in 1989.

In their efforts to adjust to this new business climate, the societies are demanding greater inventiveness and creative thinking from all staff. The management of head office functions, regional operations and branch performance now requires a range of skills and entrepreneurial attitudes that in the past has not been needed.

Branch managers probably face the greatest challenge in the new environment. In the past, they have largely performed an administrative role without the necessity to be proactive in attracting new customers. Business was essentially driven by the financial criteria dictated by regional and head offices. Since the late 1980s, however, branch managers have been urged to adopt the role of business developer, with a keener eye for new avenues of business growth and profitability. The reality now is that managers are expected to 'sell', rather than sit back and wait for business to 'walk in through the front door'. This expectation has, inevitably, heightened the importance of staff training and development which are appropriate to the transformation in culture required within the branches themselves.

The concept of 'planning' has also been catapulted into the building society world. Traditionally the societies have tended to adopt a short-term stance with regard to business planning. This primarily centred on the maintenance of the flow of investment funds to service their mortgage lending. Now, in the new climate, greater emphasis is being placed on long-term planning backed up by acute awareness of a host of relevant factors — such as demographic changes and the opportunities that these provide for new areas of business. As the UK reaches saturation point with regard to the expansion of home ownership, the societies will face even greater competition for market share in the mortgage market. Customer loyalty will be of paramount importance. It is expected that, as a result of these pressures for change, some societies will follow the Abbey National lead along the plc path. Most societies, however, are expected to remain mutual but, as we noted above, they will need to achieve a balance between the maintenance of this position and a necessary degree of commercialism in their new environment.

Table 9.6 Building society management styles, old and new

Aspects	'Old' culture	'New' culture
Objectives	Social	Commercial
Key tasks	Administration	Business development
Promotion and power	Seniority, general skills and experience	Expertise, specialisation and training — more external recruitment
Structure	Centralised and bureaucratic	Decentralised and flexible
Planning	Short term, based on tradition	Long term, based on research
Decision making	Rules and regulations	Greater personal initiative
Relationships	Status and individual roles	Job content and teamwork
Appraisal systems	Based on effort, loyalty, criticism of mistakes	Based on performance, results and praise
Staff attitudes	Loyal and proud of the society	Hopefully the same
Employment	Secure, well paid, successful and caring	Striving for achievement to ensure success, while still caring

Source: Macey and Wells, 1987.

Table 9.6 provides a diagnostic checklist of many of the aspects of management within the building society industry which are undergoing a transformation from the 'old' culture to a 'new' culture. The former was appropriate to the sort of stable, controlled environment before the 1980s, while the latter is appropriate to the dynamic, competitive environment of the 1990s. The 'winners' will be those organisations that can successfully complete the transformation and adjust to the 'new' rules.

THE IMPACT OF CHANGE ON BUILDING SOCIETY BRANCHES

So far in this chapter we have largely focused on the impact of deregulation in terms of the general business environment of building societies. However, as noted earlier, the challenge of change is probably greatest at the branch level. It is to this aspect of business activity that we now turn and report on the findings of a research project sponsored by the Cranfield School of Management involving a detailed questionnaire survey of almost 500 building society branch managers (full details are given in Nellis and Litt, 1990). The research focuses on a number of aspects of branch activity which embrace the major challenges for building societies in the 1990s. These include the following:

- the recruitment and retention of branch staff;
- staff training and development;
- salary and status of branch managers;
- the changing role of building societies;
- the authority and responsibility of branch managers;
- the measurement of branch performance.

We summarise the findings of the research under each of the above headings.

The Recruitment and Retention of Branch Staff

From the questionnaire responses, there is clear evidence that since the introduction of the Building Societies Act (1986) many branch managers have been experiencing severe difficulties with regard to the recruitment of new staff, particularly cashiers and clerks (and hence there has been a sharp increase in the number of part-time staff). It is reported that these difficulties are particularly acute in areas in the south of the UK as well as in the more affluent localities. Given these problems, the question of competitive rates of pay will have to be addressed by the societies. It was the opinion expressed by many branch managers that building society rates of pay are low compared with those of other financial institutions and that this is the principal reason for their inability to attract and retain high-quality staff. In addition, many branch managers expressed the view that they would welcome the authority to determine their staff salaries with greater flexibility in order to be able to match local salary levels.

Many societies, especially the largest ones, have had a graduate recruitment policy for some years and among the medium-sized societies it seems to be a policy that is gaining ground. As the number of graduates increases, the question of resistance on the part of existing staff whose opportunities for promotion may be reduced will clearly be a delicate matter for the societies to manage, particularly with regard to staff morale. A further potential problem is that as these graduates and the skills they acquire become more and more marketable in the changing financial climate, they will need to be offered greater incentives by the societies to retain their expertise.

The suggestion that loyalty to the society will no longer be a quality that is encouraged among building society staff adds another dimension to the problem of staff retention (see Table 9.6 above). It raises the question of the loss of investment — in terms of both time and money — in training good staff when they depart for more lucrative opportunities.

Branch managers have also expressed strong support for the introduction of early retirement schemes in the societies and, indeed, there is also likely to be a large take-up if these are offered widely. The feedback from branch managers suggests, perhaps, that some of the older branch managers may be 'finding the going tough'. Their jobs have changed almost beyond recognition from what they were in the 1960s and 1970s. While many societies may be tempted to implement more attractive early retirement schemes, they must be wary of the significant loss in experience and skills that would result. A more selective policy of staff rationalisation may be preferable.

Staff Training and Development

Today training within building societies is based on much more than product knowledge. The pressures to sell financial services are now at the top of the agenda, but it is a fact that the vast majority of branch staff have few, if any, qualifications in this area. As staff experience more and more pressure from senior managers to sell, greater emphasis must be placed on the need for appropriate training. This is an issue which stands out clearly in the responses to the questionnaire survey and seems to be one of the greatest challenges facing branches at present.

Very often the responsibility for branch training is laid at the door of the branch manager. While managers generally accept this responsibility, they believe that they themselves should be trained to train — this is a view favoured particularly by managers from the smaller societies. Looking to the future, questions will be raised as to whether or not branch managers will have the time to carry out staff training as the pressure to sell increases. On the whole, more than half the managers in the survey expressed satisfaction with their own branch training activities — this is perhaps not surprising — as well as those carried out by head offices. Despite these views, a great majority of respondents complained about the lack of time available for training purposes as a result of other pressures, while at the same time recognising that the amount of time has increased.

Since the introduction of the Building Societies Act (1986), greater emphasis seems to have been placed on self-training and audio-visual and computerised teaching, especially within the larger societies. These developments are to be welcomed, but they should not be seen as representing a comprehensive training package. They cannot bring about the major cultural shift that is urgently required within the societies since, by and large, they tend to provide skills training only.

Salary and Status of Branch Managers

From the responses received in the survey, it is clear that building societies are heading towards what may be a crisis with regard to the motivation of branch managers. It was the unanimous opinion of respondents that the salary levels of branch managers are not competitive with those of other similar professionals and are not commensurate with their perceived status. It should be stressed that no information has been obtained about the actual salary levels across the professions in question — bank managers, solicitors, stockbrokers, insurance agents, mortgage consultants, estate agents and accountants. Branch managers were only asked for their perceptions of how their salary and status compared with those of other equivalent professionals. Building societies, therefore, face a major challenge in the future — to be faced sooner rather than later — with regard to these issues and how branch managers are provided with the appropriate incentives, given the pressures which they face at the sharp end of the business.

The Changing Role of Building Societies

Another dominant theme in the research responses involves the question of whether or not building society branch managers feel that they can compete effectively in the new environment. In this respect it is notable that a large majority of respondents expressed confidence that their societies will be able to compete. Emphasis was placed on the fact that societies come from a background in which they have a good reputation, a large customer base and considerable customer loyalty. However, it was recognised that this loyalty will come under severe strain as competitors seek to attract customers away.

Some concern was expressed by branch managers that, as their societies strive to provide a full range of financial products and services, there is the danger of becoming a 'Jack-of-all-trades'. This again has implications for staffing levels in societies and at the same time highlights the need for specialists to cope with the more complex areas of business. This need for specialists is all the more important given the legal regulations under which financial institutions now operate. At the moment, few societies have ventured seriously into the new areas of business such as stockbroking, executorship and trusteeship. By and large, the focus is still on the relatively traditional areas, though there have been major inroads in the last few years into the personal loans market. Land services — estate agencies — have been prominent among the larger societies for several years now.

A majority of branch managers have expressed support for a strategic move by societies into these new business areas, although not necessarily as a substitute for their traditional business. Not surprisingly, perhaps, this support is strongest in the largest and medium-sized societies where the ability to diversify is greatest, although within the present legal framework they are limited in the extent to which they can move away from the traditional business (ie mortgages).

From the survey it appears that branch managers from those societies which have clearly identified specific strategies are the most optimistic about the future and the challenges they face. This observation has very clear implications for societies in general — it is important that clear objectives are identified and communicated to all staff. This is not only important for staff morale but also for planning purposes.

There appears to be only limited support for a move towards plc status — along the route taken by the Abbey National in 1989. While opinion is split fairly evenly among the large societies, the supporters are in the minority among managers from the smaller societies. There are fears, too, of damaging the 'caring image' which has developed under mutuality if the plc route is chosen. As noted before, a large majority of branch managers are confident that, as mutual societies, they can meet the challenges of the future effectively, given the opportunity to manage.

The Authority and Responsibility of Branch Managers

The survey results indicate strongly that branch managers regard their own efforts as being the most important factor in attracting business into the branches and they expect this role to increase in future. The importance of estate agents' and solicitors' referrals in providing new mortgage business is expected to decline, while the importance of branch promotions and referrals by local firms is expected to increase. The implication of these trends, therefore, is that branch managers expect to have a greater role to play in business development based on a more proactive approach. At the same time, branch managers expect the reputation of the society to play an increasingly important part in generating business.

Another recurrent view of branch managers is that they should be given more direct managerial responsibility. They expect that their role as decision makers, motivators and salespeople will far outweigh their declining role as administrators and that their involvement as personnel managers will increase. There are indications that there has been an increase in the extent to which authority is being delegated within branches. This is a trend that is likely to continue with the expansion in services, particularly if training programmes are intensified.

There are no false illusions among branch managers as to the pressures which they face and which are likely to increase. These pressures are coming from the greater diversity of operations, greater competition, the requirement for better performance, greater responsibility, as well as the legal regulations under which they have to operate. Acknowledgement is given of the fact that branch managers have been granted some flexibility in the mortgage limits that they can sanction and this move is welcomed. However, demand appears to be growing for improvements in a number of other areas, particularly with regard to head office support services. Much criticism has been made of head office communications with the branches, both in connection with launching new products and with respect to day-to-day problem solving. There is a widespread impression that head offices are not in tune with branch needs and that a greater awareness of the branch environment would be beneficial.

The Measurement of Branch Performance

Significant changes are taking place in the relative importance of the different indicators that are used to measure building society branch performance. The main traditional indicators are the number and value of investment balances and the value of mortgage lending. These are rapidly being overtaken by the profit and loss account. The survey responses confirm that the number and value of accounts is becoming less important as a measure of performance, although the value of mortgage lending is expected to remain high on the rankings. In addition, the importance of commission income is expected to increase significantly and to become one of the principal indicators of branch performance.

Particular problems arise for building societies in making comparisons of performance between branches that have particular local circumstances which impinge on their businesses. It makes no sense to expect a branch located in an area largely populated by young couples to have similar targets to another branch located in an area largely populated by retired people. The bottom line — that is, profits — may turn out to be very different in each case, largely due to the fact that they have different customer bases. The whole question of branch performance is one that must receive immediate attention in building societies given the greater consciousness of profitability itself. The pressures which the societies face are likely to decrease the significance given to performance based on 'numbers' of accounts — greater emphasis is likely to be placed on values such as total lending and deposits and so-called 'key customer accounts'.

CONCLUSIONS

In this chapter we have described the changes that have taken place in recent years in the nature of the business environment which building societies operate. The deregulation of the 1980s has been unprecedented in the history of the building society movement and, with the creation of the European Single Market at the start of 1993, it is likely that the pace of change will be unrelenting in the 1990s and beyond. It is inevitable that there will be further major changes in the structure of the UK and European financial services sector in the coming years. The societies, which will not be exempt from these changes, will be forced to trim their management expenses and develop effective branch management systems as the culture of the organisations moves further away from that based on mutuality to one which is focused on the achievement of a sustainable competitive edge and an adequate level of profitability.

Particular attention has been given in this chapter to the challenges faced by staff and managers operating at branch level. The analysis presented is based on the research findings from a detailed questionnaire reported in Nellis and Litt (1990). In general, it is found that branch managers look to the future with some excitement and recognise the challenges afforded by the wider range of financial products and services available to them — particularly in the larger societies. They recognise the opportunity to increase profits but appreciate the need to be ever conscious of the need to improve the quality of the services they offer. In contrast, there are no false illusions about the pressures created by the increase in competition and the pace of change within the building society movement. Further aspects of the survey results suggest that, at the personal level, branch managers perceive themselves as having strengths in a number of areas. The experience they have already accumulated in traditional building society business is seen as their main strength, but they are fully aware that they lack specialist knowledge in the new areas of business. However, in these rapidly changing circumstances qualities of flexibility, adaptability, drive and commitment are seen by many managers as their principal strengths.

Most managers welcome the opportunity to enhance their own performance and skills through their involvement with new products and services. They also recognise the opportunity this presents to enjoy a more varied career with potential rewards in the form of higher salaries and increased promotion prospects. On the other hand, there is anxiety that failure to achieve targets could threaten these promotion prospects. The threat of merger or takeover also clouds the horizons of a number of managers, so that the challenges of the future may result in less loyalty as well as less job satisfaction.

In conclusion, the evidence of the past few years suggests that, despite the enormity of the challenges which they have faced and will continue to face, building societies will remain a dominant force in the UK financial services sector for many years to come. They have demonstrated that they have the ability and confidence to compete in an aggressively competitive environment, despite the speed of transformation required of them in terms of business operation and culture. They have also demonstrated the essential benefit of their new regulatory framework to the public via a dramatic extension in the range of choice in the provision of financial services. In addition, experience so far suggests that the Building Societies Act (1986) has also contributed significantly to an increase in standards and reduction in costs of all parts of the market for personal financial services in the UK. That they have not only survived but have actually embraced the new environment positively through successful diversification demonstrates the inherent strengths of building societies to cope with the challenges of change and to adopt the appropriate role for the future.

References

Balmer, J M T and Wilkinson, A (1991) 'Building societies: change, strategy and corporate identity', *Journal of General Management*, Vol 17, No 2.
BSA (1988), *Building Societies: The Regulatory Framework*, (2nd edn), The Building Societies Association, London.

Coles, A (1992) 'Concentration and mergers in the building society industry', *Housing Finance*, No 16, November, Council of Mortgage Lenders, London.

Ennew, C T, Wright, M and Watkins, T (1990) 'New competition in financial services', *Long Range Planning*, Vol 23, No 6.

Fleming, M C and Nellis, J G (1992) 'Prospects for the UK building society branch network in the 1990s', *CBSI Journal*, September.

H M Treasury (1991) *Treasury Bulletin*, Autumn.

Johnson, C (1991) 'The outlook for financial services', *The Business Economist*, Vol 22, No 2.

Macey, R and Wells, D (1987) 'New legislation accelerates changes in building society culture', *Management Accounting*, July–August.

Nellis, J G and Litt, H M (1990) *The Challenge of Change in Building Societies — A Survey of Branch Managers' Views*, Cranfield Press, Cranfield.

10

THE FUTURE OF PROFESSIONALS IN THE RETAIL FINANCIAL SERVICES SECTOR

Jeff Watkins

OUTLINE

The aim of this chapter is to give an overview of the changing roles and work patterns of professionals in the UK retail financial services sector. It uses Toffler's (1970) 'bureaucracy-adhocracy' model as a basis for discussion and illustrates some of the main changes, including the emergence of profit centres and contract working, with examples drawn from two extensive surveys, one of human resources directors in the financial services sector (Watkins and Bryce, 1992) and the other of a wider range of professional groups (Watkins and Drury, 1992).

The following lessons are evident from this research. Financial services companies are in the early stages of a major transition in organisational structures which will cause a massive outflow of professionals from larger organisations to the fee-earning or business service sector. Service managers need to manage this transition carefully.

In particular they need to do the following:

1. Determine where value is added in the organisation. The 20 per cent of the organisation which is producing 80 per cent of the required return needs to be identified.
2. Introduce business process redesign. This entails a radical restructuring of the business processes, organisational boundaries and management systems of an organisation using the latest technologies where appropriate.
3. Blueprint the knowledge organisation. The core professionals with the required skills to drive the organisation forward need to be identified.

194

Increasingly these will be 'rounded' professionals with technical, managerial and political skills.
4. Outsource non-core professionals. Professionals whose services can be costed and measured, those whose services are not required on a full-time basis, and those who contribute relatively little to the new knowledge organisation will be outsourced to the business service sector.

In the 1970s the fairly stable world of the previous 30 years began to be replaced by one characterised by rapid changes in markets, technologies, customer attitudes and competition from emerging economies. Many UK companies recognised that they had to improve their capability profiles and encourage innovation and quick response to change in order to compete in this unstable environment. As the numbers employed in knowledge-intensive occupations — professional, managerial, technical and scientific — rose, the search for more flexible organisational structures began. These new structures aim to facilitate the creation, communication and flow of new ideas and at the same time improve efficiency and profitability.

Over the years, management writers and theorists have described flexible organisational structures of this kind in various ways. Most have much in common with the concept of the 'adhocracy' introduced by Toffler in the 1970s. Recent examples include Miles and Snow's (1986) concept of the 'dynamic network' and Handy's (1989) concept of the 'shamrock' organisation with three main strands in terms of human resources: a professional core, a contractual fringe, and a flexible labour force.

This chapter considers how far the financial services sector has progressed in implementing this kind of flexible organisational structure and examines the impact on its professionals, those in traditional professional groups such as accountants, actuaries, solicitors and underwriters and those in the newer professional groups which emerged during the 1980s in areas such as marketing, human resources and information technology.

BACKGROUND

Adhocracies

As the pace of change accelerates, competitive pressures force organisations to take on more flexible structures which facilitate speedier responses to market demands.

Traditional hierarchical structures which have evolved since the Victorian era fail to provide the kind of support and atmosphere necessary for the development of creative responses to the challenges of a very different environment. It is argued that the most effective organisational structure to deal with this kind of environment is the adhocracy. It has a network-type structure and functions as an internal market where services are bought and sold within the organisation (see Figure 10.1).

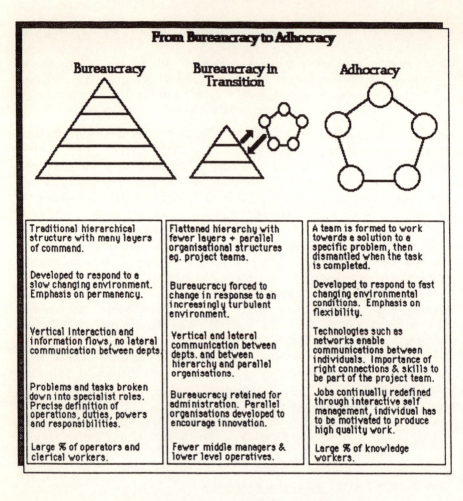

Figure 10.1 From bureaucracy to adhocracy

The main advantages of the networked adhocracy for a large organisation such as a bank, building society or insurance company are as follows:

- **It facilitates risk taking**. Adhocracies are designed to deal speedily with the unexpected. Teams of experts and other resources can be mobilised quickly and solutions designed interactively. Risks can be taken because the power to make decisions, and change them quickly as the need arises and in response to changing conditions, lies with the team. Decisions are not hampered or delayed by protocol and layers of command, hence response to the unexpected is prompt and timely, making fine tuning of solutions possible.
- **It focuses on company objectives and contribution**. Adhocracies are not without constraints — the team works as a network of responsible individuals within a framework of objectives which acts as a reference point for all.

Individual jobs focus on the objectives of the company and are defined in terms of their contribution to the objectives of the assignment.

Dynamic Networks

The concept of the adhocracy can also be extended to an industry sector. For example, the publishing and film industries are made up of a large number of small specialist firms which work both together and in competition as a dynamic network. Miles and Snow (1986) offer the film industry as a good example of such a network. After 20 years of specialisation in the industry, films are now rarely made by a single major studio. Instead the major studio acts as a financial investor and the organisation of the film production is contracted out to an independent production company which may exist solely to produce one film. The production company contracts out the different film-making functions — set design and construction, sound mixing and mastering, film processing — to specialist firms. The dynamic network has evolved as the most efficient organisational structure for this particular industry because it has the flexibility to cope with a high-risk environment. It is relevant to other service and professional organisations, especially those involved in publishing and other media-based activities but also more traditional activities such as architecture, consultancy and research, which face risks similar to those identified by Miles and Snow. They are:

- **Fluctuations in demand** — the risk associated with rapid changes in consumer preferences for increasingly differentiated products and economic cycles which have produced two major recessions in less than a decade. These factors will play an important role over the 1990s. For example, architects, after a major building boom in the 1980s, are now faced with a severe recession in which over a quarter are either underemployed or have lost their jobs.
- **Inefficiency in terms of cost and innovation** — the risk of not being able to compete because high fixed overheads and the inability to devise innovative approaches to new products and processes which match those of their competitors.

The rationale for people and service businesses to adopt this structure is clear cut. The dynamic network is a far more flexible structure than any of the previous forms, it can accommodate a vast amount of complexity while maximising specialised competence, and it provides much more effective use of human resources than has been accumulated, allocated and maintained by a single organisation.

Miles and Snow, 1986.

KEY CHANGES

In a sector such as retail financial services, which is facing a major rationalisation, we would expect to see the emergence of some of the new organisational structures described by Toffler, Miles and Snow and Handy; and some evidence of the ways in which such structural changes are affecting the work of the professionals. In our recent survey we found that the majority of companies were adopting structures between the two extremes of bureaucracy and adhocracy. This can be described as the 'bureaucracy in transition stage' (Moss-Kanter, 1983). During this stage we see a number of key developments which have serious implications for the role of the professional:

- The number of layers of command are reduced leaving the best characteristics of a bureaucracy in place to enable the organisation to continue ongoing administration and other routine tasks. Decision making is devolved.
- 'Parallel organisations' are set up such as profit centres, business units and project teams responsible for business development and special projects. These are the first stages in the creation of market-like structures within the organisation where individuals can trade resources, information, influence, skill, knowledge and ideas. Steps are taken to measure and cost the contributions made.
- Service delivery contracts based on measures of contribution are arranged between departments or business units.
- Services once provided by an internal business unit are outsourced or sub-contracted. Once the contribution and quality of a business unit or professional service can be measured, senior managers may take up the option to outsource the service, and to offer it for tender.

To survive in these new structures, a professional must have tradable skills which can be measured, costed and bought and sold within the organisation. Since communication and negotiation are key aspects of successful networking, the possession of social and personal skills is increasingly important.

> A consistent picture is now emerging of central 'professional' functions that are tighter, more professional and specialised, advisory in nature, and concerned with policy and strategy matters. The future standing of professionals is likely to depend upon the perceived relevance of their contribution, rather than their position in the organisation.
>
> Coulson-Thomas, 1988.

Handy (1989) predicts that this will lead to professionals working in larger organisations working harder and more effectively:

> There will be half the number of people paid twice as much for working three times as effectively.

EFFECTS ON PROFESSIONALS

Having identified the key features of organisational change which influence the working patterns and roles of the professional within the organisation, we go on to examine the effects of these influences with reference to examples from the financial services sector.

Organisations are changing to encourage flexible working patterns, and more and more professionals are expected to work either:

- **in a smaller centralised function which is advisory in nature**. As some of their more routine functions are devolved to line management and in some cases to associate professionals, the professional will spend more time **working in management teams**, where he or she will share responsibility for business decisions and act in an **advisory role**.
- **in profit centres and smaller business units**. Larger organisations are breaking up into smaller and smaller business units. In the private sector, this occurs as a reaction to increasingly fragmented markets, each of which has its own particular demands. Some professional functions are given cost or profit-centre status, and services are sold to internal customers at cost or on a profit basis. There may even be negotiation of internal service contracts. In some cases services are also sold on the open market.
- **on a contract or fee basis**. Many professionals will become subcontractors working for a fee for a particular service. Organisations are now shedding professional staff and employing them back on a fee basis. They will be required to provide specific advice on a periodic basis rather than work in a salaried position.

These new roles demand greater business involvement, higher levels of work, devolved decision making, high-level communications and negotiating skills, and offer rewards based on measures of contribution. These changes are meeting resistance from many professionals, but the uncertainty bred by the current economic climate is hastening an acceptance of the need for change.

The examples which follow illustrate the three trends outlined above.

Human Resources Professionals — Towards a Smaller Centralised Function which is Advisory in Nature

In the retail financial services sector, as both the structure and role of human resources departments change in response to external business pressures, the roles of its employed professionals change too. The personnel professional is taking on a new role as member of a management team which shares responsibility for business decisions.

Our research indicates a major movement over the next two years away from the large centralised function to a more devolved human resources function (see Table 10.1). The large centralised function is becoming far more service orientated — major organisational clients are provided with a personal service, eg allocating a personnel professional to cover a whole range of personnel issues for that division such as industrial relations, job evaluation, training and manpower planning.

The general trend is towards devolution: a smaller more professional human resources function which is far more strategic, less bureaucratic and linked with the business.

Table 10.1 Changing structure and role of personnel departments

	Now %	2 years' time %
Centralised Large centralised HR function with complete control over all corporate HR activities.	53	30
Devolved HR function devolved to divisional and line managers with different HR policies to deal with different environments.	29	30
Core Reduced HR function with responsibility only for core tasks, eg policy formulation, succession planning.	18	28

The process of devolution is being hastened by the introduction of new technology which, in freeing line managers from administrative tasks, gives them more time to take on some of the functions previously carried out by personnel professionals:

> In the future the role of line-managers as decision-makers, motivators and salespeople will far outweigh their declining role as administrators and their involvement in and responsibility for recruitment and personnel issues will increase substantially.

> *Chief executive in a major building society.*

This in turn frees the professional from lower level tasks, allowing him or her to take on a consultative role and to become involved, as a member of a team, in new complex areas such as business process redesign, quality management and project management, as the following comment from the banking sector illustrates:

> Our role as a facilitator and advisor to Group and individual business units is concerned with organisational development — re-engineering of work and management processes and focusing on quality issues and the flexible, cross-functional deployment of multi-skilled staff.

> *Senior personnel professional*

Many human resources professionals are not prepared to change their traditional roles and adopt these new ways of working. Without change they will be marginalised and the strategic aspects of their work taken over by other members of the senior management team, or in some cases by a breakaway and more dynamic training unit.

> The traditional role of the Human Resources Department — job evaluation, appraisal — is shifting to an organisational development and facilitating role. In our

company, senior management is taking on that role because the personnel professional is still playing the old game and does not actually have the ability to contribute on the organisation development type of facilitating role. He is being marginalised.

Human resources director in a major building society

Information Technology Professionals — Towards Profit Centres and Smaller Business Units

There is a significant trend towards profit centres in all industry sectors:

- Companies are splitting up into smaller and smaller business units, cost centres and profit centres. With the advent of better quality information systems, senior managers have far more information about where costs are incurred and where value is added, so the exact contribution of each department, branch or individual (in some cases) can be costed.
- There is a parallel trend towards the introduction of service delivery contracts between professional departments such as information technology, marketing, personnel and the business units they serve.
- Service delivery agreements are only a few short steps away from subcontracting the whole function to a third party. Once senior managers are confident of being able to measure the contribution and quality of a professional or business unit, they gain the flexibility to subcontract the service, if and when necessary. Taken to its extreme this could involve such things as franchising the whole branch network of a major bank.

The retail financial services sector is one of the largest employers of information technology professionals with large banks such as NatWest employing over 3000, large insurance companies such as Norwich Union employing over 500, and large building societies like the Halifax also employing over 500.

The results of a survey conducted among the top 50 building societies (Watkins and Bryce, 1992), to find out which stage of contracting out their IT departments had reached, showed that they are moving away from operating as a general overhead towards profit centre status (see Table 10.2). Organisations such as building societies are at a very early stage in the introduction of internal contracts, and they usually take the form of a service-level agreement which is almost always quantitatively based and relatively unsophisticated.

A similar situation exists in the banking and insurance sectors, as stressed by this response in a recent interview:

I think the whole of the technical side of running our network could be subcontracted to a third party. It is no longer cost effective for the bank to manage and maintain its own telecommunications network.

IT director of a major bank

Table 10.2 Changing status of the IT function in the building society sector

	Now %	2 years' time %
General overhead	65	3
Cost centre	31	50
Profit centre dedicated 100% to parent company	0	9
Profit centre also selling services on the open market	4	8
Total	**100**	**100**

The Growth of the Contractual Fringe — Towards Contracting Out

The number of people employed in the retail financial services sector grew rapidly in the 1980s from 646,000 in 1980 to 958,000 in 1990. The business services sector, which includes areas such as consultancy, law, accountancy, insurance intermediaries, surveying, advertising and leasing, increased from 973,000 to 1,850,000 during the same period. One of the main reasons for this was that major companies subcontracted out many of their professional services. For example:

- The software services sector expanded from 81,000 to 167,000 and much of this expansion was as a result of work subcontracted from the retail financial services sector. The software services sector employs a very high percentage (over 60 per cent) of professionals.
- A similar expansion took place in the insurance sector, where there are now over 76,000 people engaged in activities which support the big insurance companies. These include brokers, independent life intermediaries, loss adjustors and consultant actuaries, to name just a few.

Table 10.3 Growth of the business services sector in the 1980s

	1984	1990
Software services	81,000	167,000
Accountancy, management consultancy	90,000	142,000
Estate agents	90,000	157,000

Sources: Lloyds Bank Economic Bulletin, Number 145, January 1991.
Government statistics.

So during the 1980s the retail financial services sector developed a large contractual fringe of professionals including accountants, management consultants, software services, financial advisers, solicitors and surveyors (see Table 10.3).

CONCLUSIONS

Organisations in the retail financial services sector are changing in response to competitive pressures. They are introducing flexible working patterns such as adhocracies and dynamic networks. More and more professionals are expected to work in profit centres, in smaller business units or on a contract or fee basis. As a result there is reduced job security for all professionals and a professional qualification can no longer be seen as a guarantee of a job for life. As highlighted by Coulson-Thomas (1988) and Handy (1989) there will be fewer and fewer professionals working in large organisations. Those that remain will be concerned more with policy and strategy and will function in an advisory role. With the emphasis on relevance of contribution, survival as a professional in these new structures will depend on the possession of tradable skills which can be measured, costed and bought and sold within the organisation. Since communication and negotiation are key aspects of successful networking, the possession of social and personal skills is also increasingly important. These new roles also demand greater business involvement, higher levels of work, and devolved decision making. This applies in addition to the growing number of professionals working on a fee basis in the contractual fringe. Many of them are already working in the kind of dynamic network described by Miles and Snow (1986). In the near future many professionals now working in large financial service organisations will be joining them and experiencing the challenge of flexible working.

References

Coulson-Thomas, C (1988) *The New Professionals*, British Institute of Management, London.
Handy, C (1989) *The Age of Unreason*, Hutchinson, London.
Miles, R E and Snow, C C (1986) 'Organisations: new concepts for new forms', *California Management Review*, Vol XXVIII, No 3, pp62–73.

Service Sector Specific Management Issues

Moss-Kanter, R (1983) The Change Masters, Union, New York.
Toffler, A (1970) Future Shock, Bodley Head, London.
Watkins, J and Bryce, V (1992) Horatio: A Survey of Human Resources Ratios in the Retail Financial Service Sector, Bristol University/KPMG Management Consulting, Bristol.
Watkins, J and Drury, L (1992) From Evolution to Revolution: The Pressures on Professional Life in the 1990s, University of Bristol, Bristol.

204

11

QUALITY MANAGEMENT AND THE PROFESSIONAL FIRM: STANDARDS MUST IMPROVE!

Peter Barrett

OUTLINE

Most, if not all, firms are now aware of BS 5750 and third-party certification for quality assurance. As a standard rooted in manufacturing this has posed problems for many service-orientated firms. This is particularly so for professional firms and exacerbated still further when they are involved in multiple-firm projects, as is typical in construction.

This chapter reviews recent developments in international quality management standards which are highly relevant for service industry firms. Moves towards total quality management (TQM) are introduced and their potential in multiple-firm projects outlined.

The rest of the chapter seeks to identify effective strategies:

- for the implementation of quality management at the level of the *firm*;
- for the development of appropriate certification *standards*;
- for better working practices for the construction *industry* as a whole.

The following lessons are evident from the discussion in this chapter:

- Quality assurance (QA) standards do matter to firms and their clients and so it is critically important that appropriate standards are available. This means lobbying for what service industries need rather than distorting perfectly good practices to fit a manufacturing model.
- Managers should not revert to childhood whenever quality assurance comes up, either by expecting it to solve all their problems or by treating it as a

mysterious subject about which they are not qualified to comment. Quality assurance and quality management are about good management. This argues for using 'new' approaches when they make sense, but building from past experience as well. Years of experience cannot be supplanted by a single standard, but it can help reassess your own practices more objectively.

- An incremental, long-term approach to quality assurance, possibly leading to total quality management, is likely to be the most beneficial, and for small firms feasible, approach. Gaining feedback from your clients on your performance is probably the single most important thing you can do.

Some of the interviews from which this chapter draws were carried out as a preliminary part of a project financed by the Science and Engineering Research Council.

BACKGROUND TO QUALITY ASSURANCE/QUALITY MANAGEMENT 'STANDARDS'

Over the last five years or so quality assurance (QA) has become a major issue on the agendas of most firms. Professional firms are no exception. Owing to a combination of pressure from major clients and incentives via grant aid from the Department of Trade and Industry (DTI), the conditions have been very favourable; but the British Standard at the centre of developments, BS 5750 Parts 1–4 (BSI, 1987) has caused some problems for non-manufacturing firms.

These have been discussed at length elsewhere (eg Barrett, 1989a, 1989b) and will not be rehearsed here, but one conclusion is that, although the standard can be helpful especially for the manufacturing type of organisation for which it was written, for professional firms it is not really appropriate without quite considerable reinterpretation and adaptation. Even then it can lead to serious dangers, such as firms becoming inward looking and too much orientated towards paper systems.

These dangers are accentuated by the emphasis in the UK on third-party certification. This has become synonymous for many with QA, rather than being seen as one alternative, with other possibilities such as, very importantly, first-party or self-certification.

Two years ago CIRIA (1990) estimated that only 40 out of 10,000 construction-related professional firms were QA certified. From an analysis of the DTI register this has now risen to around 350. It is not possible to be more accurate because the categorisations in the register are at times difficult to interpret. So the impact of QA, in this one sector at least, is not yet widespread, although the majority of the unregistered firms are probably working on the issue or worrying about the fact that they are not!

'STANDARDS' MATTER

Management academics in the UK appear strangely disinterested in QA standards.

BS 5750 Pts 1–4 is the same as the international standard ISO 9001–4 and for many in business QA *is* BS 5750. Reviewing the papers of the British Academy of Management conference in 1991 there was barely a mention of this standard, although there were a number of papers on the more interesting facets of the subject, such as TQM and Japanese approaches. An exception was the paper by Law and Cousins (1991) in which it was noted in survey results that 100 per cent of respondents were 'contemplating registration for BS 5750'.

Although national and international standards are only part of the management of quality, possibly only a relatively small part, owing to their massive perceived importance to those in practice it is essential that their appropriateness is debated at an academic level if our research is to have *relevance*.

Drawing from a wide range of in-depth interviews, there is no doubt that for most if not all firms their interest in quality issues is driven by perceived *client demand*, or a fear of future demand from clients for QA registration to BS 5750. If the standard did not exist the clients would not be able to stipulate a requirement so clearly. So to this extent at least the standard has acted as a positive stimulus by bringing consideration of quality issues to the forefront. As a mechanism the lesson is clear, but the question remains: *does the standard actually help firms manage the quality of their work effectively?* If the answer is 'no' or even conditional, then to make good use of what is clearly an effective stimulus to action what is required are research and development to underpin appropriate 'standards'. If appropriate standards existed doubtless clients would demand their use, to the benefit of all parties.

Now is a timely point to enter the debate. A new standard has been published which differs radically at a conceptual level from the previous standard. Whereas before discussion could seem pointless given only one standard to 'choose' from, now alternatives can be considered. Another indication of a trend towards a less constrained approach can be seen in the DTI's shift in allegiance from QA to Total Quality Management (TQM); see for example the proposals for a major national TQM award (DTI, 1992). The situation is now much more fluid.

The objective should be to develop standards which channel client pressure on firms so that not only is interest in quality issues generated, but so too is effective action resulting in better quality management.

RECENT DEVELOPMENTS IN QUALITY MANAGEMENT 'STANDARDS'

Quality management (QM) or TQM are not developing in isolation. It could be said that they are, at their best, particular views on how *good* management can be achieved. In the case of the professions, the literature has blossomed over recent years as *services management* has become established as a serious subject area. Advances in this area have been reflected in developments in QM standards. International Standard 9004–2 (ISO, 1991) was published last year and is written specifically for *services*, thus confirming by implication what everyone knew: that the standards up to that date not only came from the manufacturing arena, but were intended for it. This new standard specifically mentions 'professionals' in its scope of application. It exists within the UK as the identical document, BS 5750 Part 8.

Without going into detail, it is clear that ISO 9004–2 draws from the development of new concepts in the services management literature. For example, the introduction mentions. human aspects, social processes, customer's perception, image, culture and motivation. Perhaps most importantly it stresses that: '*customer assessment is the ultimate measure of the quality of the service*' (Clause 6.3.3). In addition it states that qualitative (soft) as well as quantitative characteristics must be taken into account (Clause 4.1). Both of these aspects strongly reflect the influence of the service management theorists such as Gronroos (1983).

The coordinating diagram provided by the standard, which describes the 'service quality loop', is given in Figure 11.1.

In addition to the prominence given to the customer's assessment, there is a key 'box' shown in the diagram in which performance is analysed and *improved*.

This effectively represents the organisation learning (Argyris and Schon, 1978) and constantly improving its performance over time.

Initial press reaction to the standard described it as 'an interpretive document for BS 5750 parts 1 to 3' (*New Builder*, 10 Oct 1991). In my view this is quite wrong. One would expect an interpretive document to correspond broadly with what is being interpreted, whereas ISO 9004–2 is written in a completely different order (see Annex B of the Standard for cross-referencing).

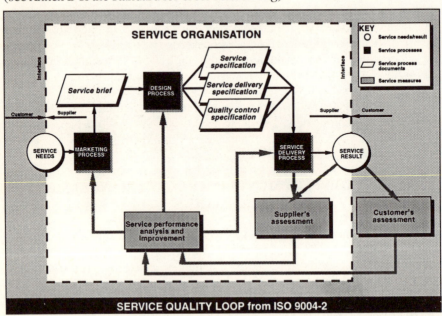

Figure 11.1 Service quality loop

So the new 'standard' marks a turning point in the development of formal standards for QA/QM. It is still paperwork orientated, but covers much more. Its underlying interactive model marks a significant advance on the exchange model underpinning the earlier 'standard'.

A PROJECT-BASED INDUSTRY

Firms involved in construction have a particular feature which raises problems: they are project orientated with many partners to each project. Thus there is a considerable integration problem. QA/QM, as encapsulated in the standards described above, focuses on the firm, not the project. So the situation could arise where the individual firms are well organised in QM terms, but the project as a whole falls apart. A simplified matrix of the possible situations is given in Figure 11.2.

Figure 11.2 QM in firms and projects

A major challenge now is to develop approaches which satisfy both organisational and project requirements. The common denominator is, of course, the client, but the historical development of construction in the UK has resulted in adversarial, contract-dominated relationships between the parties to a project, particularly when it is large.

Alternatively, in smaller conurbations oligopolistic arrangements are quite common, where the parties operate on a good deal of trust and very little formal contract.

Recent government pressure for more competition in the appointment process for professional advisers makes any move towards more cooperative working problematic, as longer-term relationships will be the inevitable casualties in the fee competition that will increasingly result.

So to achieve advances in quality management for the construction-related professions action is required on two fronts: for the individual *firms* and at an *industry* level to enhance effective project integration.

SUMMARY OF KEY ISSUES

The key issues arising from the above discussion can be summarised as follows:

- The take-up of manufacturing-orientated QA documents has been slow among the construction professions.
- For practitioners the reality of QA is encapsulated in the formal 'standards' that are available.
- Owing to a shift in government thinking towards TQM and the publication of a 'standard' specifically for services, the time is ripe for an open reassessment of QM for the construction professions.

The next section considers tentative strategies for the effective development and use of QM concepts for the construction professions.

STRATEGIES

Consideration is given to three areas: individual firms, national/international standards and the construction industry.

Individual Firms

To date firms interested in QA have typically employed a consultant with the objective of producing a set of documented procedures which will satisfy a certification body.

Drawing from Sjoholt's work in Norway (eg Hansen and Sjoholt, 1989), further analysis by this author (Barrett, 1992) and the basic principle of 'continuous improvement' which is fundamental to TQM, it is apparent that an incremental approach is most likely to provide long-term improvements. It is suggested that rather than beginning with the paperwork the following approach should, instead, be taken:

1. Referring to Figure 11.1, the initial focus should be on *feedback* from clients on current performance.
2. Immediate, key improvements should be sought to the functions of marketing, design and delivery.
3. A tight coherent framework of formal paper systems should be designed and implemented according to the principle of 'Ockham's Razor': *as much as you must and as little as you may*!
4. In parallel with 3, actions to provide *support* to staff in their work should be taken.

In essence the suggestion is to work from the client interfaces of the QM model (Figure 11.1) in towards the minimum necessary documentation, while keeping the emphasis as much as possible on providing positive support to staff.

It is common knowledge among management consultants that client surveys are a powerful way to gain leverage for change and in the context of this chapter they have the added benefit of re-orientating the firm towards the needs of its clients.

Current research by two postgraduates working with the author is focused on client requirements in two sectors: building surveying (Barrett and Hoxley, 1992) and general practice surveying (Barrett and Banks, 1992). Building from Gronroos' (1983) 'technical' (what) and 'functional' (how) factors, they have questioned clients and found considerable variation in the level of importance of various factors. Interestingly, in broad terms the 'how' factors do not rate higher than the 'what' factors, although a number are highly rated. The formulation we are moving towards parallels Herzberg's (1968) dichotomy. The clients naturally demand that the job is done properly, but equally they expect this as a matter of course. Thus the 'what' factors are like Herzberg's hygiene factors. They can upset if not present, but do not delight if found. In contrast, the 'how' factors are really of little consequence if the job goes wrong, but provided the technical aspects of the job are well done, the way the client is dealt with can make a very big impact. Thus the 'how' factors are akin to Herzberg's motivators. This research is well advanced and is throwing useful light on what clients value in a professional service. The results will be published in 1994.

National/International 'Standards'

So far the distinction between QM and QA has not been dwelt upon. The difference is quite straightforward. QM is concerned with the *internal* management of quality, whereas QA is interested in being able to demonstrate *externally* that systems and procedures have been followed.

ISO 9000–3 (BS 5750 Pts 0–3) cover QA and ISO 9004 (BS 5750 Pt4) QM for *manufacturing* operations. ISO 9004–2 covers QM for *services*. When it is listed out like this it begs the question: where are ISO 9001–2, 9002–2, etc? The answer is that 'standards' for *QA* certification specifically for services do not exist at present. If they are to exist, the question of measuring qualitative as well as quantitative variables will have to be confronted. Some relevant work in this connection has been done by Fitzgerald *et al* (1991) in their study of performance measurement in service businesses for management accountants.

If a fully viable route for firms to take is to be provided, it seems to be essential for certification standards should be developed for services, to match the QM standard which already exists.

Construction Industry

From an industry perspective the TQM emphasis on customer – supplier chains *both* within and between organisations (eg Oakland, 1989; Teboul, 1991) is perhaps the most fruitful avenue for reconciling the need to focus on the effective QM of both the firm and the project.

At least one major contractor is endeavouring to build effective customer – supplier relationships in one of the most traditionally aggressive areas, that between main and subcontractors. This firm has implemented a training programme about its procedures for subcontractors so that they can mesh better with the main contractor's operations. The subcontractors pay for the course, but if they complete it successfully they are assured of a flow of work.

CONCLUSIONS

The main conclusion of this chapter is that 'standards' *do* matter. They are a major consideration for those in practice and therefore a significant element of the dynamics of change in the quality management forum.

For professional firms the standards until recently fell short of what was really required, but there have been moves in a positive direction. It is important that the momentum created is built on and the full ramifications exposed through open debate. This should include academics with a service industry orientation and should extend to a consideration of new standards which freely accept hard and soft data in the certification of firms.

For the construction industry TQM presents a fruitful development if it can be harnessed to overcome the firm/project dichotomy.

References

Argyris, C and Schon, D (1978), *Organisational Learning: A Theory of Action Perspective*, Addison-Wesley, London.

BSI (1987) *BS 5750: Quality Systems*, British Standards Institute, London.

Barrett, P S (1989a) 'Quality assurance in the professional firm' in *Quality for Building Users Throughout the World*, Vol I, CIB, Paris.

Barrett, P S (1989b) 'Motivating to high quality work', *Implementation of Quality in Construction*, Vol II, EOQC, Copenhagen.

Barrett, P S (1992) '*Surveying Quality Management,*' RICS Research Paper No 4, RICS, London.

Barrett, P S and Banks J (1992) 'A synthesis of clients' criteria for the assessment of the professional firm', in *Proceedings of the International Symposium on Architectural Management*, University of Nottingham, 19–21 March.

Barrett, P S and Hoxley, M (1992) '*The Synthesis of an Analytical Model of the Client-Professional Relationship*', Working Paper, Department of Surveying, University of Salford, February.

CIRIA (1990) 'CIRIA launches new project on quality management for design', *CIRIA Press Release*, London, January.

DTI (1992) *Report of the Quality Award Committee on the Feasibility of a New UK Total Quality Award*, DTI, London.

Fitzgerald, L, Johnston, R, Brignall, S, Silvestro, R and Voss, C (1991) *Performance Measurement in Service Businesses*, CIMA, London.

Gronroos, C (1983) *Strategic Management and Marketing in the Service Sector*, Chartwell-Bratt, Bromley.

Hansen, R and Sjoholt, O (1989) *Quality Management: A Challenge for the Building Industry*, Norwegian Building Research Institute, Oslo.

Herzberg, F (1968) 'One more time: how do you motivate employees?', *Harvard Business Review*, Jan–Feb.

ISO (1991) *ISO 9004–2: Quality Management and Quality System Elements — Part 2: Guidelines for Services*, International Organisation for Standardization, via British Standards Institution, London, as Part 8 of BS 5750.

Law, P and Cousins, L (1991) 'Is quality market-led?', *Proceedings of the Fifth Annual Conference of the British Academy of Management*, University of Bath, 22–24 September.

Oakland, J S (1989) *Total Quality Management*, Heinemann, Oxford.

Teboul, J (1991) *Managing Quality Dynamics*, Prentice Hall, New York.

12

FROM MANAGERS TO LEADERS: THE JOURNEY METAPHORS OF VOLUNTARY SECTOR CHIEF EXECUTIVES

Colin Fletcher and Richard Kay

OUTLINE

Voluntary organisations are the most complex of all types of organisations. They have staff and volunteers, expenditure with highly uncertain incomes, 'good works' that are in neither the public nor private domain. Leadership in voluntary organisations therefore depends on bringing many points of tension together into a unitary whole with a vision of the future. Chief executives of voluntary organisations are expert witnesses in making a case for how voluntary organisations can be best understood.

This chapter reports the results of a study of the 'cream of the cream', 26 chief executives nominated as outstanding in the field. The investigation used a critical incident technique to find the images and metaphors which they used about their own organisation, as follows:

- all the images which Morgan (1986) identifies as important;
- images which Morgan does not discuss in which they give emphasis to those of 'theatre', 'game' and 'journey';
- being like a 'machine' is more important in larger organisations;
- 'being on a journey' is particularly significant;
- this 'journey' image gives focus, and describes choices;
- in the journey there are many different ideas about both the directions to be taken and the means to be used.

Business organisations are also being characterised by their journeys. However, as yet this sense or image of the journey is an especially distinctive feature of voluntary organisations because of their value base, the conflicting set of expectations which they bring together, the absence of an end-state and the rapidly changing world in which they operate. The findings show in detail why these chief executives have been chosen as the 'best of the bunch.' They are managers of many metaphors at the same time *and* they give leadership on their organisation's journey.

INTRODUCTION

This chapter takes the form of a journey, an exploration. It explores the understandings which chief executives in the voluntary sector have of their work and the 'world' of the voluntary sector. First, the significance of metaphors in general is discussed: metaphors are ways of seeing or gaining perspectives through making comparisons. Next the analysis of metaphors in organisations is briefly reviewed. Examples are given of the major metaphors identified in recent studies and the richness of the approach becomes obvious. Less obvious is the usefulness of metaphors and so this section is followed by an account of debates about the voluntary sector — a notoriously difficult field to describe.

Against this background, the research methods of a project just completed are outlined, in which 26 of the best English chief executives were interviewed about their moments of effectiveness and ineffectiveness. No two incidents were alike and yet in terms of the metaphors they used there were striking similarities. These similarities are compared with those suggested by Gareth Morgan in his hugely influential book, *Images of Organizations* (1986).

One essential difference between Morgan's 'list' and these chief executives' perspectives was immediately apparent: these chief executives spoke of the journey of 'their' voluntary organisation. Having set its sights on the 'journey', the chapter goes further and closer towards understanding the details and internal structure of this metaphor.

It is appropriate to note again that this chapter is concerned with exploration rather than explanation, with possibilities rather than proof. What the details suggest is an intriguing destination, namely that chief executives in the voluntary sector have the qualities of both leaders and managers.

To begin with, some theoretical work on metaphor will be covered. When the abstract task of setting perspectives, of adjusting the lenses of perception, has been done the search, the fieldwork, begins.

METAPHOR AND ORGANISING

The work on metaphor has been multidisciplinary and, in recent years, increasing attention has been given to its role in organisation and management theory and practice. Morris and Burgoyne (1973) noted six metaphors which inform the everyday practice of management development. These are the metaphors of building, engineering, agriculture, zoology, medicine and the military:

- laying solid foundations (building);
- stress, frictions, interfaces (engineering);
- sowing seeds, cultivating people (agriculture);
- zoologists' talk of breaking in young managers and the organisation as a jungle;
- medical metaphors: taking symptoms, organisational health and decay diagnosis;
- mobilising resources, strategy, staff, headquarters and logistics (the military).

Mangham (1986) pointed to the use of courtship, warfare and the 'wild west' as ways of organising the experience of more or less friendly takeovers. He argued that:

> We notice the colourful imagery of takeovers because it is novel and unexpected. We do not see the everyday metaphors of accounting because they have become the commonplace expressive form within which organisation activities are framed [for example, 'at the end of the day' and the 'bottom line']. Thus in research, productivity, marketing, personnel and even charity work, the terminology of finance has grown in dominance.

Mangham is emphasising here the role of language as 'creating reality in its own image' and that 'all language is metaphorical', since reality is seen through language, ie one thing is seen as if it were another. Thus, he argues, the normalisation of metaphors is a cause of their downfall as source of insight: 'where they initially clarified through the provision of a different perspective, they later obscure through their semblance to literal facticity.' He thus differentiates between creative metaphors and metaphors which have now become taken for granted.

Morgan's (1986) work, however is at a different level of abstraction. He emphasises how many of our conventional ideas about organisations build on a small number of taken-for-granted metaphors. He argues that the theories promulgated in writing on organisations and management are also 'theories-in-use':[1] they are based on metaphors which lead us to see and understand organisations in distinctive yet partial ways. In highlighting certain 'interpretations', metaphors tend to force others into a background role. Our ability to achieve a comprehensive understanding depends on the ability to see how different metaphors may coexist in a contradictory or paradoxical way: 'organisations are many things at once'. Morgan proposes five dominant metaphors structuring organisational theory:

---

1. Morgan rejects the traditional belief that theory gets in the way of practice: 'for, in recognising how taken-for-granted images or metaphors shape our understanding and action, we are recognising the role of theory. Our images or metaphors *are* theories or conceptual frameworks. Practice is never theory-free, for it is always guided by an image of what one is trying to do. The real issue is whether or not we are aware of the theory guiding our action.'

- organisation as machine;
- organisation as organism;
- organisation as brain;
- organisation as political system;
- organisation as culture.

Jelinek *et al* (1983) suggest that organisational analysis has been evolving towards more complex, paradoxical and even contradictory modes of understanding. Instead of monochromatic thinking, they suggest an interpretive framework more like a rainbow:

> a code of many colours that tolerates alternative assumptions. We need to understand organisations as having machine-like aspects, organism-like aspects, culture-like aspects and others yet to be identified. We need to encourage the tensions engendered by multiple images of our complex subject.

Most writing on organisations and management has tended to focus on the private/commercial sector. Morgan's work on metaphor has such a focus. What, then, of the voluntary sector?

THE VOLUNTARY SECTOR

Handy (1988) argues that the implicit model of the organisation in textbooks is an engineering one:

> the organisation is conceived of as a sophisticated clock or engine with interlocking parts, something which can in theory be designed to be perfect (were it not for the unpredictability of some of these human parts).

He proposes, nevertheless, that things are changing.

> New words in the organisational literature are words like 'culture', 'shared values', 'networks and alliances', 'power and influence', 'federalism', compromise and consent' and most crucially, 'leadership' rather than 'management'. These are not the metaphors of engineering but those of political theory and they symbolise a new way of thinking about organisations — as societies or communities rather than as machines or warehouses. New words are the heralds of change, and these point to a revolution in the way we think about organisations . . . The new language recognises what the voluntary world has known all along — that organisations are living communities with a common purpose, made up of free citizens with minds and values and rights of their own.

What *are* the images or metaphors-in-use in the voluntary sector? Are they different from those in the private sector which, it is proposed, tend to be the metaphors identified by Morgan as dominating organisational and management theory? Do the metaphors-in-use reflect the changing imagery proposed by Handy?

METAPHORS-IN-USE IN THE VOLUNTARY SECTOR

A methodology to identify metaphors-in-use was developed from the work of Schön (1979) and Miller (1985). Schön's article focuses on the issue of 'social problem' setting. He argues that there are 'generative' metaphors underlying how social problems are perceived and proposes that the problem's meaning can be reframed through the use of another generative metaphor.

He points to how the 'surface language' of a story offers a clue to the generative metaphors which set the problem of the story. Schön's work facilitated the development of a methodology which:

- deliberately set out to generate 'stories';
- enabled the identification of 'surface images' as clues to deep or generative metaphors.

The methodology chosen to generate stories or narrative for our research was the 'critical incident technique' (Flanagan, 1954; Fivars, 1980). This was used to elicit narratives from a purposive sample of 26 chief executives/directors of voluntary organisations, providing services directly or indirectly to children and/or young people. These were selected by 'peer acclamation' as particularly effective, in order to analyse the 'sense making' of the chief executives. Six experts in the field were asked to nominate highly effective chief executives. Those who were nominated three or more times were interviewed.

The purpose of the research was *not* to study issues of effectiveness; it is recognised that effectiveness can be conceptualised in many ways. The aim here was to identify the 'cream' of chief executives.

The critical incident technique was used as a window into the world of the chief executives' experience as chief executives and their use of metaphors/images of organising. Each chief executive was asked to recount four incidents in the preceding 12 months, two in which they believed they had been particularly effective and two ineffective. Not all the chief executives could recount four incidents; however, in total 94 incidents were described. The full transcripts of the interviews were then analysed for surface/satellite images of core metaphors. The concept of 'image' was used for the term which was said to be a 'satellite image' of a particular core metaphor. It was recognised that any identification was tentative and so a second person was used to negotiate the allocation of images to particular metaphor categories. Morgan's metaphor categories were used initially, but it was quickly recognised that other metaphors were in use.

Table 12.1 gives examples of the allocation. It shows examples of the nouns, verbs and phrases that have been identified as images of particular metaphors. They will be seen to be nouns and verbs that are embedded in everyday language as well as phrases that stand out as more, even becoming prominent as clichés. It is argued that these *all* have significance as they are used in the 'sense making' of the chief executives.

Table 12.1 Examples of allocation of terms/images to metaphor categories

Term/image	Metaphor
Plan, objectives, authority, accountability, hierarchy	Machine
Staff, strategy, targets	Military
Organisational and personal needs, groups, boundaries, environment, health	Organism
Power, influence, conflict, negotiation	Politics
Values, traditions, norms, principles	Culture
Decisions, information, communication	Brain
Crossroads, directions, stages, travel	Journey
Role, performance, drama, juggling	Theatre
Keep balls in the air, team, keeping cards close to one's chest	Game
Money, budget, deficit	Business
Regional, national, local, field	Territory

Table 12.2 shows the metaphors identified by Morgan (1986) and those in use by these chief executives.

Table 12.2 Metaphors of organising

	Morgan's metaphors	Voluntary organisation metaphors
'The dominant metaphors of organisational theory.'	Machine	Machine
	Organism	Organism
	Political system	Politics
	Culture	Culture
	Brain	Brain
	Psychic prison	Military
		Business
	Flux and transformation	Journey
		Game
	Instruments of domination	Theatre
		Territory

Morgan did not identify the 'journey', 'game' and 'theatre' metaphors, probably because he concentrated at the organisational level. His was a top-down approach. He also developed his work from an analysis of academic work and *not* from theories-in-use. Our research, however, was into the metaphor use by chief executives who are sense making both at a personal and institutional level, making manifest what Schön (1979) calls their 'theories-in-use'.

The research showed that, contrary to what Handy (1988) is proposing, the 'machine' metaphor is extensively used in voluntary organisations and *coexists* alongside the other metaphors. The chief executives are multiple metaphor users and voluntary organisations are seen as many things at once. An analysis of the *quantitative* use of metaphors showed the 'brain' metaphor predominated with 10 chief executives, 'organism' with 6 'politics' with 6 and the 'machine' metaphor with 4. Table 12.3 identifies the frequencies of metaphors-in-use for the 26 chief executives.

There is no suggestion here that a chief executive had one particular dominant metaphorical style, ie that one metaphor will *always* predominate. Instead, we suggest that a metaphor will dominate at a particular time, ie 'be on top' and reflecting the chief executive's current interactive relationship with his or her experience.

Table 12.3 Frequencies of metaphors-in-use

Metaphor	Usage frequency (%)
Brain	21.4
Machine	17.7
Organism	16.8
Politics	15.4
Business	7.9
Culture	6.5
Journey	4.4
Military	3.9
Territory	2.0
Images of change	1.1
Theatre	0.9
Game	0.8

A further analysis was undertaken of comparative metaphor use by the chief executives of the 11 largest organisations (200 staff or more — 10 of the 11 were also the most experienced as chief executives). They were shown to have a comparatively high use of the 'machine' metaphor when compared with the other chief executives.

This would suggest that the size of the voluntary organisation does correlate with the extent of the use of the 'machine' metaphor (Meyer's study (1982) supports the thesis that the larger the organisation the more formality). However, greater size did *not* correlate with greater comparative use of the 'machine' metaphor. The 4 largest organisations' chief executives (2000+ staff) used the machine imagery *less* than the 7 other chief executives of this group of large organisations. There is *choice, not determinism*. It was noticeable that 10 of these largest 11 shared another pattern in their use of the 'culture' metaphor. The comparative analysis showed that 10 of the chief executives (the 10 who were the most experienced) made comparatively high use of the 'culture' metaphor.

Thus what was evident was that the large organisations (and most experienced chief executives) do not *replace* the 'machine' imagery with the 'culture' imagery (or vice versa). This exemplifies both/and thinking and not either/or thinking. There is not a move away from 'machine' imagery to other imagery, as Handy (1988) appears to be proposing. *The chief executives are multi-metaphor users.* From the *quantitative* analysis of metaphors the research shows that there does *not* appear to be any difference between the private and voluntary sectors as regards different metaphor *use*. However, it is proposed that two metaphors did have a particular *qualitative* significance for the voluntary sector:

- the 'journey' metaphor;
- the 'culture' metaphor.

In this chapter we concentrate on the detail and significance of the journey metaphor.

THE JOURNEY METAPHOR-IN-USE IN VOLUNTARY ORGANISATIONS

The use of the verb 'to organise' places emphasis on process, identifying the dynamic nature of organising or managing. Morgan (1986) introduces a metaphor of 'organisation as flux and transformation' as a way of emphasising change; of creating new means of thinking about change and dealing with change in organisations. However, the analysis of our research data identified a different dominant metaphor of process in use, that of 'journey'. The analysis also showed a rich and varied range of images in the 'journey' metaphor.

A detailed analysis of the transcripts of the 26 chief executives was undertaken to identify the use by the chief executives of the 'journey' metaphor, the form of the metaphor having the content of a range of 'satellite images'. These images were extracted from the text with the sentence context in which they were found. The statements were those when the speaker was in some way emphatic. They were the kind of 'now look here' statements, 'nitty-gritty' statements when the voice is harder, more firm and more controlled. Put another way, they were not statements about what the chief executive did but what he or she thought. They were direct expressions of the chief executive's 'theories-in-use'.

Thus one chief executive stated:

Again it is like a typical voluntary sector, where you are never quite sure who is *driving* whom . . . who is *on the bridge of the Queen Mary*.

In this sentence there is a satellite image, 'driving', and also 'on the bridge of the Queen Mary'; both images are of the means/vehicle of a journey.

Similarly, another chief executive stated:

> being able to keep one's organisation roughly in the right *direction* having best guessed where the world was *going*; to be ahead of events as one can . . . given all these imponderables, one has to be *quick on one's feet*.

A further example is the statement:

> My job is mainly about the long term *direction* of the organisation; the corporate thing, yet at the same time trying to keep in touch with the day-to-day issues, otherwise you will come to be in a world of your own.

There is again the use of the satellite image of '*direction*'. Thus in these statements we have images of:

- *direction*, emphasising the process aspect of the metaphor;
- images of the *means/vehicles* of the journex,ncdn'onnomdnQueen Mary' (ship); other examples of the means/vehicle were identified: 'bus', 'aircraft', 'ferry', 'horse rider'.

A closer analysis of these examples also suggested a further classification. It is possible to identify an image of difficulty or problem: 'where you are never quite sure who is driving whom'. A much more dramatic example of the image of problem is:

> I feel like continually going through a hurricane; battered all the time; driven off course; somehow I don't sink, it gets close. The hurricane image also gives an image of being alone in that process, blinded by rain and the continual feeling of not enough energy to accomplish all those tasks. The hurricane is predominantly outside the organisation.

The image of the means/vehicle, *of the ship* can be seen again, identified through the phrase 'driven off course', and consonant with that means/vehicle image is an image of a hurricane highlighting the difficulty/problem.

This difficulty/problem imagery can be contrasted with a later statement made by the same chief executive: 'a fairly tranquil lake and I am the ferryman, and taking people with me on the ferry and crossing the waters on new adventures.' The 'tranquillity' image is very evidently contrasted with the 'hurricane', yet there is also the use of a similar image of a ship/ferry, an image of a means/vehicle of the journey. The reference to being the 'ferryman' focuses on the chief executive and on the means or vehicle of the journey. Examples were also found where the focus was on the 'institution' (see Table 12.5). The journey imagery appears to have value in being able to be used at both levels anthropomorphically. A close examination of: 'You were on your own, you had to trust your own judgement' reveals an image of prescription: 'you had to trust your own judgement'; it is an image of either/or thinking. 'Trust your own judgement' prescribes action in one form only.

Therefore it is possible to classify prescriptive statements into either/or, both/ and and a third *choice* where the chief executive intimates a sense of choice.

These various examples show it is possible to classify the 'journey' metaphor-in-use in the journey matrix as in Table 12.4.

Table 12.4 Directions in the journey metaphor: examples

Focus	
Difficulties/ problems	I am torn between a maze and wading through treacle, they both have something about them. The maze being the confusion. Here I am at the crossroads, do I turn left or right; if I turn left I might be back in the middle again. If I turn right I might find my way out. The treacle being the glutinous quality of it.
Prescriptive	
1. Either/or	Once you have gone through this interdisciplinary door there is no coming back.
	The CEO must be able to march in step with the trustees. If he can't stop them and they go down a road you have advised them against it may be a resignation issue.
2. Choice	The danger is that there is so much information giving and decision making that there isn't time to take a step or two back, looking around and 'there be deeps and here be dragons', so what do we need to start working towards in the next two to three years to prepare for these 'waters'?
3. Both/and	The approach of the staff lurching from one peccadillo to another is probably unhelpful, in terms of the totality of things it is unhelpful. It is a balance between the big and the little things and the little things ought to be, in part, the working out of wider objectives. Yet too much prissiness about the little things clutters up and people lose their way.

THE SIGNIFICANCE OF THE 'JOURNEY' METAPHOR

The exploration into the 'journey' metaphor-in-use, a metaphor of process, has, it is argued, demonstrated its qualitative significance for the voluntary sector.

While Morgan (1986) makes no reference to the 'journey' metaphor, do other writers on organisation and management theory?

Table 12.5 Means and vehicles in the journey metaphor: examples

---

Focus

Difficulties/ problems	If you have been around as long as we have you tend to be like the Queen Mary, full ahead on automatic pilot with the throttle jammed open and you suddenly find you lose power and steerage as we did in the 1960s about our actual role in life.

Prescriptive

1. Either/or	I put in my report to the Governors and said we must never allow ourselves to drift into something of that nature.
2. Choice	The Queen Mary analogy is not a very good one since we have to dump a speed boat over the side, go for the resources and head for goal.
	It is the opportunity to develop practice towards that vision not just doing something that happens to be on offer. You don't quite know how you are going to make the journey, by bicycle or by Rolls-Royce. You don't want to be diverted.
3. Both/and	Helicopter management, your role is to stay up in the helicopter taking an overview of what is going on but if you see trouble you have to be able to zoom down and deal with it quickly. The problem is if you spend too long on the ground you get caught there, then you can't see where you are going, you need to get in and deal with things and get back up again.

A review of the literature indicates that journey imagery is being increasingly used by writers on leadership and is often used to compare the manager with the leader. Golzen and Garner (1990) wrote: 'Managers are concerned with efficiency, marshalling the physical resources of the organisation. Leaders have gifts of inspiring people with a vision of *the direction* in which the organisation or even just their bit of the organisation is going.' (Emphasis ours in this and following quotations.)

Bennis and Nanus (1985) state that: 'Effective leadership can *move* organisations from current to future states . . . Leaders concern themselves with the organisation's basic purpose and general direction.'

Adair (1987) argues: 'Leadership is action, not position; one of the distinctive features of leader will find a way *forward*. He/she will generate a *sense of direction.*'

A much more explicit and extended use of the 'journey' metaphor is made by Kouzes and Posner (1987). They write:

> We use the metaphor of the journey as the most appropriate metaphor for discussing the task of the leaders. That is because the root origin of the word 'lead' is a word meaning 'to go'. This root origin denotes *travel from one place to another*. Leaders can be said to be those *who go first*.
>
> They are those who *step out* to show others the *direction in which to head*. They begin the quest for a new order. In this sense leaders are *pioneers*, they are people *who venture into unexplored territory*. They guide us to new and often unfamiliar *destinations* . . . A main difference between managers and leaders can be found in the root meaning of the two words, the difference between what it means to handle things and what it *means to go places*. The unique reason for having leaders — their differentiating function — is to *move us forward*, leaders *get us going somewhere*.

What about the world of business? Is the 'journey' metaphor used in practice?

Hayes (1985) quotes a comment from the chief executive of Diamond Shamrock:

> Why has our vision been narrowed? Why has our flexibility been constricted? To my mind, there is one central reason: our strategies have become too rigid . . . a detailed strategy is *like a road map, telling us every turn* we must take to get to our goal . . . The entrepreneur, on the other hand, views strategic planning not *as a road map* but as a compass and is always looking for a new road.

All these writings indicate that the presence of the journey imagery is *not* a *distinctive* feature of voluntary organisations. However, our research highlighted how the discourse of the chief executives of voluntary organisations contains a rich, varied and extensive use of the imagery of the 'journey' metaphor. Why? A number of reasons are suggested:

1. Voluntary organisations are better depicted as social value institutions because of the importance of social values to the sector. As an image of process, the metaphor of journey has particular *qualitative* significance for the voluntary sector, in that the process emphasises action and the operationalisation of the values of the institution, the *direction and journey to achieve the valued purpose*. Examples of a striking use of the journey to achieve this valued purpose is the use of the term 'movement' for institutions of social change, which many voluntary organisations are. A second example is from one of the voluntary organisations participating in this research. They had recently issued a new statement of purpose and values. They placed emphasis on their 'Christian *pilgrimage*', 'faith in action'. It is suggested that the self-image of members of voluntary organisations is more likely to be that of traveller or pilgrim, rather than 'machine' or 'organism'.

2. The essential 'value-based' and intangible nature of much of the work of voluntary organisations, and the lack of any suitable overall performance measure analogous to 'return on capital' in industry, has been emphasised by authors such as Handy (1988). In a similar vein, the ambiguous and often conflicting nature of the 'goals' of public organisations, including not-for-

profit organisations, has been identified by Nutt and Backoff (1992). They point to the demands of interest groups, flux in missions and manipulation by important shareholders and third parties creating a complex and confusing set of expectations that are frequently conflicting. They note the difficulty with which not-for-profit organisation funders may require efficient operations; clients want personalised care; staff want continual improvement of resources; and trustees want prestige and tranquillity:

> These expectations produce conflicting goals as well as vague and hard-to-interpret requirements and priorities . . . strategy development in situations that involves ambiguous goals is difficult, if not impossible. This ambiguity provides a sharp distinction between strategic management in public as compared to private organisations.[2]

The theory-in-use of the chief executives of the voluntary organisations to cope with this issue of ambiguous and often conflicting goals is the emphasis of the imagery of journey towards the achievement of the social purpose(s) of the organisation, while managing the tensions of conflicting interests and expectations. The imagery content of the metaphor thus allows for flexibility and change, while there is still a sense of 'direction' to the purpose of the journey.

3. The social value purposes, often emphasising social as well as individual change, and frequently not totally achievable, at least in the time of the present staff and/or members. Similarly, a purpose to keep all young people out of custody, while providing focus and purpose, will not be achieved by one voluntary organisation; only a small number of young people will be kept out and even then many other factors may impinge on that achievement. The 'distance' (journey imagery) and uncertainty of the achievement of the social purpose can be creatively conceptualised through the rich and varied imagery of the 'journey' metaphor. Yet even though this uncertainty and distance can lead to confusion, and drift (journey imagery), the 'journey' metaphor also has an image of direction.

   So, even though there will be uncertainty and difficulty, tensions and pressures, the leader using the 'journey' metaphor needs to ensure the institution has direction. 'It is better to travel with hope . . .' As an allegory, for example in Bunyan's *Pilgrim's Progress*, the 'journey' metaphor has been used to highlight direction, yet also difficulty and uncertainty.

4. The 'journey' metaphor's imagery of uncertainty and change is also useful in depicting the context in which voluntary organisations' action takes place. The context of voluntary organisations today is that of turbulence, change and uncertainty. It has been proposed by Adair (1987) that this is why leadership has once again come to the fore. 'Leaders like change, it is their chosen element . . . he or she find a way forward, generate a sense of direction . . . building a team which is able to ride out storms.

---

2. Nutt and Backoff use Bozeman's notion of publicness (1987) to draw attention to the degree to which the public authority affects how organisations act.

In summary, the 'journey' metaphor may be a qualitatively distinctive feature of the voluntary sector. Whether this is the case would need to be tested out in comparative research with private as well as public sector organisations.

CONCLUSION

This chapter does not give the whole story. Two further arguments have been advanced elsewhere. First, these voluntary sector chief executives are using metaphors creatively; they extend expressions *and* bring images of metaphors together in exciting and challenging combinations. Secondly, the distinctiveness of the voluntary sector lies in the qualitative significance of the combination of images from *both* the journey metaphor *and* the culture metaphor (Kay, 1992). However, there is one generalisation which we would like to make, based on our appreciation of the insightful intelligence of the chief executives who were the subjects of this research. The generalisation has to do with the value of metaphorical expression in leadership and in the leadership of voluntary organisations. Most accounts of metaphor open with a quotation from Aristotle. For us it is a fitting point of arrival:

> . . . the greatest thing by far is to be master of metaphors. It is the one thing that cannot be learned from others; and it is also a sign of genius since a good metaphor implies an intuitive perception of similarity of dissimilars. Through resemblance, metaphor makes things clearer.

References

Adair, J (1987) *Not Bosses but Leaders*, Kogan Page, London.

Bennis, W and Nanus, B (1985) *Leaders: The Strategies for Taking Charge*, Harper and Row, New York.

Bozeman, B (1987) *All Organisations are Public: Bridging Public and Private Organisational Theories*, Jossey Bass, San Francisco.

Fivars, G (1980) *The Critical Incident Technique: A Bibliography*, Psychology Laboratory, Palo Alto.

Flanagan, J C (1954) 'The critical incident technique', *Psychological Bulletin*, Vol 51, pp 327–358.

Handy, C (1988) *Understanding Voluntary Organisations*, Penguin, London.

Hayes, R M (1985) 'Strategic planning: forward in reverse', *Harvard Business Review*, November–December.

Golzen, G and Garner, A (1990) 'The special gifts that make a leader', *Sunday Times*, 1 October.

Jelinek, M L, Smircich, L and Hirsch, P (1983) 'Introduction: a code of many colours', *Administrative Science Quarterly*, Vol 28, pp 331–338.

Kay, R (1992) 'The Metaphors of the Voluntary Non Profit Sector Organizing!', Cranfield School of Management Working Paper SWP 13/92.

Kouzes, J M and Posner, B Z (1987) *The Leadership Challenge — How to Get Extraordinary Things Done in Organisations*, Jossey Bass, San Francisco.

Mangham, I L (1986) *Power and Performance in Organisations*, Blackwell, Oxford.

Meyer, A D (1982) 'How ideologies supplement formal structures and shape responses to environments', *Journal of Management Studies*, Vol 19, No 1.

Miller, D F (1985) 'Social policy: an exercise in metaphor', *Knowledge: Creation, Diffusion, Utilisation*, Vol 7, No 2.

Morgan, G (1986) *Images of Organizations*, Sage Publications, Beverley Hills, CA.

Morris, J and Burgoyne, J (1973) *Developing Resourceful Managers*, IPM, London.

Nutt, P C and Backoff, R W (1992) *Strategic Management of Public and Third Sector Organisations*, Jossey Bass, San Francisco.

Schön, D A (1979) 'Generative metaphor: a perspective on problem-setting in social policy' in Ortony, A (ed) *Metaphor and Thought*, Cambridge University Press.

INDEX

crucial role in the success of the
    function 103
global/international 45, 47
intangibles 117, 129
internal 98-115
legitimacy 126
mixed 99, 110-13, 125-7
network 116, 120, 124, 125, 126, 127-9
relationship 32, 124, 125
self-employed practices 122
'stranger' 122, 123-5, 126
transactions 32, 120
value of trust in service sector 116-30
Marketing (Special Report) 157, 165, 168
markets 106-7
    convergence of 44-5
    demands 143
    diversification 58
    domestic 41, 42, 45, 51, 60, 61
    employee 33
    entry 124
    Eurobond 179
    evolution of 43
    financial 47, 48, 180
    food 169-70
    global/international 41, 43, 44-7, 53, 54,
        60
    homogenisation of 43, 44-7
    influencer 33
    internal 33, 99
    internationalisation of 182
    larger, organic growth in 170
    lead times for securing 47
    mass 156
    mortgage 178
    national, smaller 156
    niche 55, 123, 160
    orientation 104, 105
    penetration 43
    reaching saturation point 167
    referral 33
    regional 60
    regulated 104
    split 125
    supplier 33
    target 47, 75, 120
    world, expansion into 43

see also labour markets; market
    research; market segmentation;
    market shares; marketing
Marks & Spencer 51, 157
Martin, L 141
Mathe, Herv 21, 72
Mathur, S S 31
Mercury 67
mergers 47, 48, 51, 100, 155
    threat of 192
Meshovlam, I 101
metaphors 214-28
Metcalf, H 133
METRA (Metropolitan Authorities'
    Recruitment Agency) 139-40
Meyer, A D 220
Midland Bank 143-4
Miles, R E 195, 197, 203
Miller, D F 218
Miller, P 113
Mingay, A 133
Minimum Lending Rate 179
Mintel 160
mission statement 99, 107-8
mistakes 91-2
    ability to recover from 82, 87
    actions taken to recover from 93
    one-off 94
moments of truth 36, 55
money transmission services 182, 183
monitoring sales 59
monopolies 68, 104
monopsonistic power 162, 163
Moores, John 146
morale 107
Morgan, G 214, 215, 216-17, 218-20, 221,
    223
MORI 166
Morris, J 215
mortgages 178, 179, 181, 182, 186
Moscow 67
Moss-Kanter, R 198
motivation 38, 66, 68, 134, 143
MTBF (mean time between failures) 96
multinational service providers 71, 74, 78
multisite development 56
Murphy, P A 103
mutuality 175, 186

Winterthur 65, 69
Withington Hospital 141, 142
WNC (Women's National Commission)
    134
women 141, 168
    retirement age equalised and raised for
        147
    returners 132, 143, 144
Women's Institute 147
Wood, S 133, 136, 137
Woolwich 178n
word of mouth 117, 124, 125, 126, 128
workforce 145
    see also employees; labour markets;
        staff
WPP 52

Yip, G 42

Zeithaml, V A 35
Zemke, R 42